JESSE LIBERTY'S
from scratch
PROGRAMMING SERIES

e-Commerce Applications Using Oracle8i and Java

from scratch

Meghraj Thakkar

A Division of Macmillan USA
201 West 103rd Street, Indianapolis, Indiana 46290

e-Commerce Applications Using Oracle8i and Java from Scratch

Copyright © 2000 by Que Corporation

International Standard Book Number: 0-7897-2338-7

Library of Congress Catalog Card Number: 00-100251

Printed in the United States of America

First Printing: April, 2000

02   01   00   4   3   2

Trademarks

Warning and Disclaimer

Associate Publisher
Tracy Dunkelberger

Acquisitions Editor
Michelle Newcomb

Development Editor
Bryan Morgan

Technical Editor
Karen Edge-Clere

Managing Editor
Matt Purcell

Project Editor
Pamela Woolf

Copy Editor
Megan Wade

Indexer
Greg Pearson

Proofreader
Benjamin Berg

Team Coordinator
Cindy Teeters

Media Developer
Michael Hunter

Interior Designer
Sandra Schroeder

Cover Designer
Anne Jones
Maureen McCarty

Copywriter
Eric Borgert

Production
Stacey Richwine-DeRome
Ayanna Lacey
Heather Hiatt Miller

Overview

Contents

Introduction

This book is part of the *from Scratch* series, which uses the philosophy of learning by working on a project. Most of the books that teach you database application development focus on teaching you a lot of syntax and programming techniques throughout the book. In such books, parts of a sample application are demonstrated to reinforce the skills. This book is different.

In this book we go through the various phases of developing a Web-enabled database application using Java and Oracle8i. We will look at the requirements, analysis, design, implementation, testing, and deployment of an Online Coffee Shop from scratch. This book is ideal as a meeting point for people from two streams of the IT industry:

- IT professionals familiar with Oracle who want to Web-enable their database using the Java features available in Oracle8i
- Java developers who want to implement e-commerce applications using Oracle8i

This book shows you the project development from scratch—without any assumptions of Oracle knowledge or Java knowledge. However, a basic programming background in any 3GL would be helpful. Although we will use a simple application and implement its core features, the book will give you enough exposure to the Internet capabilities of Oracle8i to implement more complex applications or enhance the Online Coffee Shop project used in the book.

This book is not intended to be an exhaustive repository of Oracle syntax or Java programming techniques. Neither will this book teach you all the nuts and bolts of the Java language. There are numerous books available for that purpose. What we do want to focus on, however, are things such as

- What features are available in Oracle8i for e-commerce?
- How can I use Java in Web-enabling my database applications?

- What issues should I worry about when using Java for database programming?
- How can I use the Oracle8i Internet capabilities?
- What are the issues in developing a Web-enabled database from scratch?

These and other such questions will be answered by this book using a hands-on approach.

How This Book Is Organized

This book doesn't make assumptions about prior Oracle or Java background and therefore will give you the opportunity to learn what you need to know about Oracle8i and Java for the purpose of performing Java database programming using Oracle8i. The main focus of the book is to understand the issues in such a project and how to use the Internet capabilities of Oracle8i to resolve these issues. Unlike other books on programming languages, this book won't show you a very long code listing and try to explain it all at once. This is because the application development project is multitiered. We will see code sections used in the various tiers such as database development, code to connect the browser to the database, and so on.

The chapters are organized as follows:

- Chapter 1, "Introduction to the Internet Capabilities of Oracle8i," shows you the Oracle architecture and provides an overview of the Oracle Java Virtual Machine. The project is introduced in this chapter.
- Chapter 2, "Creating and Populating the JavaStop Database," discusses the issues involved in developing a Web-enabled database application. We also will see how an Oracle8i database can be created and populated using Oracle tools such as SQL*Loader and Export/Import. The JSTP database used throughout the book will be designed and created in this chapter.
- Chapter 3, "Manipulating the JavaStop Oracle Database Using SQL," shows you how to use SQL and PL/SQL to manipulate the Oracle database.
- Chapter 4, "Java Basics for Developing JavaStop," shows you how to use Java to develop the basic infrastructure for Web-enabling the application.
- Chapter 5, "Using JDBC to Connect to JavaStop," uses JDBC to connect to and interact with the database.
- Chapter 6, "Using JDBC to Perform Data Manipulation in JavaStop," shows you how to manipulate JavaStop using JDBC.
- Chapter 7, "Implementing Clean and Compact Code Using SQLJ," uses SQLJ to write efficient database applications.
- Chapter 8, "Handling Exceptions in JavaStop," deals with JDBC error messages and exceptional handling in the project.

- Chapter 9, "Writing Java Stored Procedures for JavaStop," shows you how to store Java code in the database using Java stored procedures.
- Chapter 10, "Diagnosing Problems and Debugging JavaStop Code," shows you the various techniques available for debugging your applications.
- Chapter 11, "Securing JavaStop Using Database Security and Firewalls," uses Oracle security to secure the database from unauthorized usage.
- Chapter 12, "Improving the Scalability of JavaStop," shows you how to enable the application to work with a large number of concurrent users.
- Chapter 13, "Optimizing JavaStop Performance," focuses on improving the performance of JavaStop by identifying the sources of performance problem and reducing them. We will primarily focus on tuning Oracle8i and Java performance.
- Chapter 14, "Testing JavaStop to Improve Quality," deals with stress testing your application.
- Chapter 15, "Enhancing JavaStop Using EJBs and CORBA," discusses different ways in which you can enhance the basic application that has been developed so far. We understand how Enterprise JavaBeans and CORBA can be used for distributed computing.

Each chapter first looks at the issues and then shows you ways in which to resolve them. Also, we first identify the action that needs to be taken and then learn the skills to complete the task.

Conventions Used in This Book

Some of the unique features in this series include

 Geek Speak—An icon in the margin indicates the use of a new term. New terms will appear in *italics*.

EXCURSIONS

Excursions are short diversions from the main topic being discussed, and they offer an opportunity to flesh out your understanding of a topic.

With a book of this type, a topic might be discussed in multiple places as a result of when and where we add functionality during application development. To help make this clear, we've included a Concept Web that provides a graphical representation of how all the programming concepts relate to one another. You'll find it on the inside cover of this book.

Notes offer comments and asides about the topic at hand, as well as full explanations of certain concepts.

 Tips provide great shortcuts and hints on how to program in Java more effectively.

 Warnings help you avoid the pitfalls of programming, thus preventing you from making mistakes that will make your life miserable.

In addition, you'll find various typographic conventions throughout this book:

- Commands, variables, and other code appear in text in a special `computer font`.
- In this book, I build on existing listings as we examine code further. When I add new sections to existing code, you'll spot it in **`bold computer font`**.
- Commands and such that you type appear in **boldface type**.
- Placeholders in syntax descriptions appear in an *`italic computer font`* typeface. This indicates that you will replace the placeholder with the actual file name, parameter, or other element that it represents.

Getting Project Code

The code is available for download from this book's Web site at `http://www.mcp.com/product_support`. When you locate the URL, enter 0789723387 for the book's ISBN, and then click the Search button to go to this book's information page. You will find the links to the code to help you get the most out of this book. The source code on the Web is organized by chapter. Check back periodically for new information.

Chapter 1

Introduction to the Internet Capabilities of Oracle8i

The explosion of the Internet has opened numerous opportunities for IT professionals. These new ventures have also posed significant challenges that were not encountered before, such as

- Handling of complex data types such as audio, video, HTML, and so on
- Protecting data from unauthorized use over the Internet
- Performance issues when working with the Internet
- Connecting to the database from the Web browser

These and other such issues will be discussed throughout this book using Oracle8i as the Internet database of choice.

What Is a Database?

Several definitions are used for the word *database*, but for our purpose we will refer to it as an organized collection of data. The data collection is organized because the data is stored and accessed in a consistent manner. An example of a database is a contact book that contains the phone numbers and addresses of various people. Information stored in this database includes

- Name of the person
- Phone number
- Address

It doesn't contain irrelevant information such as the age, height, weight, and other physical attributes of the person. Information stored in the database could be of various types and not simply restricted to numeric or text data. In fact, most of the modern applications require that the data stored in the database be quite complex, such as pictures, video, audio, and so on.

Most of the time, a database stores information for a specific purpose—for example, a database storing information for an order-entry system or a database for student enrollment in a university. In the earlier days, the need for using a database arose from several requirements:

- Programmers needed a persistent store where data was retained between the various program runs.
- Complex applications required analysis of data over a long period of time and the amount of data involved warranted that there be an efficient mechanism for data storage and retrieval.

Usually a database is used for a small group of people, such as a workgroup or department. Frequently, a database can also serve a large number of people such as a whole organization, in which case it is referred to as an enterprise database. You might create a database where you keep information useful only to you, whereas a payroll database might contain information relevant to everyone in the organization.

Another term commonly used is a *data warehouse*. A data warehouse is essentially a data store containing information that can be used by various smaller operational databases. In Internet applications, these data warehouses are commonly used as a back end for Web browser front ends.

Another term loosely used is a *data mart*. A data mart is similar to a data warehouse, but it is generally used to integrate departmental or workgroup databases instead of enterprise databases.

Very large databases (VLDB) are often used interchangeably with data warehouses, but there is a difference. A *very large database* is a database that has grown in size due to a variety of reasons:

- It might be storing historical data or
- It might be storing large data such as images or
- It might be storing data at a very high rate

On the other hand, a data warehouse serves the needs of other smaller databases. Data warehouses might contain historical data, provide decision support, summarize data, or act as a central repository for other applications.

As mentioned earlier, a VLDB is simply a large database, and the qualification of such a database has changed over time. A few years ago when data storage was a critical component of any system, a database was considered large if it was greater than 10GB. Nowadays, a database is considered large if it is greater than 100GB.

Database Management Systems (DBMS)

Often the terms database and DBMS are used interchangeably. However, a database management system is a software product that manages a database. Several important features are desired from a DBMS and most modern databases provide some mechanisms for these features:

- It should be easy to store and retrieve data
- It should provide security for the data stored
- It should provide some method for concurrent access to the database and control of this concurrency
- There should be some method to recover the database in case of a database crash
- Data consistency and integrity should be retained
- Metadata should be available. *Metadata* refers to the data that provides information about the stored data. In other words, a data dictionary or a system catalog should be available that provides information about the name, location, and type of all data stored in the database

Database Management System Models

Several database models have been commonly used but they all satisfy, in one way or another, the requirements to be a DBMS. The various database models are

- **Flat-file**—These are not even real databases because they store the data in flat files. Storing data in this model is very cumbersome and makes the data difficult to access.
- **Network**—This model stores data in a network structure. An example of this database model is IDMS.
- **Hierarchical**—This model stores data in a hierarchical structure. An example of this database model is IMS.

  Many legacy databases used in minicomputers and mainframes still make use of the network and hierarchical database models.
- **Relational**—These databases, which have been dominant since the 1970s, make use of a mathematical concept of relations and store information in tables. Examples of this model include Oracle, Sybase, and Informix.

- **Object-oriented**—This model has become popular recently due to the limitations of traditional relational DBMS in handling complex data in a non-transactional manner. In addition, these databases have found a niche in applications such as CAD/CAM and multimedia.

Vendors such as Oracle have improved upon traditional RDBMS by adding features to compete with object-oriented models. These features include

- The ability to handle complex data types such as audio, video, text, and spatial data
- User-defined types
- REFs
- Object methods
- VARRAYs and nested tables
- Multidimensional data

Some applications such as behavioral science use highly indexed complex data that cannot be efficiently implemented in traditional RDBMS.

Oracle has provided Oracle Express as a layered product to compete with such object-based technologies also.

Understanding the Relational Model

A *relation* is a mathematical concept that describes how elements of two sets relate to one another. A relational model has some basic characteristics:

- Data is stored in tables, and only tables that relate to one another.
- Operations on these tables yield only relations.

Everyone accessing the database views information as a table. A relational table consists of

- A set of named attributes called columns. These columns represent the attribute of the object being represented.
- A set of tuples or rows that describe one particular instance of the object.

The intersection of a row and column is typically referred to as a *cell*. Columns have domains or data types associated with them that limit the type of information stored in them. For example, an employees table (shown in Table 1.1) might contain information such as employee ID, name, salary, department number, and so on.

Table 1.1   A Sample Employees Table

Emp_id	Emp_name	Sal	Position	Dept_no
1001	John Doe	50000	Engineer	2
1002	Jane Doe	60000	Engineer	2
1003	Charles Stone	85000	Architect	3
1004	Paul Nguyen	75000	Engineer	3
1005	Steve Smith	70000	Programmer	2
1006	Dave Hansen	95000	Manager	1
1007	Tim Floyd	80000	Architect	4

A relational table has several characteristics:

- Data stored in a cell is atomic. This is, however, a design choice and might not be followed in real life depending on storage and data usage considerations. For example, the preceding employees table makes use of the Emp_name column. Information in the Emp_name column is not really atomic because we are storing both the last name and first name in the same cell. This design might work for some situations but might not work for others where, for instance, you want to know only the last name of everyone in department 2.

- All data stored in a column is of the same data type.

- Each row is uniquely identifiable.

- Columns do not use any ordering.

- Rows do not use any ordering.

- Columns have unique names.

- Data integrity is maintained across tables. In other words, you should get the same data irrespective of how you get to it. Two different access paths to the same data should not give you different values.

 Note   Mathematical set operations such as unions and joins can be applied on relational tables.

There are two fundamental integrity rules associated with relational databases that should be understood. These are the entity integrity rule and the referential integrity rule. In order to understand these rules we need to understand two terms:

- **Primary key**—A primary is a column or set of columns whose values are used to uniquely identify the rows or records of a relational table. For example, in the employees table, the emp_id is a primary key for that table because by knowing the emp_id of an employee you can easily locate the record of an employee. Primary keys that consist of multiple columns are referred to as composite keys or concatenated keys.

- **Foreign key**—A foreign key is a column or set of columns whose values serve as primary keys in some other relational table. For example, the employees and department tables (shown in Table 1.2) have a common column—dept_id. The dept_id column is a primary key in the department table. In the employees table, the main purpose of the dept_id column is to link the two tables. This enables us to perform queries that gather information from both tables by performing a join operation using this common column. The dept_id is therefore a foreign key in the employees table. An example of such a query would be to find the salary of all the employees in the accounting department.

Table 1.2   A Sample Department Table

Dept_no	Dept_name	Location
1	Accounting	Los Angeles
2	Finance	Los Angeles
3	Information Technology	San Francisco
4	Payroll	Seattle
5	Human Resources	Seattle

 Note

In your database, for any given table there might be more than one possibility for a primary key. A database designer should choose one of these as a primary key, and the others should be considered as candidate keys or alternative keys.

The entity integrity rule states that the primary key must satisfy the following conditions:

- **No Null**—It should not be totally or partially null or empty.

- **No Duplicate**—The primary key values should be unique so that they can unambiguously find a record in the table.

- **No Change**—Even though you can change the primary key values, you should not do so because by changing the primary key value you are effectively changing the identity of the record.

The referential integrity rule states that the foreign keys should satisfy the following conditions:

- It should be NULL or
- It should match exactly the primary key value of some other table that it references

Dr. Codd's rules

Dr. E.F. Codd has made several important contributions to the early days of relational databases and has proposed the following 12 rules that a DBMS should follow in order to be considered fully relational (these original rules were updated and detailed in a later release):

1. Information should be represented as data stored in cells.
2. Each data item should be accessible using the following combination:

   table name

   primary key

   column name

3. NULLs should be used consistently for missing data and not contain any values. If a value is desired, such as for missing numeric or missing character values, then a default should be used.
4. An active, online data dictionary should be available and stored as relational tables accessible using standard data access language.
5. The data access language should be the only way of accessing the data in the DBMS.
6. Any view that can be updated should be updateable.
7. Set-level inserts, updates, and deletes should be supported.
8. Applications should be independent of the physical attributes of the data. For example, if a file representing a table is moved from one disk to another, it should not require a change in the application.
9. Applications should be independent of the logical attributes of the data. For example, if a table is split into two, there must be some way to still access the data and re-create the original values.
10. Integrity rules such as primary key constraints and foreign key constraints should be stored in the data dictionary.
11. It should be possible to distribute the database—both locally as well as on remote systems.
12. Any low-level access such as the backup or load utilities should not be able to bypass the regular security implemented for the database.

> **Note** The discussion in the rest of this chapter will be better understood if you have an Oracle8i database installed on your machine or if you have access to an Oracle database instance on another machine. Please refer to the Oracle installation manuals for your particular platform for specific installation instructions.

Oracle8i Architecture

The Oracle RDBMS architecture is comprised of two parts:

- **The Oracle instance**—This consists of the background processes (threads) and memory structures such as the shared global area (SGA) and program global area (PGA). A unique system identifier is used to identify each Oracle instance. We will be discussing each of these components in detail later.

- **The Oracle database**—This consists of the physical components such as data files, control files, redo log files, initialization files, and archive logs. It also consists of the logical components such as tables, constraints, procedures, views, and so forth. We will be discussing each of these components in detail later.

Running Oracle on Windows NT

On Windows NT, Oracle uses the Windows NT multithreaded model by running the Oracle server executable as a process and running the background processes as threads. As a result, when you run multiple instances of Oracle on Windows NT, there will be one server process for each instance.

While running Oracle on Windows NT, you might encounter a limitation in the number of concurrent users because Windows NT reserves 2GB of address space for each process, and system resources use 2GB (which is shared by all processes). Each Oracle instance (which runs as a process on Windows NT) therefore has 2GB of address space. Furthermore, for every thread, the stack consists of two components: the reserved space and the committed space. The number of concurrent connections is directly related to the stack space and the type of work performed by the threads. By default, each thread uses 1MB reserved space and Oracle on Windows NT is linked in the default way. Consequently, the number of threads that would concurrently run is limited.

Thread—The smallest entity of work that can be scheduled by the operating system.

While running Oracle8i on Windows NT you can increase the number of concurrent connections per Oracle instance by using one of the following methods:

- **Multi-Threaded Server (MTS)**—Allows many user threads to share very few server threads. Each client request goes through a dispatcher that redirects it to an available server thread. The server thread processes the request and sends the result back to the client via the dispatcher.

- **Connection Manager**—Concentrates multiple clients into a single multiplexed data connection. This technique is possible even if the clients use different protocols.

- **Connection pooling**—Places idle users in suspended mode and reassigns their physical connections until they become active again.

- **Orastack**—Is a utility provided for Windows NT that allows customers to change the amount of default reserved stack space used by each Oracle thread. This utility should be used carefully because it potentially can make the system unstable.

 Note   On Windows NT, Oracle instances run as services and can therefore interact with the operating system. This characteristic also enables Oracle databases to be started automatically without any users logging on to the system.

Background Processes and Threads

 **Note**   On Windows NT, Oracle background processes run as threads, which Windows NT uses for scheduling purposes. The fast context switching that can occur between threads can improve performance.

An Oracle instance consists of several required background processes and other optional processes. It also includes memory structures such as SGA. The processes that comprise an Oracle instance include

- **System Monitor (SMON)**—A required process responsible for performing instance recovery, coalescing free extents, and reclaiming space used by temporary segments.

- **Process Monitor (PMON)**—A required process responsible for performing process recovery for failed processes and release system resources held by these processes, rolling back aborted transactions, and restarting shared servers and dispatchers.

- **Database Writer (DBWR)**— A required process responsible for writing modified database buffers from the database buffer cache to the data files on disk, reducing disk I/O, improving the cache hit ratio by using a least recently used (LRU) algorithm to retain frequently accessed database blocks, and performing checkpoint.

- **Log Writer (LGWR)**

> **Note**
>
> Log Writer is a required process responsible for writing redo log buffers to redo log files when a commit is issued or as specified by the initialization parameters:
>
> - LOG_CHECKPOINT_INTERVAL—It sets the threshold for the number of redo log buffers that need to be filled, after which a checkpoint occurs.
> - LOG_CHECKPOINT_TIMEOUT—It specifies the amount of time that must elapse before a checkpoint occurs.

- **Recovery process (RECO)**—This is an optional process responsible for the recovery of failed distributed transactions. It resolves in-doubt transactions.
- **Archiver process (ARCH)**—This is an optional process responsible for the archiving of redo log files to archive logs on disk or tape.
- **Checkpoint process (CKPT)**—This is an optional process responsible for updating the data files and control files with the new log file control number. This process causes all the database files to be in sync with each other. In the absence of a CKPT process, this task is performed by the LGWR process.
- **Lock process (LCKn)**—This is an optional process that communicates with the distributed lock manager in a parallel server environment to maintain concurrency control.
- **Parallel query process (Qnnn)**—This is an optional process used during the execution of parallel operations.
- **Snapshot process (SNPn)**—This is an optional process used for refreshing snapshots.
- **Shadow process**—Whenever a user connects to the database, a shadow process is created for the user connection. This shadow process performs all the database tasks on behalf of the user connection.

The following is performed during a checkpoint:

- LGWR signals DBWR to write the modified database buffer blocks to the data files on disk.
- CKPT or LGWR updates the headers of all data files and control files to indicate that a checkpoint has occurred.

The following situations cause a checkpoint to automatically occur:

- A log switch
- An online backup
- The database is shut down
- A tablespace is taken offline
- As specified by the settings of LOG_CHECKPOINT_INTERVAL and LOG_CHECKPOINT_TIMEOUT initialization parameters

Oracle Instance Memory Structures

The Oracle instance comprises two important memory structures: SGA and PGA.

 The *shared global area* (SGA) consists of several components:

- A fixed part containing the internal Oracle structures.
- A variable part that contains the data dictionary cache and shared and private SQL areas. The shared SQL area (also referred to as the *library cache*) contains parsed SQL statements and their execution plan.

 The initialization parameter SHARED_POOL determines the size of the shared pool.

- A database buffer cache that contains the database buffers. Information that's read from or written to the database is stored in the database buffer cache.

 The DB_BLOCK_SIZE and DB_BLOCK_BUFFERS parameters determine the size of the database buffer cache.

- A redo log buffer that records all changes made to the database. It functions in a circular manner and is used during database recovery. The redo log buffer also keeps track of checkpoints that have occurred.

 The size of the redo log buffer is determined by the LOG_BUFFER initialization parameter.

The *program global area* (PGA) is a fixed size structure in memory that's created when a user connects to the database. It contains the user stack space and private SQL area. If Multi-Threaded Server is used, the PGA is part of the SGA.

Figure 1.1 shows the Oracle8i architecture.

Figure 1.1

Oracle8i architecture.

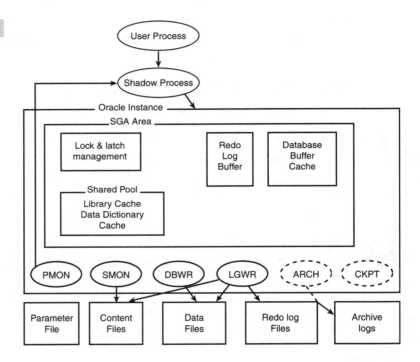

Physical Database Structure

The physical structure of an Oracle database consists of several file types: the initialization file, control files, redo logs, archive log files, and data files.

Initialization File

When the database starts up, it is initialized by using the parameters in the initialization parameter file (init*SID*.ora). This file is read only during database startup. In order for changes made to the initialization file to take effect, the database must be restarted.

The following sample initialization file shows you what it contains:

```
#Name of the database
db_name = test
#Name of the instance
```

```
instance_name = test
#Maximum number of database files
db_files = 2048
#Location of control files
control_files = ("c:\database\test\control01.ctl",
➥" c:\database\test \control02.ctl")
#Number of database blocks read for one I/O operation during a table scan
db_file_multiblock_read_count = 8
#Number of database buffers in the database buffer cache
db_block_buffers = 6400
#Size of the shared pool
shared_pool_size = 120000000
#Specifications for determining how often to perform a checkpoint
# Perform a checkpoint after 10000 database blocks have been read
log_checkpoint_interval = 10000
# Log_checkpoint_timeout not used
log_checkpoint_timeout = 0
#Number of processes
processes = 50
# Maximum number of parallel processes
parallel_max_servers = 5
#Size of the redo log buffer
log_buffer = 32768
# Limit of trace files generated
max_dump_file_size = 10240
#Dump destinations
background_dump_dest = c:\database\test\bdump
user_dump_dest = c:\database\test\udump
#Database block size
db_block_size = 8192
#Password file is shared
remote_login_passwordfile = shared
# Compatibility setting
compatible = 8.1.5.0.0
#Sort area size
sort_area_size = 100000
```

Control Files

The control file associated with a database contains pointers to the location of other files (such as data files and redo log files) that make up the database. Without a valid control file, the database won't know how to locate the data files and it is therefore very important that you mirror your control file.

The control file includes the following information:

- System change number (SCN)
- Location of data files
- Location of redo log files

- Database name
- Database size

Redo Logs

Redo logs record all the changes made to the database and the checkpoint information. Redo logs should be multiplexed, and the redo log groups should be placed on separate disks so that you have more than one copy in case there's a problem with one set of redo logs.

Archived Log Files

Redo logs are written in a circular fashion and unless they are archived, they eventually will be overwritten. Redo logs can be archived by running the database in the archive log mode. Running the database in the archive log mode copies the redo log files before they are overwritten. Archive log mode also allows you to make hot backups. *Hot backups* refers to the process of making backups with the database open. It is important to understand that if you are archiving the redo log files, the archive process should be fast; otherwise, the LGWR might have to wait for the archiving process to complete before proceeding—resulting in database activity stopping.

Data Files

The data files associated with a database contain data, including tables and indexes. One of the most important decisions made during the physical design of the database is to ensure that the data files are spread across all the available disks, ensuring that the tables and indexes are separate so that the I/O is balanced.

You should follow some naming conventions for your data files so that they can be easily managed. The following optimal flexible architecture (OFA) guidelines can be useful:

- It should be possible to distinguish data files from other files on the system.
- Files belonging to one database should be distinguished from files of other databases.
- Data files should be able to be associated with their tablespaces.

Logical Database Components

We have seen that the physical components of the database comprise various files. Logically, however, the database consists of data blocks, extents, segments, and tablespaces.

Data Blocks

An Oracle *database block* is a set of contiguous operating-system blocks. A *data block* is the smallest unit of data storage and can't span data files.

 **Note**   Each block in the database buffer is the size of a data block.

If you want to change the database block size of a database after it is created, you will have to re-create the database; otherwise, the database might become corrupt.

When choosing the size of a data block you should consider the type of database environment. For example, is it a DSS or OLTP environment? In a data warehousing environment, where you perform many long-running queries, use a large data block size. For an OLTP system, where you have a large number of small transactions, you will benefit by using a small data block size.

Extents

An *extent* is a collection of contiguous data blocks that can't span data files. Oracle allocates space in terms of extents. In other words, when a table, index, rollback segment, or temporary segment is created or needs more space, it is assigned a new extent.

When determining the size of an object such as a table or an index, it is very important to determine the storage parameters of the extents. The storage parameters that can be specified include the following:

- Size of the initial extent
- Size of subsequent extents
- Percentage by which subsequent extents are greater than the previous extents
- Maximum number of extents that can be created for the object

Segments

A *segment* is a chain of extents allocated for a specific database object such as a table, an index, a rollback segment, or a temporary segment. Segments can span data files because they are non-contiguous. Four segment types can be associated with an Oracle database:

- **Data segment**—Contains data and is associated with tables and clusters.
- **Index segment**—Contains indexes that can be used to improve database performance by eliminating full table scans and improves the database's performance.
- **Rollback segment**—Contains rollback information and is used during recovery to provide read consistency and to roll back uncommitted transactions.
- **Temporary segment**—Contains temporary objects used during operations such as joins and sorts.

Data and Index Segments

User-created objects such as tables and indexes are referred to as *data segments*. In addition to these, your database might have two other segment types—temporary segments and rollback segments. The temporary segment tablespace and rollback segment tablespace can be created by an administrator or a user with the appropriate privileges. These segments are referred to as system segments.

Tables

Tables are the database segments that hold data. They consist of one of more columns, with each column representing an attribute of the entity described by the table. Columns are assigned a name and datatype. Commonly used datatypes in Oracle8i are described in Table 1.4.

Table 1.4 Commonly Used Oracle8i Datatypes

Datatype	Description	Max Size
CHAR	Fixed-length character field, padded with trailing blanks	2000 bytes
VARCHAR2	Variable-length character field	4000 bytes
LONG	Variable-length character data	2GB
NUMBER	Variable-length numeric data	1×10^{-130} to 9.99×10^{125}
DATE	Data time values	Dec 31, 9999
RAW	Variable-length raw binary data	2000 bytes
LONG RAW	Variable-length raw binary data	2GB
ROWID	Row ID variable type	6 bytes

Information about tables and their columns can be obtained by querying the data dictionary views `dba_tables` and `dba_tab_columns`.

Indexes

Indexes are data segments that are used to speed up the retrieval of data from tables. They consist of one or more columns of a table and the `ROWID` for the corresponding column values.

Several types of indexes are available in Oracle:

- **B*-Tree index**—Uses a variation of standard tree traversal by guaranteeing that any leaf node can be reached in the same number of tree traversals. Essentially, the tree is balanced and contains sufficient empty space in the tree nodes to allow for expansion.
- **Cluster index**—Is built on the columns shared by tables in the cluster. Before any DML operations can be performed against the cluster, a cluster index must be created.
- **Bitmap index**—Creates a bitmap from the column values in the indexed table and stored in the index rather than the actual column values. Bitmap indexes result in more efficient usage of space compared to B*-Tree indexes. Bitmap indexes are ideal for columns where the number of unique column values is very small.

The data dictionary views `dba_indexes` and `dba_ind_columns` can be queried to obtain information about indexes in the database.

Table Clusters

A *table cluster* is a database object that physically stores groups of tables within the same data block. Usually you would place tables that are used together, such as those used during join operations, in a cluster. Table clusters can result in improved I/O performance when the tables comprising the cluster are used together.

Hash Clusters

Hash clusters are used to store table data by applying a hash function to the primary key values of the table. In order to retrieve data from this table, a hash function is applied to the key value being requested and the result is used to obtain the Oracle data block in the hash cluster.

Views

Views are database objects that can be used to simplify and customize the retrieval of information. Views are stored SQL statements and obtain their result from underlying base tables. Using views provides several advantages:

- **Security**—A view can be built on base tables such that it only displays information relevant to the user. For example, if the employee table contains employee details such as name, address, salary, and position. You can create different views for different employees so that some employees can obtain all the information from the employees table; while others can see only the names and positions of employees.
- **Hide distributed data**—A view can be based on remote database objects and thereby hide the details about the physical location of the tables.
- **Display derived values**—A view can be used to display information derived from base tables so that such calculated values are not stored in the base tables.

Packages, Procedures, and Functions

A *stored procedure* is a unit of code that performs some task. Arguments can be passed to a stored procedure and it can return values. A *stored function* is also a unit of code that performs some task. Arguments can be passed to a function but it returns only one value. A *package* is a collection of variables, functions, and procedures that are logically grouped together. Functions, procedures, and packages are stored in the data dictionary along with their source code.

The data dictionary views `dba_objects` and `dba_source` can be used to obtain information about functions, procedures, and packages.

Triggers

Triggers are database objects that are associated with tables. They are similar to stored procedures in that they are stored units of code that perform some task. They are different from stored procedures in that they are automatically fired when certain events occur. The event that can fire a trigger can be an insert, an update, a delete, or any combination of these actions on a table. Triggers can be fired for each row or statement. Generally, you would use a trigger to enforce a complex business rule or constraint that cannot be easily implemented by using other data integrity constraints.

The data dictionary view `dba_triggers` can be used to obtain information about triggers.

Sequences

Sequences are database objects that are commonly used to generate unique values such as surrogates for primary key columns. When creating a sequence you have to specify its starting value, increment, and maximum value.

1

Sequences are used by selecting the CURRVAL or NEXTVAL pseudocolumns from it. For example, if you have a sequence called project_seq

- Select project_seq.currval from dual. This returns the current value of the sequence.
- Select project_seq.nextval from dual. This returns the next value of the sequence and increments the current value of the sequence.

Information about sequences used in the database can be obtained by querying the `dba_sequences` data dictionary view.

Synonyms

Synonyms are database objects that are used as pointers to other database tables. When creating a synonym, you have to specify a synonym name and the object that it references. When a synonym is referenced in a SQL statement, Oracle automatically replaces the synonym name with the object it references. Synonyms can be either private or public. *Private synonyms* are created in a specific schema and are accessible only by that schema. *Public synonyms*, however, are owned by the PUBLIC schema and can be referenced by all database schemas.

The following order is used for resolving object names in a SQL statement:

1. First, a table or view with that name is checked for existence in the issuing user's schema. If a table or view with that name doesn't exist, step 2 is performed; otherwise, the table or view is used.
2. The existence of a private synonym with that name is checked. If one exists, it is used; otherwise, step 3 is performed.
3. The existence of a public synonym with that name is checked. If one exists, it is used; otherwise, an error "ORA-942: Object does not exist" is returned.

Information about synonyms can be obtained by querying the data dictionary view `dba_synonyms`.

Database Links

Database links are used in a distributed database environment to access remote database objects. A *database link* is a stored database definition of a connection to a remote database object.

Information about database links can be obtained by querying the data dictionary view `dba_db_links`.

Rollback Segments

Rollback segments are the database objects responsible for providing read-consistency. They store the before-image of the data that is changed by transactions but not yet committed. When a data change is made, the data is changed in the database buffer cache and the before-image is copied to the rollback segment. If another session requests this data, the information is obtained from the rollback segment (this is also referred to as consistent read). After the data is committed, the rollback segment entry is made invalid.

Each rollback segment consists of at least two extents. When a transaction starts, the user session obtains an exclusive lock on an available extent in an available rollback segment. When this extent becomes full, another extent is used until the rollback segment has no more extents left. New extents can be allocated as needed, with the maximum number set by the storage parameters for the rollback segment. When a rollback segment cannot extend because the maximum number of extents has been reached or because there is no more space then the transaction is rolled back and an error occurs.

Information about rollback segments can be obtained by querying the data dictionary view `dba_rollback_segs`.

 Note   Rollback segments can be shared by multiple transactions.

The Oracle Data Dictionary

The Oracle data dictionary is a repository of information about all the objects in the database. It also contains information about database security such as users, privileges, roles, auditing, and so on. The data dictionary is read-only, and you should not attempt to make direct modifications to it. The data dictionary contains four parts: internal tables (x$ tables), data dictionary tables, dynamic performance views (v$ views), and data dictionary views.

Internal Tables (x$ Tables)

x$ tables are the heart of the Oracle RDBMS and contain information required by the database to function. These x$ tables have cryptic names and are undocumented because you are not supposed to manipulate them directly. However, after you are comfortable with the Oracle RDBMS as a DBA, you will find a lot of valuable information in these x$ tables that won't be available anywhere else.

x$ tables contain several internal statistics and configuration information not available anywhere else.

Data dictionary tables obtain all their information from these x$ tables. In order to find out which x$ table supplies information to a particular data dictionary table, you can perform an auto trace on that data dictionary table. For example

1. Log in to SQL*PLUS as SYS (or an account that has been granted access to the x$ and v$ tables). The password for the SYS account is change_on_install.

2. At the SQL prompt, issue the command set autotrace on

    ```
    SQL> set autotrace on
    ```

3. Issue a query against the desired data dictionary table

    ```
    SQL> select * from v$sysstat where 0 = 1;
    no rows selected
    Execution Plan
    ----------------------------------------------------------
       0      SELECT STATEMENT Optimizer=CHOOSE
       1    0    FILTER
       2    1      FIXED TABLE (FULL) OF 'X$KSUSGSTA'


    Statistics
    ----------------------------------------------------------
             0   recursive calls
             0   db block gets
             0   consistent gets
             0   physical reads
             0   redo size
          1081   bytes sent via SQL*Net to client
           560   bytes received via SQL*Net from client
             3   SQL*Net roundtrips to/from client
             1   sorts (memory)
             0   sorts (disk)
             0   rows processed
    ```

As seen in the preceding, the X$KSUSGSTA table is used to obtain information displayed by the v$sysstat data dictionary table.

In order to be able to use the autotracing facility you might have to run the SQL script utlxplan.sql found in the $ORACLE_HOME/rdbms/admin directory.

Data Dictionary Tables

The *data dictionary tables* are a collection of tables that store information about the database objects such as tables, views, indexes, and so on. These tables are owned by SYS and are created during database creation by automatically running the SQL.BSQ script. These tables are easily identified by a trailing dollar sign at the end of their name—for example, tab$, seq$, and so on. Most of the information in the data dictionary tables can be viewed through the data dictionary views.

 **Note**   The SQL.BSQ script is located in the $ORACLE_HOME/dbs directory.

Dynamic Performance Views (V$ Views)

The dynamic performance views (V$ views) are a very powerful set of views that can be used by the DBAs. Database administrators often rely on these views to obtain performance and diagnostic information. These views contain runtime performance and statistic information on a large number of database activities. Information about these views can be obtained from the "Oracle Server Reference" manual that came with your Oracle software.

Dynamic performance views are public synonyms to actual V$ views that are owned by SYS. As a result, it is often necessary to reference or grant permissions on the base V$ views when writing stored procedures and functions. Generally these V$ views are based on internal tables, which have similar names but are prefixed with V_$.

Data Dictionary Views

Data dictionary views are built on X$ tables and data dictionary tables. End users and DBAs should normally use the data dictionary views to query the data dictionary. Data dictionary views are placed in three categories:

- **DBA_ views**—These views show information about all the objects in the database. For example, `dba_tables` shows information about all the tables in the database.

- **ALL_ views**—These views show information about all the objects in the database that can be accessed by the user querying the data dictionary view. For example, `all_tables` shows information about all the tables that can be accessed by the user querying `all_tables`.

- **USER_ views**—These views show information about all the objects in the database that are owned by the user querying the data dictionary view. For example, user_tables shows information about all the tables that are owned by the user querying all_tables. Some useful data dictionary views are shown in Table 1.5.

Table 1.5   Useful Data Dictionary Views

Data Dictionary View	Information It Contains
DBA_CATALOG	All the database tables, views, and sequences
DBA_CONSTRAINTS	Constraints on the database tables
DBA_INDEXES	All the indexes in the database
DBA_SEQUENCES	All the sequences in the database
DBA_TABLES	All the tables in the database
DBA_USERS	All the users of the database
DBA_VIEWS	All the views in the database
DBA_DATA_FILES	All the data files and tablespaces in the database
DBA_EXTENTS	All the database extents
DBA_ROLLBACK_SEGMENTS	Rollback segments
DBA_FREE_SPACE	Free space available in the database
V$SESSION	Current sessions running against the database
V$DATABASE	Database information such as database name, archive log mode, and so forth
V$LOCK	Locking information
V$PARAMETER	Database parameters in effect
V$LOGFILE	Redo log files

Let us consider some examples that demonstrate how to make use of the data dictionary. The following examples use SQL*PLUS. Connect to the database using the account system with the password manager:

1. Determine when a database is created and whether it's in archive log mode:

Input/Output

```
SVRMGR> select name, created, log_mode
from v$database;
NAME      CREATED    LOG_MODE
--------- ---------- -----------
ORCL      02-JUL-99 ARCHIVELOG
1 row selected.
```

2. Find out information about the rollback segments:

Input

```
Svrmgr> select segment_name, owner,
            Tablespace_name, status
        From dba_rollback_segs;
```

Output

```
SEGMENT_NAME          OWNER   TABLESPACE_NAME      STATUS
-------------------   ------  --------------------  ---------
SYSTEM                SYS     SYSTEM               ONLINE
RB0                   PUBLIC  RBS                  ONLINE
RB1                   PUBLIC  RBS                  ONLINE
RB2                   PUBLIC  RBS                  ONLINE
RB3                   PUBLIC  RBS                  ONLINE
5 rows selected.
```

3. Find information about the data files associated with the database:

Input

```
Svrmgr> select file_name, file_id, tablespace_name
            Status, autoextensible
        From dba_data_files;
```

Output

```
FILE_NAME                      FILE_ID  TABLESPACE_NAME  STATUS      AUT
----------------------------   -------  ---------------  ---------   ---
C:\ORANT\ORCL\SYSTEM01.DBF  1  SYSTEM                    AVAILABLE YES
C:\ORANT\ORCL\RBS01.DBF     2  RBS                       AVAILABLE YES
C:\ORANT\ORCL\USERS01.DBF   3  USERS                     AVAILABLE YES
C:\ORANT\ORCL\TEMP01.DBF    4  TEMP                      AVAILABLE YES
C:\ORANT\ORCL\INDX01.DBF    5  INDX                      AVAILABLE YES
5 rows selected.
```

4. Find the dump destinations and the maximum dump file size:

Input

```
SVRMGR> select name, value, description
        From v$parameter
        Where name like '%dump%';
```

Output

```
NAME                VALUE               DESCRIPTION
------------------  ------------------  ------------------------
background_dump_dest c:\orant\orcl\bdump Detached process dump directory
user_dump_dest      c:\orant\orcl\udump User process dump directory
max_dump_file_size  10240               Maximum size (blocks) of
                                        ➥dump file

3 rows selected.
```

> **Note**
>
> The alert log is in the location specified by the background_dump_dest, and the trace files generated by the user processes go in the location specified by the user_dump_dest.

Tablespaces

A *tablespace* is a set of segments.

> **Note**
>
> A tablespace can consist of one or more data files, but a data file is owned by only one tablespace.

Several types of tablespaces are allowed:

- **System tablespace**—It must be available all the time and is necessary for the database to be operational. The system tablespace contains the data dictionary, stored procedures, triggers, and system rollback segment.

- **Data tablespace**—It can be used to store user data in tables and indexes. User data tablespaces don't need to be online all the time for the database to be operational. However, they should be online in order to access the data contained in them.

- **Temporary tablespace**—It is used by operations, such as sorting and joins, that take up temporary space.

Managing Transactions

A *transaction* is the smallest unit of work. Either all the statements that are part of a transaction should be completely successful or none of them should be successful. It uses the concept of all-or-none. When a transaction completes, it is called *committed* and its changes are applied to the database. When a transaction doesn't complete successfully, it is rolled back. Rolling back a transaction undoes any modification that might have been made by the transaction to the database. Transactions are also used as a unit of recovery. A log is maintained in the database of all the transactions that have occurred against the database so that, if needed, transactions can be rolled back or rolled forward. *Rolling back* a transaction refers to the process of undoing it, whereas *rolling forward* refers to the process of redoing the transaction.

A transaction might need to be rolled forward if changes made by a committed transaction couldn't make it from the memory to the disk because of some hardware or software failure.

Locking is usually used as a concurrency control mechanism and provides multiuser access to the database. Generally speaking, the smaller the granularity of a lock the better it is for concurrency because it allows more users to simultaneously access the database. Row-level locking is the smallest unit of locking and is ideal for small transactions. Some DBMS also use block-level or even page-level locking.

Oracle uses row-level locking.

The Starter Database

During Oracle8i's installation, you can choose to install the starter database. This is just a sample database that you can work with to learn more about Oracle8i and practice. The starter database contains the following:

- User accounts

Account	Description
INTERNAL (password: ORACLE)	This isn't a true account, but an alias for the SYS account and SYSDBA privilege. In addition to administrative tasks, it allows you to perform database startup and shutdown.
SYS (password: change_on_install)	This DBA account has the following privileges: CONNECT, RESOURCE, DBA, AQ_ADMINISTRATOR_ROLE, AQ_USER_ROLE, DELETE_CATALOG_ROLE, EXECUTE_CATALOG_ROLE, EXP_FULL_DATABASE, IMP_FULL_DATABASE, RECOVERY_CATALOG_OWNER, SELECT_CATALOG_ROLE, SNMPAGENT, CTXADMIN, CTXAPP, and CTXUSER.

SYSTEM	This account has the DBA database role.
(password: manager)	

It is recommended that upon the installation of Oracle8i, you change the password of SYS and SYSTEM for security reasons.

User name SCOTT (password: tiger)	This user has CONNECT and RESOURCE privileges.
User name DEMO (password: demo)	This user has CONNECT and RESOURCE privileges.
DBSNMP (password: DBSNMP)	This account, used as the Oracle Enterprise Manager account, has the CONNECT, RESOURCE, and SNMPAGENT database privileges.
CTXSYS (password: ctxsys)	This account, used as the Context Administrator, has the CONNECT, RESOURCE, and DBA database privileges.

- Tablespaces

Tablespace	*Description*
System	Contains the data dictionary
User_data	Contains the application data
Temporary_data	Contains the temporary tables or indexes created during the operations that need temporary storage such as join and sort operations
Rollback_data	Contains the rollback segments

- Data files located in the ORACLE_HOME directory

Datafile	Location
SYS1ORCL.ORA	System tablespace
USR1ORCL.ORA	User_data tablespace
TMP1ORCL.ORA	Temporary_data tablespace
RBS1ORCl.ORA	Rollback_data tablespace

- The INITORCL.ORA initialization file in the %ORACLE_HOME%\ database directory
- The LOG1ORCL.ORA and LOG2ORCL.ORA redo logs in the % ORACLE_HOME%\database directory
- The CTL1ORCL.ORA control file in the %ORACLE_HOME%\database directory

Web-enabling Oracle Database Applications

Java is a very powerful language that's quickly gaining acceptance in the development community for deploying enterprise applications, and Oracle recognizes its importance. Java has several important features that make it so popular:

- It's an object-oriented language.
- It allows the development of applications using an open standard.
- It enables the development of portable applications.
- It allows the reuse of code by means of JavaBeans and Enterprise JavaBeans (EJB), resulting in improved productivity.
- It can execute in browsers, application servers, and databases.
- It allows applications to be deployed in two-tier and multi-tier configurations.

Oracle's Java Strategy

Oracle has implemented Java into Oracle8i by providing

- An enterprise-class Java server platform that allows fast access and manipulation for online transaction processing systems and decision support systems, support for a large number of concurrent users, high availability, and fast failover. It also integrates with other tools such as the Oracle Enterprise Manager. The biggest feature, however, is the integrated Java Virtual Machine.
- A set of Java tools that can be used to quickly develop efficient Java applications. These include

JDBC drivers that provide database connectivity from Java

A SQLJ translator, which allows the use of embedded SQL in Java

JDeveloper, an integrated development environment (IDE) that allows the development of Java programs and integrates JDBC and the SQLJ translator into a complete development environment

CORBA connectivity

Oracle Application Server

Support for JavaBeans and EJB

Figure 1.2 shows that Java is a key component of Oracle8i's Internet strategy.

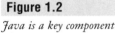
Figure 1.2

Java is a key component of Oracle's Internet strategy.

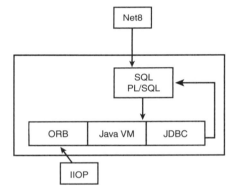

Working with Java Database Connectivity (JDBC)

JDBC is a standard set of classes that allow application developers to access and manipulate relational databases from within Java programs. Oracle provides two types of JDBC drivers, which you can use for different types of applications:

- **Thin JDBC driver**—This driver is written completely in Java and is only 300KB, making it ideal for Java applets that can be used with a browser. When you download an applet from an HTML page, the thin JDBC driver is downloaded with it. A direct Net8 connection is established between the applet and database. Scalability is provided with the use of Net8 connection manager.

- **JDBC/OCI driver**—This driver makes use of Oracle client libraries such as OCILIB, CORE, and Net8 to provide OCI calls to access the database. You have to perform client installation of the JDBC/OCI driver because it is not downloadable. It can be used for client/server Java applications, as well as middle-tier Java applications running in a Java application server.

> **Note**
>
> Irrespective of which driver you use, the Java code you write to access Oracle is the same. The particular driver used only affects the connect string.

The JDBC drivers provided by Oracle have several important features:

- Oracle7 and Oracle8 object-relational data types are supported.
- Manipulation of LOB data is supported.
- Performance enhancement features such as array interface, prefetching, and batch SQL statement execution are provided.
- PL/SQL and Java stored procedures can be accessed.
- All Oracle character sets are supported.

Using SQLJ to Embed SQL in Java

SQLJ enables developers to write efficient and compact programs. SQLJ is built on top of JDBC and enables application developers to embed SQL statements in Java programs. A preprocessor is used to translate SQLJ to Java code that makes JDBC calls to the database. Oracle's JDeveloper, which is a standard Java development tool, can be used to develop and debug SQLJ programs. Use of SQLJ improves the productivity and manageability of Java code for several reasons:

- It provides code that's significantly compact compared to JDBC.
- Typed cursors enable the use of strong-typed queries.
- SQL statements are checked at compile-time, allowing for early detection of errors.

Listings 1.1 and 1.2 show a JDBC program and its equivalent SQLJ program. These examples demonstrate that SQLJ programs are significantly compact compared to JDBC programs. At this stage you might not understand all the code listings, but there is no need to worry about it because we will be discussing them in a lot more detail in subsequent chapters.

Listing 1.1   A Sample JDBC Program

```
Java.sql.CallableStatement stmt;
Connection conn;
ResultSet res;

/* Declare the objects for a callable statement,
connection, and the result set*/

Conn = DriverManager.getConnection("jdbc:default");
```

```
/* Initialize the connection object with the default connection */
Stmt = conn.prepareStatement
("SELECT empno, ename FROM emp WHERE sal > ? AND deptno = ?");

/* Prepare the statement to execute */

Stmt.setString(1,sal_p);
Stmt.setInteger(2,deptno_p);

/* Use positional parameters to set the variables*/

Res = stmt.executeQuery();

/* Execute the query and store the results in the result set */
```

Listing 1.2   Equivalent SQLJ Program

```
ResultSet res;

/* Define an object to store the result set */

#sql res = (SELECT empno, ename FROM emp
        WHERE sal > :sal_p AND deptno = :deptno_p);

/* Pass the program through the SQLJ translator and execute the program.
The result set is stored in "res" */
```

 **Note**   A SQLJ translator is embedded in Oracle8i's Java virtual machine.

Oracle's Java Virtual Machine

Oracle's Java Virtual Machine (JVM) provides high performance and scalability while running Java applications. The components of the Java Virtual Machine are shown in Figure 1.3. Several important features include:

- 100% JDK 1.1.6 compliant.
- Support for shared Java byte codes and lightweight Java threads.
- Provides a memory manager and garbage collector that optimizes the use of the SGA and the operating system's virtual memory manager.
- Able to store Java classes in the database as database library units.
- Provides support for both JDBC driver and SQLJ translator.
- Provides the NCOMP Java compiler to translate Java byte code to the more efficient C executables.
- Standard Java libraries such as Java.lang, Java.io, and Java.util are supported.

- Allows the use of Java stored procedures and triggers.
- Provides utilities to load and unload Java programs in the database.
- Provides a CORBA 2.0–compliant ORB (Object Request Broker).
- Allows the use of Enterprise JavaBeans (EJB 1.0 compliant).
- Efficiently makes use of the Oracle Multi-Threaded Server (MTS). The Net8 Connection Manager can multiplex both CORBA/IIOP connections as well as Net8 connections.
- Supports efficient load balancing on SMP and MPP architectures.
- Integrated with the Oracle Enterprise Manager.
- Existing database security mechanisms, such as roles and grants for PL/SQL, also can be used with Java stored procedures. In addition, it allows the use of invoker rights.

Figure 1.3

Components of Oracle's Java Virtual Machine.

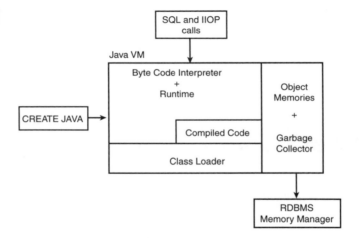

Enterprise JavaBeans

A component-based model can be used for implementing Java systems. This is made possible with the help of Enterprise JavaBeans (EJBs). EJBs offer several advantages:

- They are simple to program because they use a high level of abstraction.
- They can be completely developed in Java.
- They are compatible with CORBA, D/COM, and so on.
- Transactional applications can be used as modular components.
- They can be deployed using execution containers such as databases, Transaction Processing monitors, and application servers.

CORBA

A CORBA 2.0–compliant Object Request Broker (ORB) provided with Oracle8i allows applications to access Java stored procedures and EJBs through the IIOP protocol. Also, Java applications can be written to call out of the database and communicate with other ORBs through IIOP.

Java Stored Procedures

Java database applications can be built by using three methods:

- Writing Java stored procedures and triggers
- Implementing CORBA servers in the database
- Developing Enterprise JavaBeans

Oracle8i enables you to write stored procedures using PL/SQL and Java. The traditional method of writing stored procedures is to use PL/SQL because it is seamless with SQL. However, using Java provides an open, general-purpose platform to develop and deploy applications.

OLTP applications can benefit tremendously with the use of Java stored procedures:

- Result sets can be processed on the database server and only the results are sent across the network. This allows network traffic to be reduced.
- A variety of configurations such as client/server and multi-tier configuration are supported.
- Use of Java in the development of stored procedures enables them to be portable because they result in an ANSI/ISO-compliant standard environment.
- Use of SQLJ enables the embedding of SQL in Java.
- Business rules can be enforced centrally and by allowing Java stored procedures to be replicated between, say, the headquarters and the branch offices.
- Java stored procedures can be replicated between Oracle8i servers and from Oracle8i servers to mobile clients by using Oracle Lite.

Several simple steps are used to develop Java stored procedures:

1. Develop a Java program that you want to make a stored procedure. This can be done using any standard Java development tool—including JDeveloper, which is provided by Oracle.
2. Load the Java program into Oracle8i's JVM. Java source text can be loaded as standard Java .class files or as Java .jar files.
3. Register the Java program with SQL by exposing the top-level entry point. These exposed entry points are the only calls that SQL can make to this Java program.

4. Grant appropriate rights to the users, allowing them to call and run this procedure.

5. The Java stored procedure can now be called from SQL DML, PL/SQL, or triggers.

The standards compliance for Java stored procedures in Oracle8i provides the following specifications:

Part 0   SQLJ specification. This allows you to develop efficient applications by embedding SQL statements in Java programs.

Part 1   Java stored procedure specification. This provides standard DDL extensions to publish or register Java programs with SQL, thereby allowing Java Stored Procedures to be callable from SQL. In addition, extensions to standard DML are provided so that Java can be called from SQL.

Introducing the Project

Every project is the result of a vision. A group of people sit down and think about a very cool idea. Usually there is only one individual who is a true visionary and the others help in conforming or disputing the issues involved in making it a reality. Most of the time, however, the requirements of the project are not crystal clear. A core set of requirements are known before the project starts. Changes are made to this set of requirements, new requirements are added, and so on as the project progresses. This book describes the requirements, analysis, design, and implementation of an Online Coffee Shop using Oracle8i and its Java features.

Online Coffee Shop—The Vision

A small coffee shop—JavaStop—has gained tremendous popularity in your neighborhood. The owner desires to go global and sell the popular brands of coffee to customers all over the world. The shop has made arrangements with a reliable courier service that will help them in transporting the orders to customers efficiently. All they need is a user-friendly way in which customers can place their orders. The coffee shop, being in its early stages of growth, has another set of important requirements—to keep track of how the various brands of coffee are selling, the most popular brands, and their biggest customers.

Mr. Bean (the owner of JavaStop) has determined that the best way to make this vision a reality is to develop a Web-based application that can serve as an order-entry system.

Requirements Analysis

The first phase of the project consists of an analysis of the core requirements of the project. Oracle8i is a very popular e-commerce database and we will use it for our project. The requirements analysis begins with understanding the domain of our problem. In this project, it happens to be an order-entry system where the orders are placed for a specific product, coffee. Customers would place their orders using the Internet and this information would be placed in an Oracle8i database. Java—the popular Web development language—will be used for implementing the necessary reporting and other functionality desired from the database. Issues might arise such as security and concurrent access to the Web site; however, we will hold on to these issues for now. We will discuss them in a later phase of the project in another chapter. For now we are simply focused on getting the core requirements finalized.

After long hours of discussion with everyone in the company related to the project, the following requirements have been agreed upon by everyone:

- Store, maintain, and retrieve information about all the products and their brands
- Store, maintain, and retrieve information about all the customers
- Store, maintain, and retrieve information about all the orders
- Obtain a list of the top ten customers based on the dollar value of their orders
- Obtain a list of the top five popular brands of coffee
- Obtain a list of customers by country
- Obtain a list of customers by states within the USA
- Obtain a list of orders by month
- Provide a high level of security for transactions
- Allow for at least 50 customers to place orders concurrently
- Enable customers to use any Web browser for accessing the wWeb site—no specific requirements should be place on the client side

Next Steps

After knowing these core requirements we can now proceed to designing and implementing the database using Oracle8i. In Chapters 2, "Creating and Populating the JavaStop Database," and 3, "Manipulating the JavaStop Oracle Database Using SQL," we will be working more with the database aspects of the project: creating the database objects (tables, indexes, and so on), populating the database, and using SQL to manipulate the data. After Chapter 3 we will be making use of Java and the Internet capabilities of Oracle8i to Web-enable our database.

In this chapter

- *Making Use of Java as a Strategic Component*
- *Issues with Web-enabling JavaStop*
- *Tasks Prior to Database Creation*
- *Choosing Initialization Parameters for JSTP*
- *Populating the Database Using Oracle Utilities*
- *Working with Export/Import Utilities*

Chapter 2

Creating and Populating the JavaStop Database

By now you should have gained enough information about the Oracle environment and the project requirements. Now is the time to create the *database* that will be used to store all the data related to the project.

Database—A collection of data organized so that its contents can be easily accessed, updated, and managed.

The following are general steps for creating an Oracle database, all of which will be performed while we create our database. We will call our database JSTP for the purpose of this project.

1. Create the init*SID*.ora parameter file.
2. Create an *OFA*-compliant directory structure.

OFA—Optimal Flexible Architecture. It is a recommended design strategy used by Oracle for placement of database files so that they can be easily managed.

3. Choose a method of database creation and an operating system platform.
4. Create the database instance/service.
5. Create the database, using the desired method.
6. Run post-database creation scripts.
7. Create the supporting database objects.
8. Secure the default accounts.
9. Update any relevant configuration files.

Making Use of Java as a Strategic Component

Java is rapidly gaining popularity for developing enterprise-level Internet, *intranet*, and *extranet* applications. Java will form a strategic part of our project strategy.

 Intranet—A private network that is contained within an enterprise. The main purpose of an intranet is to share company information and resources among employees.

 Extranet—A private network that uses Internet protocols and public telecommunication systems to share information between vendors, suppliers, customers, and other businesses. It can be viewed as part of a company's intranet that is extended to users outside the company.

Many people have the misconception that Java is suitable only for developing cool Web pages. Even though Java is useful for developing client-side components, it is equally useful for server-side and distributed computing. We also can use JDBC for connectivity and EJB for reusable and portable components. In Chapter 1, "Introduction to the Internet Capabilities of Oracle8i," we have seen the Java features available in Oracle8i. Figure 2.1 shows how we will be using Java in our project.

Figure 2.1

Using Java for Web-enabling JavaStop.

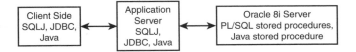

As seen in Figure 2.1, we will use Java as follows:

- JDBC/SQLJ on the client side.
- SQL execution only on the server side.
- PL/SQL and Java stored procedures on the server. Also, methods of Oracle8 data types and object type bodies can be implemented using Java.
- Communication protocols such as IIOP.

Using Oracle8i, the Oracle application server, and Java provides us with improved performance and scalability because of the following features:

- Highly scalable cartridge architecture
- Connection pooling, multiplexing, and multithreaded server architecture
- Dynamic load balancing
- Highly configurable Oracle8i memory architecture

Dedication

This book is dedicated to my father.

Acknowledgments

Thanks to my wife, Komal, for her undying support and my son, Varun, for his smiles and showing me what really matters.

I would also like to thank the wonderful and always supportive staff at Macmillan—Michelle, Tracy, Bryan, Pamela, Megan, Cindy, Eric, Matt, Ben, Dan, and everyone else that I forgot to mention. It is a pleasure working with you all.

A special thanks to Jesse Liberty for the great idea of the *From Scratch* series and allowing me to contribute to this unique effort.

- Excellent IDE, namely, JDeveloper for hiding the complexity of the development process
- 100% JDBC-compliant Java Virtual Machine

Designing and Building the Application

It is common during the designing phase to decide a lot of things but not record half of them. Designing includes many important aspects:

- **Developing a logical data model**—This is probably the most important part of the designing phase. No matter how small the project, an *entity-relationship diagram* should be created using a tool such as the Entity-Relationship diagrammer in Designer/2000 or LogicWorks's ERwin. These tools can help you create the logical model, generate the database, and document the data being stored in the database.

ER (Entity-Relationship) diagram—A diagram that provides a logical model of the database. It shows the various database entities and how they relate to each other.

- **Choosing a development tool**—Usually this is done by considering the various client machines and platforms that will be used. Java is ideal for our purpose because of its platform independence.

- **Implementing the functionality in stages**—It is important to have various "releases" of your product so that users can have a preview of it, as well as make suggestions about whether it has the features that they are expecting. The designing phase should consider this sequential development and identify the core objects.

- **Using reusable components**—Identify existing components that you will be able to use and also identify components in your project that you might be able to use later.

- **Using a configuration management tool**—A configuration management tool should be used to perform version control and a backup/recovery strategy should be decided on.

- **Identifying users and their roles**

- **Choosing a consistent user interface**

- **Determining a testing plan**

- **Implementing a diagnostic plan for troubleshooting the application**

Database table—An entity consisting of rows and columns that will contain data. Each column represents an attribute of the object being defined and each row represents a record.

Designing the JavaStop Database

The requirements of JavaStop described in Chapter 1 show that we will have in our database the following basic *tables* to keep track of our information:

- **Products**—This table will keep track of all the products sold by JavaStop. Information stored in this table includes

  `product_id` specifies a unique ID for each product and serves as the primary key for this table.

  `Description` specifies the details of each product.

- **Price**—This table will store the pricing information about each product. We might be giving special discounts for important customers and therefore the pricing information should be both the list price as well as the special price. Information stored in this table includes

  `product_id` refers to the product_id column of the products table. It acts as the foreign key for this table.

  `list_price` specifies the list price of the product.

  `min_price` specifies the minimum or the special price of each product.

  `start_date` specifies the start date for the special price.

  `end_date` specifies the end date for the special price.

  For each product, there can be one or more records in the price table because the product might have different prices at different dates.

- **Customers**—This table will keep track of the customers of JavaStop. Information stored includes

  `customer_id` specifies a unique ID for each customer and acts as the primary key for this table.

  `name`

  `address`

  `city`

  `state`

  `country`

  `zip_code`

  `area_code`

  `phone_number`

  `comments` specifies particular customer needs, characteristics, and so on.

Foreword

Welcome to *Jesse Liberty's Programming from Scratch* series. I created this series because I believe that traditional primers do not meet the needs of every student. A typical introductory computer programming book teaches a series of skills in logical order and then, when you have mastered a topic, the book endeavors to show how the skills might be applied. This approach works very well for many people, but not for everyone.

I've taught programming to over 10,000 students: in small groups, in large groups, and through the Internet. Many students have told me that they wish they could just sit down at the computer with an expert and work on a program together. Rather than being taught each skill step-by-step in a vacuum, they'd like to create a product and learn the necessary skills as they go.

From this idea was born the *Programming from Scratch* series. In each of these books, an industry expert will guide you through the design and implementation of a complex program, starting from scratch and teaching you the necessary skills as you go.

You might want to make a *From Scratch* book the first book you read on a subject, or you might prefer to read a more traditional primer first and then use one of these books as supplemental reading. Either approach can work: Which is better depends on your personal learning style.

All the *From Scratch* series books share a common commitment to showing you the entire development process, from the initial concept through implementation. We do not assume you know anything about the subject: *From Scratch* means from the very beginning, with no prior assumptions.

Although I didn't write every book in the series, as series editor I have a powerful sense of personal responsibility for each one. I provide supporting material and a discussion group on my Web site (www.libertyassociates.com), and I encourage you to write to me at jliberty@libertyassociates.com if you have questions or concerns.

Thank you for considering this book.

Jesse Liberty

Jesse Liberty

From Scratch Series Editor

About the Author

Megh Thakkar currently works as a senior software engineer at Quest Software. Before this, he worked at Oracle Corporation as a Technical Specialist. Megh has several industry vendor certifications, including OCP, MCSE, Novell Certified ECNE, SCO UNIX ACE, and Lotus Certified Notes Consultant. He is a regular presenter at Oracle OpenWorld and various Oracle user groups all over the world. He is the author of *Sams Teach Yourself Oracle8i on Windows NT in 24 Hours* and has co-authored several books, including *Special Edition Using Oracle8/8i*, *Oracle8 Server Unleashed*, *C++ Unleashed*, *COBOL Unleashed*, *Oracle Certified DBA*, and *Using Oracle8*. Megh is a renowned Oracle specialist and has performed Oracle development, consulting, support, and DBA functions all over the world during the past nine years.

- **Orders**—This table is used to store orders placed by customers. Information stored includes

  `order_id` is a unique ID for an order and serves as the primary key for this table.

  `order_date` specifies the date when the order was placed.

  `customer_id` refers to the `customer_id` column of the customers table.

  `ship_date` specifies the date when the order was filled.

  `total` specifies the total dollar value of the order placed.

  Each customer can place multiple orders.

- **Items**—This table specifies details of products ordered. Information stored includes

  `order_id` refers to the `order_id` column of the orders table.

  `item_id` is the ID of each item in a particular order.

  `product_id` refers to the `product_id` column of the products table.

  `actual_price` specifies the actual price paid by the customer for the particular product.

  `quantity` specifies the quantity of the product ordered.

  `total` specifies the total dollar amount of the item ordered.

The entity-relationship diagram for the JSTP database is shown in Figure 2.2.

Figure 2.2

Entity-relationship diagram for the JSTP database

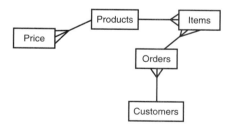

Relationships in JavaStop

Several types of relationships are possible between database tables:

- **One-to-one**—In a one-to-one relationship, each record of one table is related to exactly one record of the other table. This relationship is commonly used to split information in a large table into two or more tables. The splitting is a vertical splitting.

- **One-to-many**—In a one-to-many relationship, a record in one table is related to one or more records in another table. An example of this is the relationship between orders and the items table. For each order, there can be one of more items ordered.

- **Many-to-many relationship**—In a many-to-many relationship, a record in table X is related to one or more records in table Y. Likewise, a record in table Y is related to one or more records in table X. Normally, a many-to-many relationship is implemented with the help of a third table that has the columns from both tables in order to implement the relationship. The third table references the primary keys of both tables.

Issues with Web-enabling JavaStop

During the process of Web-enabling JavaStop, we face several issues similar to the ones experienced when Web-enabling any application. These issues include how we would achieve the following in our environment:

- **Develop applications for the Web**—This issue involves choosing the IDE for development and the database technology. We have chosen Oracle8i and JDeveloper for Java development, because of reasons mentioned earlier.

- **Performance.**

- **Security.**

- **Availability.**

- **Concurrency.**

- **Scalability.**

- **Deployment of applications.**

- **Communication protocols to use.**

These and other issues will be discussed throughout this book.

Tasks Prior to Database Creation

Before creating an Oracle database, you must configure the operating system.

In addition to configuring the operating system, you will have to make some decisions regarding the database usage and configuration. These decisions should include the following:

- **Database sizing**—In order to obtain an optimally tuned database, it is important to set the initialization parameters appropriately.

- **MTS configuration**—The Multithreaded Server can be used in Oracle databases to increase the number of concurrent connections to the database. This feature can help increase concurrency in our project.

- **Set environment variables**—The `ORACLE_SID`, `ORACLE_HOME`, and `path` variables should be set to the correct values so that the correct instance can be accessed. This will become important if your machine is hosting multiple database instances.

> If you are planning to use Windows NT, the settings of `ORACLE_SID` and `ORACLE_HOME` should be done in the *Registry*.

Windows NT Registry—A hierarchical structure that is used to store all the configuration information.

- **Create an OFA-compliant directory structure**—Optimal Flexible Architecture (OFA) is the Oracle standard for creating and configuring your Oracle environment. It is a set of rules and guidelines, the use of which can improve the manageability of your database. Cary Millsap of Oracle Corporation wrote the OFA standard in the early 1990s. A copy of his white paper can be obtained from Oracle Metalink. Listings 2.1 and 2.2 show a sample OFA implementation that can be used for JSTP.

- **Back up all existing databases**—It is recommended that you make a complete backup of all your existing databases to protect them against accidental modifications or deletions of existing files during the creation of the new database.

- **Mirroring control and redo log files**—The control and redo log files are important components of your database and you should mirror these files. Keep at least two copies of the control file on different physical devices. The redo log files should be multiplexed, and the redo log groups should be placed on different physical devices. The directory choices made here will be reflected in the initialization file.

Oracle extent—A collection of contiguous data blocks.

Segment—A chain of extents allocated for a specific database object such as a table, index, and so on.

Tablespace—A set of segments.

- **Organize the database contents in multiple *tablespaces***—Proper distribution of database objects will help in minimizing contention. Table 2.1 shows several tablespaces that you should create (other than the system tablespace).

Table 2.1   Minimize Contention by Separating Database Objects

Tablespace	Contents
TEMP	Temporary segments
RBS	Rollback segments
APPS_DATA	Production data
APPS_IDX	Indexes

Listing 2.1   UNIX Sample OFA Implementation for JSTP

```
/                          Root Directory
    u01                        u01 Mount Point
app                     Application directory
oracle                  Oracle Application directory
            admin           Administrative directory
            JSTP             JSTP database directory
             Pfile           Initialization parameter file
             Bdump           Background dump files
             Udump           User dump files
             Cdump           Core files
             Create           Database creation scripts
             Sql               SQL scripts
            TEST             Test database directory
            [...]           Same directory structure as JSTP
            oradata     Oracle database files
            JSTP     JSTP database files
            TEST     TEST database files
        U02                      u02 mount point
            Oradata     Oracle database files
    JSTP     JSTP database files
            TEST     TEST database files
```

Listing 2.2   Windows NT Sample OFA Implementation for JSTP

```
C:                   Drive specification
        Oracle          Oracle software directory
        Home            Oracle home directory
         [...]             Contents of ORACLE_HOME
        oradata            Oracle database files
        JSTP             JSTP database files
        TEST             TEST database files
        admin        Administrative directory
        JSTP             JSTP database directory
         Pfile           Initialization parameter file
         Bdump           Background dump files
         Udump           User dump files
         Cdump           Core files
         Create           Database creation scripts
         Sql               SQL scripts
```

```
         TEST              Test database directory
         [...]             Same directory structure as JSTP
  D:                       Drive specification
     Oracle                Oracle software directory
        oradata               Oracle database files
        JSTP                  JSTP database files
        TEST                  TEST database files
```

Choosing Initialization Parameters for JSTP

The initialization file (init*JSTP*.ora) should be created. It will provide the parameters used during database startup. If you have created the sample database ORCL during installation then you should have a file called initorcl.ora that can be edited as desired and saved as initJSTP.ora. However, if you chose not to create ORCL during installation then you can get initorcl.ora from the Oracle CD-ROM. In any case, the *initialization file* can be edited using any text editor, such as Notepad (for Windows NT) or vi (for UNIX).

Initialization file—A file containing database configuration parameters that are read when the database instance starts up.

> **Note**
>
> The default initialization parameters aren't ideal for most systems, and therefore you should customize these parameters with your database environment in mind.

Table 2.2 shows some initialization parameters that should be modified for our project.

Table 2.2   Initialization Parameters That You Should Modify for JSTP

Parameter	Description
DB_NAME	Database identifier. This should be unique for every database, and if you try to mount two databases with the same name, you will get the error ORA-01102: cannot mount database in EXCLUSIVE mode during the second mount. Set this to JSTP.
CONTROL_FILES	Full path of the control files. It is important to change this setting when reusing another existing initSID.ora file. Otherwise, other database files might get overwritten, making them unusable.
DB_BLOCK_SIZE	Oracle database block size in bytes. The JSTP database is a hybrid environment, and therefore a good value to start with is 8KB.

continues

Table 2.2   Continued

Parameter	Description
SHARED_POOL_SIZE	Shared pool size in bytes. In our project a large shared pool will help performance because of the number of concurrent connections that are expected. A starting value of 15MB should be sufficient.
BACKGROUND_DUMP_DEST	Location of background trace files.
USER_DUMP_DEST	Location of user trace files.
DB_BLOCK_BUFFERS	Number of buffers in the database buffer cache. This will determine the size of the buffer cache and eventually the buffer cache hit ratio. A starting value of 8192 should be sufficient.
COMPATIBLE	Specifies the server version with which this instance is compatible. Set this to 8.1.5.0.0.
IFILE	This is an optional parameter that specifies another parameter file that has additional parameters used during startup.
MAX_DUMP_FILE_SIZE	Maximum size (in OS blocks) allowed for trace files. It is a good idea to limit the size of these files in order to prevent storage problems. We could set this to 5120. Because our db_block_size is 8KB, this will limit the trace files to 5120×8KB.
PROCESSES	Maximum number of OS processes that can simultaneously connect to this instance. We will be allowing about 50 concurrent connections. A good starting value should be twice the number of concurrent connections, therefore set this to 100.
ROLLBACK_SEGMENTS	The rollback segments allocated to this instance. It is recommended that you create private rollback segments to avoid contention for the system rollback segment. We will create two rollback segments for JSTP: r01 and r02.
LOG_BUFFER	Size of the redo log buffer (in bytes). A good starting value is 65536.
LOG_ARCHIVE_START	Enables archiving if the database is in ARCHIVELOG mode. Set this to true. Archiving of the database will allow us to take hot backups.
LOG_ARCHIVE_FORMAT	Filename format to be used by default for archived logs. This can be set to "%%jstp%%T%TS%S.ARC".
LOG_ARCHIVE_DEST	Location of archived redo log files.
LICENSE_MAX_SESSIONS	Maximum number of concurrent sessions that can be used against the instance. Set this to 50.
Java_pool_size	It specifies the size in bytes of the java pool. It can be set to 20MB because our Java stored procedures will be using it.

The following is a sample init.ora file for JSTP on Windows NT:

```
db_name = JSTP
db_domain = WORLD
db_files = 1020
control_files = (C:\oracle\oradata\JSTP\ctl1JSTP.ora,
➡C:\oracle\oradata\JSTP\ctl2JSTP.ora)
db_file_multiblock_read_count = 16
db_block_buffers = 8192
shared_pool_size = 15000000
log_checkpoint_interval = 4000
processes = 100
dml_locks = 200
log_buffer = 65536
background_dump_dest = C:\oracle\admin\jstp\bdump
user_dump_dest = C:\oracle\admin\jstp\udump
db_block_size = 8192
compatible = 8.1.5.0.0
sort_area_size = 65536
log_checkpoint_timeout = 0
remote_login_passwordfile = shared
max_dump_file_size = 5120
java_pool_size = 20971520
license_max_sessions = 50
log_archive_start = true
log_archive_dest_1 = "location=D:\Oracle\oradata\jstp\archive"
log_archive_format = "%%jstp%%T%TS%S.ARC"
rollback_segments = (r01, r02)
```

Organizing Database Objects

Database objects should be grouped and separated according to their usage and fragmentation propensity. This will minimize contention and fragmentation.

Table 2.3 shows the amount of fragmentation expected for various types of objects.

Table 2.3   Amount of Fragmentation Expected by Segment Type

Segment Type	Expected Fragmentation
Data dictionary	Zero
Rollback segments	Medium
Temporary segments	High
Application data	Low

The following guidelines can be used for grouping objects. These object groups should be placed on different disks as well as different tablespaces:

- **Segments with different backup needs**—In JSTP, the products and customers table are changed less frequently compared to the orders and items tables and would consequently be backed up less frequently.

- **Segments with different security needs**—Information about customers is more secure than information about products.

- **Segments belonging to different projects**—The customers table may be shared by different projects such as the marketing staff as well as the order-entry system.

- **Separating large segments from smaller segments**—The orders and items tables would be growing at a much faster rate compared to the products table.

- **Rollback segments.**

- **Temporary segments.**

- **Data segments.**

- **Index segments.**

> Choose the character set during database creation.
>
> The database character set that you choose should be the same as or a superset of all the character sets that would be used to access the database. It is important to make this decision early because changes to the character set after database creation will require database re-creation.

Setting Environment Variables

Several environment variables should be set so that the database instance runs properly:

- ORACLE_SID specifies the default instance to connect to. Set this to JSTP.

- ORACLE_HOME specifies the full pathname of the Oracle system home directory. Set this to the directory in which the Oracle software is installed. This is a mandatory configuration parameter and is used by many Oracle executables to locate shared code, configuration files, and so on.

- PATH specifies the search path and should include the ORACLE_HOME directory.

- ORA_NLS specifies the location of the language object files. If the database is started with languages and character sets other than the database defaults, and ORA_NLS isn't set properly, they won't be recognized. This is important when working with multiple languages and character sets.

Methods for Database Creation

The database can be created using a variety of methods:

- **Using the Oracle Installer**—The Oracle Installer enables you to create a seed database that can be used as a template for creating other databases.

- **Using the Database Configuration Assistant**—A GUI tool that simplifies the creation of Oracle databases.

how tōō prō nouns' it	GUI is pronounced as GOO-E.

- **Using database creation scripts**—Oracle provides database creation scripts— namely, `Build_all.sql` and `Build_db.sql`. You can modify these scripts as desired to customize the creation of your database. After making the desired changes, run the scripts to create your database. Listings 2.3, 2.4, and 2.5 show a script-based approach to database creation.

- **Using the CREATE DATABASE command**—The CREATE DATABASE command can be manually run to create the database (refer to the Oracle SQL reference manual for the complete syntax). This method is the most flexible of all the methods and we will use it to create JSTP. The basic syntax of this command is shown in the following and Table 2.4 describes its parameters.

```
CREATE DATABASE database
    [CONTROLFILE [REUSE]]
    [LOGFILE filespec[, ...]]
    MAXLOGFILES integer
    MAXLOGMEMBERS integer
    MAXLOGHISTORY integer
    DATAFILE filespec[, ...]
    MAXDATAFILES integer
    MAXINSTANCES integer
        ARCHIVELOG¦NOARCHIVELOG
    EXCLUSIVE
    CHARACTERSET charset
```

Table 2.4 CREATE DATABASE **Parameters**

Parameter	Description
database	Name of the database to create.
CONTROLFILE	Location of control files.
REUSE	Allows the reuse of existing control files.

continues

Table 2.4   Continued

Parameter	Description
LOGFILE	Specifies one or more redo log file groups. Redo log file groups containing one or more redo log file members are specified by each *filespec*. By default, two redo log file groups are created.
MAXLOGFILES	Specifies the maximum number of redo log file groups that can be created for this database.
MAXLOGMEMBERS	Specifies the maximum number of members for a redo log file group.
MAXLOGHISTORY	Specifies the maximum number of archived redo log files for automatic media recovery. This parameter is commonly used with the PARALLEL SERVER option.
DATAFILE	Specifies one or more data files for the database.
MAXDATAFILES	Specifies the maximum number of data files that can be created for this database.
MAXINSTANCES	Specifies the maximum number of instances that can simultaneously mount and open this database.
ARCHIVELOG or NOARCHIVELOG	Specifies whether the database is in archive log mode or not. By default, the database is in NOARCHIVELOG mode.
EXCLUSIVE	Specifies that the database is running in exclusive mode. In this mode, only one instance can mount the database.
CHARACTERSET	Specifies the character set used by the database to store the data.

When the CREATE DATABASE command is run, it performs the following functions:

- Creates the specified data files and erases any existing data files.
- Creates and initializes the specified control files.
- Creates and initializes the specified redo log files.
- Creates the SYSTEM tablespace and the SYSTEM rollback segment.
- Specifies the character set that will be used by the database.

Listings 2.3, 2.4, and 2.5 show the complete code for the creation of the JSTP database and the database objects.

Listing 2.3 shows the main script that calls all the other scripts.

Listing 2.3   Master Script for Creating the JSTP Database

```
-- This script can be used to create the JSTP database.
-- It calls other scripts as needed.
-- Author: Megh Thakkar
-- Script name: buildjstp.sql
-- Assumptions:
--   (1) You are creating the database on Windows NT
--   (2) The Oracle home directory is c:\oracle
--If the above assumptions are not valid then you can edit the
➥script accordingly


-- Spool the output of the database creation process
spool c:\Oracle\ADMIN\JSTP\CREATE\build.log
SET TERMOUT OFF
SET ECHO OFF
-- Connect using the internal account
connect internal
-- Create the JSTP database
@@blddb.sql
-- The post-database creation steps start here
-- Run catalog.sql to create the data dictionary views
@c:\Oracle\Ora81\RDBMS\admin\catalog.sql
-- Run catsnmp.sql to create an SNMPagent role to access the v$ tables
@c:\Oracle\Ora81\RDBMS\admin\catsnmp.sql
connect internal
-- Run catexp7.sql to create version7 style export/import views
-- This will allow you to run version7 export/import against
➥the version8 database
@c:\Oracle\Ora81\RDBMS\admin\catexp7.sql
-- Run catproc.sql to create the support for the procedural option
@c:\Oracle\Ora81\RDBMS\admin\catproc.sql
-- Run megh.sql to create the user 'megh' and the database objects
➥to support JSTP
@@buildobj.sql
connect system/manager
-- Run catdbsyn.sql to create private synonyms for the DBA-only
➥data dictionary views
@c:\Oracle\Ora81\RDBMS\admin\catdbsyn.sql
-- Run pupbld.sql to create the product and user profile tables
@c:\Oracle\Ora81\dbs\pupbld.sql
connect internal
alter rollback segment rbs_temp offline;
shutdown;
spool off
```

Listing 2.4 shows the script for creating the database.

Listing 2.4   Contents of Script `blddb.sql`

```
-- This script can be used to create the JSTP database
-- Author: Megh Thakkar
-- Script name: blddb.sql
-- This script is called by buildjstp.sql
-- Assumptions:
--   (1) You are creating the database on Windows NT
--   (2) The Oracle home directory is c:\oracle
--   (3) The file is run out of the directory containing the
--       initialization file
-- If the above assumptions are not valid then you can edit the
➥script accordingly

-- Startup nomount the database instance
startup nomount pfile=c:\oracle\admin\jstp\pfile\initjstp.ora

--   Create the database

create database jstp
      logfile
    GROUP 1
    ('C:\oracle\oradata\jstp\redo01a.ora',
     'D:\oracle\oradata\jstp\redo01b.ora') size 10M reuse,
    GROUP 2
    ('C:\oracle\oradata\jstp\redo02a.ora',
     'D:\oracle\oradata\jstp\redo02b.ora') size 10M reuse
        datafile 'C:\oracle\oradata\jstp\data1.ora' size 80M reuse
➥autoextend on
                  next 10M maxsize 200M,
              'D:\oracle\oradata\jstp\data2.ora' size 80M reuse autoextend on
                  next 10M maxsize 200M
        character set WE8ISO8859P1;

create rollback segment rbs_temp
 storage (initial 100k next 100k
         minextents 4 maxextents 121)
 tablespace system;


-- Create additional tablespaces ...

CREATE TABLESPACE temp
   DATAFILE 'c:\oracle\oradata\jstp\tempjstp.dbf' SIZE 20M
   DEFAULT STORAGE (INITIAL 10K NEXT 50K
                     MINEXTENTS 1 MAXEXTENTS 999)
   ONLINE;


CREATE TABLESPACE tools
   DATAFILE 'c:\oracle\oradata\jstp\toolsjstp.dbf' SIZE 20M
   DEFAULT STORAGE (INITIAL 10K NEXT 50K
```

2

```
                         MINEXTENTS 1 MAXEXTENTS 999)
   ONLINE;

CREATE TABLESPACE rbs_01
   DATAFILE 'c:\oracle\oradata\jstp\rbs01jstp.dbf' SIZE 10M
   DEFAULT STORAGE (INITIAL 10K NEXT 50K
                       MINEXTENTS 1 MAXEXTENTS 999)
   ONLINE;

CREATE TABLESPACE rbs_02
   DATAFILE 'c:\oracle\oradata\jstp\rbs02jstp.dbf' SIZE 40M
   DEFAULT STORAGE (INITIAL 10K NEXT 50K
                       MINEXTENTS 1 MAXEXTENTS 999)
   ONLINE;

CREATE TABLESPACE rbs_03
   DATAFILE 'c:\oracle\oradata\jstp\rbs03jstp.dbf' SIZE 80M
   DEFAULT STORAGE (INITIAL 10K NEXT 50K
                       MINEXTENTS 1 MAXEXTENTS 999)
   ONLINE;

CREATE TABLESPACE user_data1
   DATAFILE 'c:\oracle\oradata\jstp\ud1stp.dbf' SIZE 40M
   DEFAULT STORAGE (INITIAL 10K NEXT 50K
                       MINEXTENTS 1 MAXEXTENTS 999)
   ONLINE;

CREATE TABLESPACE user_data2
   DATAFILE 'c:\oracle\oradata\jstp\ud2jstp.dbf' SIZE 100M
   DEFAULT STORAGE (INITIAL 10K NEXT 50K
                       MINEXTENTS 1 MAXEXTENTS 999)
   ONLINE;

CREATE TABLESPACE user_index
   DATAFILE 'c:\oracle\oradata\jstp\uidxjstp.dbf' SIZE 20M
   DEFAULT STORAGE (INITIAL 10K NEXT 50K
                       MINEXTENTS 1 MAXEXTENTS 999)
   ONLINE;

-- Bring the temporary rollback segment online
alter rollback segment rbs_temp online;

-- Change the password of SYS and SYSTEM accounts

alter user sys identified by new_sys_password;

alter user system identified by new_system_password;


-- Create additional rollback segments
```

continues

Listing 2.4 Continued

```
create rollback segment r01
 storage (initial 100k next 100k
         minextents 4 maxextents 121)
 tablespace rbs_01;

create rollback segment r02
 storage (initial 1M next 1M
         minextents 8 maxextents 121)
 tablespace rbs_03;

alter rollback segment r01 online;

alter rollback segment r02 online;
```

Listing 2.5 shows the script for creating the database objects. It also calls the script for populating the database.

Listing 2.5 Contents of Script `buildobj.sql`

```
-- This script can be used to create a sample schema for the JSTP database
-- Author: Megh Thakkar
-- Script name: buildobj.sql
-- This script is called by buildjstp.sql
-- Assumptions:
--  (1) You are creating the database on Windows NT
--  (2) The Oracle home directory is c:\oracle
-- If the above assumptions are not valid then you can edit the
➥script accordingly

SET TERMOUT OFF
SET ECHO OFF

-- Create a user megh and assign the necessary privileges
CREATE USER megh identified by megh;
GRANT CONNECT,RESOURCE,UNLIMITED TABLESPACE TO megh;
ALTER USER megh DEFAULT TABLESPACE user_data1;
ALTER USER megh TEMPORARY TABLESPACE temp;

-- Connect to the database using the account megh
CONNECT megh/megh

-- Create the database tables for JSTP
DROP TABLE PRODUCTS;
CREATE TABLE PRODUCTS (
        PRODUCT_ID              NUMBER (6),
        DESCRIPTION             VARCHAR2 (30));

DROP TABLE PRICE;
CREATE TABLE PRICE (
        PRODUCT_ID              NUMBER (6),
```

```
        LIST_PRICE              NUMBER (8,2),
        MIN_PRICE               NUMBER (8,2),
        START_DATE              DATE,
        END_DATE                DATE);

DROP TABLE CUSTOMERS;
CREATE TABLE CUSTOMERS (
        CUSTOMER_ID             NUMBER (6),
        NAME                    VARCHAR2 (45),
        ADDRESS                 VARCHAR2 (40),
        CITY                    VARCHAR2 (30),
        STATE                   VARCHAR2 (2),
        COUNTRY                 VARCHAR2 (20),
        ZIP_CODE                VARCHAR2 (9),
        AREA_CODE               NUMBER (3),
        PHONE_NUMBER            NUMBER (7),
        COMMENTS                LONG);

DROP TABLE ORDERS;
CREATE TABLE ORDERS   (
        ORDER_ID                NUMBER (4),
        ORDER_DATE              DATE,
        CUSTOMER_ID             NUMBER (6),
        SHIP_DATE               DATE,
        TOTAL                   NUMBER (8,2));

DROP TABLE ITEMS;
CREATE TABLE ITEMS   (
        ORDER_ID                NUMBER (4),
        ITEM_ID                 NUMBER (4),
        PRODUCT_ID              NUMBER (6),
        ACTUAL_PRICE            NUMBER (8,2),
        QUANTITY                NUMBER (8),
        TOTAL                   NUMBER (8,2));

-- Grant select permissions on the tables to PUBLIC
GRANT SELECT ON PRODUCTS TO PUBLIC;
GRANT SELECT ON PRICE TO PUBLIC;
GRANT SELECT ON CUSTOMERS TO PUBLIC;
GRANT SELECT ON ORDERS TO PUBLIC;
GRANT SELECT ON ITEMS TO PUBLIC;

-- Place comments on the tables for ease of readability
COMMENT ON TABLE PRODUCTS IS 'The various brands of coffee available';
COMMENT ON COLUMN PRODUCTS.PRODUCT_ID IS 'Unique 6 digit number
➥assigned to all coffee brands.';
COMMENT ON COLUMN PRODUCTS.DESCRIPTION IS 'Description of the coffee brand';

COMMENT ON TABLE PRICE IS 'Prices of the various coffee brands';
COMMENT ON COLUMN PRICE.PRODUCT_ID IS 'Refers to the product_id
➥column of the products table';
```

continues

Listing 2.4   Continued

```
COMMENT ON COLUMN PRICE.LIST_PRICE IS 'Undiscounted price (in U.S. dollars).';
COMMENT ON COLUMN PRICE.MIN_PRICE IS 'Lowest price (in U.S. dollars)
➥that can be offered.';
COMMENT ON COLUMN PRICE.START_DATE IS 'Date which standard and minimum
➥prices go into effect.';
COMMENT ON COLUMN PRICE.END_DATE IS 'Date which standard and minimum
➥prices expire.  This value can be
 left NULL.';

COMMENT ON TABLE CUSTOMERS IS 'Customer information';
COMMENT ON COLUMN CUSTOMERS.CUSTOMER_ID IS 'Unique 6 digit number
➥assigned to all customers.';
COMMENT ON COLUMN CUSTOMERS.NAME IS 'Name of the customer';
COMMENT ON COLUMN CUSTOMERS.ADDRESS IS 'Customer address.';
COMMENT ON COLUMN CUSTOMERS.CITY IS 'Customer city';
COMMENT ON COLUMN CUSTOMERS.STATE IS 'Customer state';
COMMENT ON COLUMN CUSTOMERS.ZIP_CODE IS 'Customer zip code';
COMMENT ON COLUMN CUSTOMERS.COUNTRY IS 'Customer country';
COMMENT ON COLUMN CUSTOMERS.AREA_CODE IS 'Area code of phone
➥number for customer.';
COMMENT ON COLUMN CUSTOMERS.PHONE_NUMBER IS 'Customer phone number';
COMMENT ON COLUMN CUSTOMERS.COMMENTS IS 'Special notes about the customer';

COMMENT ON TABLE ORDERS IS 'Sales order information. Item details
➥ can be found in the items table.';
COMMENT ON COLUMN ORDERS.ORDER_ID IS 'Unique 4 digit number
➥assigned to all orders.';
COMMENT ON COLUMN ORDERS.ORDER_DATE IS 'Date when order was placed';
COMMENT ON COLUMN ORDERS.CUSTOMER_ID IS 'Refers to the customer_id
➥column of the customer table.';
COMMENT ON COLUMN ORDERS.SHIP_DATE IS 'Date when order was fulfilled';
COMMENT ON COLUMN ORDERS.TOTAL IS 'Total dollar amount of the order';

COMMENT ON TABLE ITEMS IS 'Details of orders found in the orders table.';
COMMENT ON COLUMN ITEMS.ORDER_ID IS 'Refers to the order_id column
➥of the orders table.';
COMMENT ON COLUMN ITEMS.ITEM_ID IS 'Number of item within the
➥particular sales order.';
COMMENT ON COLUMN ITEMS.PRODUCT_ID IS 'Refers to the product_id
➥column of the products table';
COMMENT ON COLUMN ITEMS.ACTUAL_PRICE IS 'Actual price paid by the customer.';
COMMENT ON COLUMN ITEMS.QUANTITY IS 'Quantity ordered';
COMMENT ON COLUMN ITEMS.TOTAL IS 'Total price of the particular item order.';
-- Now run the script to populate the database tables
-- We will look at this script in more detail in Chapter 3
@populate.sql
-- Now run the script to create indexes and constraints
-- We will look at this script in more detail in Chapter 3
@cr_idx.sql
@cr_constr.sql
```

2

Using the CREATE DATABASE Command to Create JSTP

JSTP can be created using the following specifications:

- Use two data files sized 80MB each, and allow them to autoextend.
- Redo log files are multiplexed and 10MB each.
- Character set is WE8iSO8859P1.

The following steps can be used for this purpose. We will use the OFA structure specified in Listing 2.2:

1. Copy the `initorcl.ora` file to `c:\oracle\admin\jstp\pfile\initjstp.ora`.
2. Edit `initjstp.ora` as specified in Table 2.1.
3. Create the database instance. Database instance creation is one of the most misunderstood tasks of database creation. On UNIX platforms, the Oracle instance is not a permanent structure but rather it is created each time the database is started. The instance is named using the ORACLE_SID environment variable and is created using the initialization parameters. However, on Windows NT, you need to create a Windows NT service for the new database. This is achieved by using the ORADIM utility. For example, from a DOS prompt, type

```
C: > oradim -NEW -SID JSTP -INTPWD password -STARTMODE AUTO
    -PFILE c:\oracle\admin\jstp\pfile\initjstp.ora
```

4. Set the environment variable ORACLE_SID to JSTP. If you are using Windows NT, start the ORACLESERVICEJSTP service from the control panel. Otherwise, go to the next step.
5. Connect to the database as the internal account by using Server Manager:

```
C:\ > svrmgrl
C: \> connect internal/password
```

6. Start the database in the NOMOUNT state:

```
SVRMGR> STARTUP NOMOUNT PFILE= c:\oracle\admin\jstp\pfile\initjstp.ora
```

7. Run the CREATE DATABASE command from Server Manager:

```
create database jstp
        logfile
          GROUP 1
              ('C:\oracle\oradata\jstp\redo01a.ora',
               'D:\oracle\oradata\jstp\redo01b.ora') size 10M reuse,
          GROUP 2
              ('C:\oracle\oradata\jstp\redo02a.ora',
               'D:\oracle\oradata\jstp\redo02b.ora') size 10M reuse
          datafile 'C:\oracle\oradata\jstp\data1.ora' size 80M reuse
➥autoextend on
```

```
                       next 10M maxsize 200M,
              'D:\oracle\oradata\jstp\data2.ora' size 80M reuse autoextend
⇒on
                       next 10M maxsize 200M
             character set WE8iSO8859P1;
```

8. Run CATALOG.SQL to generate the data dictionary:

   SVRMGR> **@%RDBMS81%\ADMIN\CATALOG.SQL**

9. Run CATPROC.SQL to generate the objects used by PL/SQL:

   SVRMGR> **@%RDBMS81%\ADMIN\CATPROC.SQL**

10. Run additional scripts as desired, such as CATREP8M.SQL for advanced replication.

11. The default password for SYS is CHANGE_ON_INSTALL, and the default password for SYSTEM is MANAGER. These user accounts perform administrative tasks and their passwords should be changed as soon as possible.

    SVRMGR> **alter user sys identified by new_sys_password**
    SVRMGR> **alter user system identified by new_system_password**

Post-Database Creation Tasks

In the preceding database creation procedure, steps 9 through 12 are actually post-database creation steps. These and several other steps need to be performed after creating a database:

- Run the post-database creation procedures. These procedures include catalog.sql (creating the data dictionary), catproc.sql (creating the database objects for pl/sql), and any other scripts that are needed for the database options you plan to use.
- Change the password of the administrative accounts SYS and SYSTEM.
- Update the system configuration files tnsnames.ora and listener.ora so that the database can be reached via SQL*NET.
- Create the supporting database objects.

After a basic database has been created, we can create the additional database objects, such as rollback segments, so that it can support our production workload. After the database is created, it will have a system rollback segment in the system tablespace. This system rollback segment cannot be dropped or taken offline and is used for transactions involving objects in the system tablespace. Using the following command, create a temporary rollback segment (please refer to the Oracle SQL reference guide for a complete syntax of the CREATE ROLLBACK SEGMENT command):

```
Svrmgr> create rollback segment rbs_temp
2     storage (initial 100k next 100k
3              minextents 4 maxextents 121)
4     tablespace system;
```

The following command would bring the rollback segment online:

```
Svrmgr> alter rollback segment rbs_temp online;
```

Now create the production tablespaces that will be used, as shown in Table 2.5.

Table 2.5   Tablespace Usage in JSTP

Tablespace Name	Usage
TEMP	Stores temporary database segments
TOOLS	Stores third-party and in-house database tool objects
RBS_01	A small rollback segment
RBS_02	A medium-sized rollback segment
RBS_03	A large rollback segment
USER_DATA1	Stores user data that doesn't change frequently, such as customers and products
USER_DATA2	Stores user data that changes frequently, such as the orders and items tables
USER_INDEX	Index tablespace

```
Svrmgr> CREATE TABLESPACE temp
2     DATAFILE 'c:\oracle\oradata\jstp\tempjstp.dbf' SIZE 20M
3     DEFAULT STORAGE (INITIAL 10K NEXT 50K
4                      MINEXTENTS 1 MAXEXTENTS 999)
5   ONLINE;


Svrmgr> CREATE TABLESPACE tools
2     DATAFILE 'c:\oracle\oradata\jstp\toolsjstp.dbf' SIZE 20M
3     DEFAULT STORAGE (INITIAL 10K NEXT 50K
4                      MINEXTENTS 1 MAXEXTENTS 999)
5   ONLINE;

Svrmgr> CREATE TABLESPACE rbs_01
2     DATAFILE 'c:\oracle\oradata\jstp\rbs01jstp.dbf' SIZE 10M
3     DEFAULT STORAGE (INITIAL 10K NEXT 50K
4                      MINEXTENTS 1 MAXEXTENTS 999)
5   ONLINE;

Svrmgr> CREATE TABLESPACE rbs_02
2     DATAFILE 'c:\oracle\oradata\jstp\rbs02jstp.dbf' SIZE 40M
3     DEFAULT STORAGE (INITIAL 10K NEXT 50K
4                      MINEXTENTS 1 MAXEXTENTS 999)
```

```
5   ONLINE;

Svrmgr> CREATE TABLESPACE rbs_03
2    DATAFILE 'c:\oracle\oradata\jstp\rbs03jstp.dbf' SIZE 80M
3    DEFAULT STORAGE (INITIAL 10K NEXT 50K
4                     MINEXTENTS 1 MAXEXTENTS 999)
5   ONLINE;

Svrmgr> CREATE TABLESPACE user_data1
2    DATAFILE 'c:\oracle\oradata\jstp\ud1stp.dbf' SIZE 40M
3    DEFAULT STORAGE (INITIAL 10K NEXT 50K
4                     MINEXTENTS 1 MAXEXTENTS 999)
5   ONLINE;

Svrmgr> CREATE TABLESPACE user_data2
2    DATAFILE 'c:\oracle\oradata\jstp\ud2jstp.dbf' SIZE 100M
3    DEFAULT STORAGE (INITIAL 10K NEXT 50K
4                     MINEXTENTS 1 MAXEXTENTS 999)
5   ONLINE;

Svrmgr> CREATE TABLESPACE user_index
2    DATAFILE 'c:\oracle\oradata\jstp\uidxjstp.dbf' SIZE 20M
3    DEFAULT STORAGE (INITIAL 10K NEXT 50K
4                     MINEXTENTS 1 MAXEXTENTS 999)
5   ONLINE;
```

Now, create your production rollback segments. You should have at least one roll-back segment for each of the following purposes:

- **OLTP operations**—The rollback segment used for this purpose should be relatively small with a large number of extents.

- **Bulk data loads**—The rollback segment used for this purpose should be relatively large and contain a small number of extents.

```
Svrmgr> create rollback segment r01
2    storage (initial 100k next 100k
3             minextents 4 maxextents 121)
4    tablespace rbs_01;

Svrmgr> create rollback segment r02
2    storage (initial 1M next 1M
3             minextents 8 maxextents 121)
4    tablespace rbs_03;
```

These rollback segment can now be brought online:

```
Svrmgr> alter rollback segment r01 online;

Svrmgr> alter rollback segment r02 online;
```

After you have created the production rollback segments, they can be added to the rollback_segments parameter in the initialization parameter file.

When all these tasks have been finished, the temporary rollback segment created earlier can be dropped:

```
Svrmgr> drop rollback segment rbs_temp;
```

 Note The initialization parameter is read only during database startup. Therefore, whenever you edit the initialization parameter file, you have to shut down and start up the database in order for the changes to be effective.

Populating the Database Using Oracle Utilities

Oracle databases can be populated with information from a variety of sources. Oracle provides several utilities that can help in loading and unloading data from the database:

- **SQL*Loader**—This utility can be used to load data from a flat file into an Oracle database. Information in the flat file can come from various sources, such as other Oracle databases, non-Oracle databases, and spreadsheets.

- **Export utility**—This utility backs up the entire database, entire schema, or specified tables into a proprietary binary file that can be read by only the Import utility.

 **Note** Data can be exported from the database incrementally. This can be useful for very large databases.

- **Import utility**—This utility performs the reverse function of the export utility and can be used to restore data backed up with the Export utility.

Using SQL*Loader to Load Data

Oracle provides SQL*Loader to load data into the database from various sources. The incoming data should be available in an ASCII text file. SQL*Loader also can be used to process the data before loading it into the database.

SQL*Loader's Files

Several files are used by SQL*Loader to perform a data load. These files work together to indicate to SQL*Loader how to load the data.

SQL*Loader's Control File

SQL*Loader's control file contains the necessary DDL to indicate the location of the input files, log file, and bad file. Data mappings also can be included in the control file.

The DDL used by the control file consists of reserved words, shown in Table 2.6. Please refer to the Oracle Utilities manual for a complete description of each of these keywords. Some of the reserved words are required, while the others are optional.

 Note   The control file isn't case sensitive.

Table 2.6   Reserved Words Used in the Control File

AND	DISCARDFILE	LOAD	RESUME
APPEND	DISCARDMAX	LOG	SEQUENCE
BADFILE	DISCARDS	MAX	SKIP
BDDN	DOUBLE	NEXT	SORTNUM
BEGINDATA	ENCLOSED	NO	SQL/DS
BLANKS	EXTERNAL	NULLCOLS	STREAM
BLOCKSIZE	FIELDS	NULLIF	SYSDATE
BY	FIXED	OPTIONALLY	TABLE
CHAR	FLOAT	OPTIONS	TERMINATED
CONCATENATE	FORMAT	PARALLEL	THIS
CONSTANT	GENERATED	PART	TRAILING
CONTINUE_LOAD	GRAPHIC	PIECED	UNLOAD
CONTINUEIF	INDON	POSITION	VARCHAR
COUNT	INDEXES	PRESERVE	VARGRAPHIC
DATA	INFILE	RAW	VARIABLE
DATE	INSERT	RECLEN	YES
DECIMAL	INTEGER	RECNUM	ZONED
DEFAULTIF	INTO	RECORD	WORKDDM
DISCARDDN	LAST	REPLACE	

The manner in which data is loaded is specified by the following keywords:

- INSERT—Requires that the table not have any data.
- APPEND—Adds rows to the table. The table may already contain data.
- REPLACE—Replaces the table's current data with the new data. This keyword maintains the referential integrity constraints.
- TRUNCATE—Replaces the table's current data with the new data. Any referential integrity constraints on the table should be disabled before using this keyword.

SQL*Loader's Data File

The data to be loaded is contained in the input file (also referred to as the SQL*Loader data file). Every line in this file is treated as a physical record to be loaded. However, a table with a large number of columns can be loaded by using several physical records composed into one logical record.

Two formats are allowed for the data records:

- *Fixed* **format**—Requires that a data column be of the same size for all the logical records. When using this format, columns are delimited by position and length.
- *Variable* **format**—Requires that each column be delimited in one of two ways: terminated by a character such as a comma or period, or enclosed by a special character such as quotation marks before and after the column.

SQL*Loader's Log File

Detailed information about any messages and errors that occur during the SQL*Loader run are placed in the SQL*Loader log file.

SQL*Loader's Bad File

Records that were loaded unsuccessfully into the target table during a SQL*Loader run are placed in the SQL*Loader bad file. Several situations might cause the records not to be loaded properly:

- Invalid record format.
- Data violates referential integrity constraints.
- Incompatible data type with the target table.

SQL*Loader's Discard File

During a SQL*Loader run, records might be discarded because they didn't meet the conditional DDL statements specified in the control file. Such discarded records are placed in the SQL*Loader discard file.

Loading Data

SQL*Loader allows you to load data using one of two methods:

- **Conventional data load**—This technique uses SQL*Loader as a normal background process, which competes with other processes for system resources.
- **Direct path data load**—This technique bypasses the SQL engine and enables faster processing.

 **Note**   Direct path data load has certain restrictions that can preclude its use.

Performing a Conventional Data Load

By default, data is loaded using the conventional method. During a conventional data load, data is processed by using the SGA buffer cache and INSERT statements with a bind-array buffer. A conventional data load can be used even while other activities (such as inserts and updates) are occurring on the target table.

Performing a Direct Path Load

Performance of a data load can be improved by using a direct path load instead of the conventional method. This method uses the DIRECT=TRUE option of SQL*Loader:

```
C:\> sqlldr scott/tiger control=customers.ctl DIRECT=TRUE
```

A direct path load doesn't use an INSERT statement, but instead formats the data in the Oracle data block configuration and loads it directly into the database file.

 **Note**   In order to perform a data load—conventional or direct path—the user ID specified in the control file must have insert privileges on the target table. This user ID also requires the DELETE privilege on the table if the REPLACE option is used.

Direct path data load has several restrictions:

- Clustered tables can't be loaded.
- Active transactions can't be occurring on target tables during the load.
- The control file shouldn't contain SQL functions.
- If the target table contains indexes then even SELECT statements can't be executed against them during a data load. After a direct path load, indexes might get placed in the direct load state. These indexes should be dropped and re-created.
- Referential integrity constraints are disabled during the load but re-enabled after the load.
- Default column values aren't used.

Several options can be used to further improve the performance of a direct-path load operation:

- UNRECOVERABLE—Prevents the generation of redo during the data load.
- SORTED INDEXES—Improves performance if the target table has an index and the data is presorted in the order of the index.
- PARALLEL—Allows multiple parallel SQL*Loader sessions to be run concurrently.
- PIECED and READBUFFERS—Can be used to load long datatypes.

Enhancing SQL*Loader Performance

If the performance of a data load using SQL*Loader is not acceptable then the following tips can help:

- Remove the indexes on the target table before the data load, load the table, and then re-create the indexes.
- Set the ROWS parameter and perform commits less frequently. If this technique is used, make sure that you have a large rollback segment.
- Perform the data load during periods of the least database activity.
- When using a variable format for the data load, use the RECLEN parameter and specify the maximum possible logical record size. This will enable SQL*Loader to preallocate the buffer and improve performance.
- Set the bind array size (BINDSIZE) parameter as high as possible:

  BINDSIZE = *(maximum row size in bytes)***(number_of_rows)*

- Reduce the amount of redo generated by using UNRECOVERABLE.
- If the target table has an index and the data is presorted in the order of the index, you can use the SORTED INDEXES clause.
- Use the PARALLEL clause to perform multiple SQL*Loader sessions simultaneously.

Working with Export/Import Utilities

The Export/Import utility combination is provided by Oracle to perform data transfer between Oracle databases. Export generates an Oracle proprietary file that contains the necessary data and information to perform the data transfer. This dump file is in a binary format and you should not try to edit it. This dump file can be read by only the Import utility.

Editing the export dump file can make the file unusable.

Export/Import can be used to transfer data between databases on different platforms as well as between different Oracle versions because they are neither version-specific nor operating-system specific. However, when transferring dump files across different platforms, make sure to transfer them in binary format, not ASCII.

Using Export/Import you can transfer information as follows:

- Between databases on the same version of Oracle
- Between databases on different versions of Oracle
- Between databases on different operating system platforms
- From one schema to another schema
- From one tablespace to another tablespace
- The entire database

Export can be performed at three levels:

- **Incremental export**—Backs up data that has changed since the last incremental backup.
- **Cumulative export**—Backs up data that has changed since the last cumulative backup.

 Cumulative backups can be used to condense incremental backups.

- **Complete export**—Backs up the entire database.

The following scenario can be used to understand how the various backup types interrelate:

Sunday	Complete export
Monday	Incremental export
Tuesday	Cumulative export
Wednesday	Incremental export
Thursday	Cumulative export
Friday	Incremental export
Saturday	Incremental export

This strategy takes a complete export every Sunday (longest), incremental exports (fastest and shortest) daily, and cumulative exports on Tuesdays and Thursdays.

If recovery is needed on Tuesday (before the Tuesday cumulative export), you can apply the following:

- Full export from Sunday
- Incremental export from Monday

If recovery is needed on Thursday (before the Thursday cumulative export), you can apply the following:

- Full export from Sunday
- Cumulative export from Tuesday
- Incremental export from Wednesday

If recovery is needed on Friday (before the Friday incremental export), you can apply the following:

- Full export from Sunday
- Cumulative export from Thursday

Oracle Export and Import Parameters

While using the Export and Import utilities, you can make use of various parameters to influence the data transfer process. Several parameters are common to both utilities, whereas others are unique to one utility.

The following parameters can be used with Oracle's Export utility:

- BUFFER specifies the size in bytes of the data buffer used for the export run:

  ```
  Buffer_size = maximum_row_size*num_rows_in_array
  ```

  The larger the buffer, the faster the export. In any case, make sure that it is as large as the longest row of data to be exported; otherwise, an error will be generated.

- Setting COMPRESS to Y causes segments in multiple extents to be compressed into one initial extent.

- CONSISTENT specifies whether Export will use the SET TRANSACTION READ ONLY setting to ensure a read-consistent export.

- CONSTRAINTS specifies whether constraints should be exported.

- DIRECT allows you to perform a direct path export.

- FEEDBACK specifies whether Export should provide a progress meter in terms of dots per specified number of rows exported.

- FILE specifies the name of the file that will contain the export.
- Setting the FULL parameter to Y enables you to perform full database export. A full database export requires that you have the EXP_FULL_DATABASE role assigned to you. It can't be used with the TABLES or OWNERS parameter.
- GRANTS specifies whether object grants should be exported.
- HELP displays a help message describing the export parameters.
- INCTYPE specifies the type of export: COMPLETE, CUMULATIVE, or INCREMENTAL.
- INDEXES specifies whether indexes should be exported.
- LOG specifies the file in which information and error messages during export should be written.
- OWNER specifies a list of users whose objects need to be exported. When used with the TABLES parameter, it signifies a user mode export. It can't be used with the FULL parameter.
- PARFILE specifies the full path of the parameter file that supplies the export parameters.
- RECORD specifies whether an incremental or cumulative export should be recorded in the database tables SYS.INCVID, SYS.INCFIL, and SYS.INCEXP.
- RECORDLENGTH specifies the length of the file record in bytes.
- ROWS specifies whether the data rows of the table are to be exported.
- STATISTICS specifies the type of optimizer statistics to generate when the data is imported: NONE, ESTIMATE, or COMPUTE. These statistics are used by the optimizer while choosing the execution plan.
- TABLES specifies a list of tables to export. It can't be used with the FULL=Y parameter.
- USERID specifies the username and password of the user who will perform the export.

The following parameters can be used with Oracle's Import utility:

- BUFFER specifies the size in bytes of the data buffer used for the import run:

  ```
  Buffer_size = maximum_row_size*num_rows_in_array
  ```

  The larger the buffer, the faster the export. In any case, make sure that it is as large as the longest row of data to be imported; otherwise, an error will be generated.
- Setting COMMIT to Y specifies that Import should commit after each array insert. By default, a commit occurs only after an entire object is loaded.

- DESTROY specifies whether existing data files should be reused. If tablespaces have been pre-created for the database, you should leave DESTROY=N; otherwise, the pre-created tablespaces will be lost.

- FEEDBACK specifies whether Import should provide a progress meter in dots per specified number of rows imported.

- FILE specifies the name of the file to be imported.

- FROMUSER specifies a list of usernames whose objects are to be imported. It can't be used with the FULL=Y parameter. The following is considered when this parameter is used for importing:

  If the TOUSER clause isn't specified, the specified objects are imported into the FROMUSER schema.

  If the specified user doesn't exist in the target database, the objects are imported into the schema of the importer.

- Setting the FULL parameter to Y enables you to perform a full database import. A full database import requires that you have the IMP_FULL_DATABASE role assigned to you. It can't be used with the TABLES or OWNERS parameter.

- GRANTS specifies whether object grants should be imported.

- HELP displays a help message describing the import parameters.

- IGNORE specifies the handling of object creation errors during the import process. If IGNORE=N, object creation errors are displayed, and then Import proceeds to the next object. On the other hand, setting IGNORE=Y causes these errors to be ignored.

- INDEXES specifies whether indexes should be imported.

- INDEXFILE specifies a file to be used to write the index creation statements that are part of the export file. The associated table and cluster creation statements are also placed in this file as comments. This file can be edited later and used as a standard SQL script for re-creating indexes.

- LOG specifies the file in which information and error messages during import should be written.

- RECORDLENGTH specifies the length of the file record in bytes.

- ROWS specifies whether the data rows of the table are to be imported.

- TABLES specifies a list of tables to import. It can't be used with the FULL=Y parameter.

- TOUSER specifies a list of usernames to whose schema the data will be imported. This parameter, along with the FROMUSER parameter, can be used to import to a user different than the original owner.

- USERID specifies the username and password of the user to perform the import.

Optimizing Database Exports

At times the database export could be slow because of the amount of data being exported or some other load on the system. The following tips can help in improving the speed of a database export:

- Place the export dump file on a disk separate from the disk containing the data files. This will minimize the contention for I/O.
- Break the export into smaller exports, and then run each export in parallel.
- Determine what is really supposed to be exported. The following should not be exported every time:

  Indexes that can be easily re-created.

  Roles, profiles, and so on that don't change very often.

  Read-only data. However, make sure that the read-only tablespace wasn't read-write during the last export and has not switched to read-only since that time.

- Use high-speed disks instead of tapes as the destination for database exports.
- Increase the buffer size by increasing the BUFFER parameter.
- Schedule the export during periods of the least database activity.

Optimizing Database Imports

At times the database import could be slow because of the amount of data being imported or some other load on the system. The following tips can help in improving the speed of a database import:

- Increase the buffer size by increasing the BUFFER parameter.
- Don't use COMMIT=Y.
- Use a large rollback segment, and offline other rollback segments to ensure that the import uses a large rollback segment.
- Put the database in NOARCHIVELOG mode because an import generates a lot of redo that doesn't need to be recorded.
- Speed up the index creation process by increasing the value of SORT_AREA_SIZE.
- Pre-create the tables without the indexes and constraints, load the data, and then create the indexes and constraints.
- Schedule the import during periods of the least database activity.

Exporting Between Different Oracle Versions

The CATEXP.SQL script provided by Oracle is used to create several views. These views are used by the Export utility to organize the data that will be sent to the export dump file.

2

It is important to understand that the export views aren't the same across Oracle versions. They are changed to reflect the changes in the data dictionary between the different Oracle versions.

When exporting to an older version database, follow these steps to avoid errors during data transfer:

1. Run the older `catexp.sql` script on the source database.
2. Use the older export executable to export the source database and create an export dump file.
3. Use the older import executable to import to the target database.
4. Run the newer `catexp.sql` on the source database to update its export views.

When exporting to a newer version database, follow these steps to avoid errors during data transfer:

1. Run the newer `catexp.sql` script on the source database.
2. Use the newer export executable to export the source database and create an export dump file.
3. Use the newer import executable to import to the target database.
4. Run the older `catexp.sql` on the source database to update its export views.

Issues with Sequences During Export/Import

Special care has to be taken when exporting sequences. Sequences might be lost during an export/import procedure under the following conditions:

- Users are accessing the sequence while the export is running.
- Cached sequences are used. Export will skip them and get the sequence value from the data dictionary.

If one or both of the preceding conditions are true, the end result depends on how the column that is using the sequence gets its values:

- If a front-end application accesses the sequence to insert values in the column, the column values that exist in the dump file are used during the import. Sequences are not re-accessed.
- If an `INSERT` trigger populates the columns by using `sequence.nextval` and the trigger is enabled during the import, the trigger fires during the import and re-accesses the sequence.

 **Note**   Re-accessing a sequence during import can result in sequence values that are different from their original values.

Next Steps

This chapter demonstrated how an Oracle database can be created and populated. We used a detailed script-based approach to see the various steps involved in this process. It should be noted that you also could have used a GUI approach for database creation, which would be simpler but wouldn't have explained to you what goes on behind the scenes during database creation.

Now that we have created and populated JSTP (the JavaStop database), the next chapter will show you how to use SQL to manipulate the database by inserting, updating, deleting, and selecting data from the database.

Chapter 3

Manipulating the JavaStop Oracle Database Using SQL

Introduction

Structured Query Language (SQL) is used by a majority of relational databases (including Oracle) as a way to communicate with the database. In this chapter, we will look at the most commonly used SQL commands and understand how our JavaStop sample application can be manipulated using SQL.

Accessing the Database

A database is useless without an efficient mechanism to create and maintain it. Likewise, we need an efficient method for manipulating the database contents. In other words, we need an efficient method of talking to the database. A number of programming languages have been developed and used over the years, and most computer professionals are literate with the usage of some 3GLs (third generation languages) such as BASIC, C, and so on. However, the 3GLs are general purpose and are not meant for any particular application. As a result, 3GLs are not very efficient for specific applications and might not contain the commands to perform a specific task. This gave popularity to 4GLs (fourth generation languages), which are designed for specific applications. A DBMS's 4GL is designed to perform database tasks and build database applications effectively. DBMS 4GLs can be of three types:

- **Proprietary languages**—These languages are particular to one DBMS only. Paradox application language (PAL) used by Borland's Paradox DBMS is an example of such a proprietary language.

- **De-facto standard languages**—These are languages that started out as proprietary but are now popularly used by other DBMSs. dBASE is a common example of a language that started out with the original dBASE products by Borland. It is now also used by other DBMSs, such as Microsoft's FoxPro.

- **Standardized languages**—SQL (Structured Query Language) is an example of a language that is standardized. It can be used by any DBMS and is not specific to any application. The SQL standard describes the basic components of the SQL language and also what each component should do. SQL was first standardized by ANSI in 1986, and this version is referred to as the ANSI SQL-86 or ANSI SQL Level 1. In 1989, a revised standard was made and it is referred to as ANSI SQL-89 or ANSI SQL Level 2. The ANSI SQL Level 2 also includes an addendum called "Integrity Enhancement Addendum" that describes commands used for referential integrity.

SQL is commonly used by the majority of RDBMSs as the default application programming language. However, the standard SQL language is quite limited in what it can really do, and therefore it is common for individual vendors to provide an extension to the standard SQL language so that efficient applications can be written against their specific database.

Different vendor-specific extensions to SQL might be incompatible with each other, and you should therefore be careful when developing database applications.

Oracle was the first commercial RDBMS to make use of SQL and since 1979 (when it was first released) it has continued to use SQL as its native language. In addition to extending SQL by providing additional commands such as built-in mathematical and character-string manipulation functions, Oracle also provides PL/SQL (Procedural Language/SQL) as a superset of the native SQL. PL/SQL allows for procedural programming such as looping, branching, and other program-logic and transaction control commands.

Oracle is ANSI SQL Level 2 compliant.

SQL Commands

SQL commands can be broken down into three categories based on the type of database functions they perform:

- Data Definition Language (DDL)
- Data Manipulation Language (DML)
- Data Control Language (DCL)

A fourth SQL subset called Embedded SQL (EMB) is also supported by Oracle. We will discuss the most commonly used commands in this chapter. For a complete and detailed description of the various SQL commands, please refer to the *SQL Language Reference* manual that came with your Oracle Server software.

Data Definition Language

Data Definition Language refers to the commands that are used for creating and manipulating the schema or structure of a database. Table 3.1 shows the commonly used DDL commands.

Table 3.1　Commonly Used DDL Commands

Oracle SQL's DDL Command	*Usage*
Alter database	Change the characteristics, maintain or recover an existing database
Alter sequence	Change the minimum, maximum, increment, and behavior of a sequence
Alter table	Change the attributes of a table
Create database	Create a new database
Create database link	Create a new database link
Create index	Create an index
Create sequence	Create a sequence
Create synonym	Create a synonym
Create table	Create a table
Create procedure	Create a procedure
Create view	Create a view
Drop <object>	Drop the specified object
Rename <object>	Rename the specified object
Validate Index	Validate the structure of an index

As seen from Table 3.1, DDL commands are usually quite self-explanatory and are used to create, drop, or modify database structures. Refer to Listings 3.2 and 3.3 for a demonstration of how DDL commands can be used to create indexes and constraints in JavaStop.

Data Manipulation Language (DML)

Data Manipulation Language commands are used to insert, update, delete, or retrieve data from the database. Some of the commonly used DML commands are described in Table 3.2.

Table 3.2   Commonly Used DML Commands

Oracle SQL's DML Command	Usage
Select	Retrieve data from the database
Insert	Insert data into the database
Update	Modify data in the database
Delete	Delete data from the database

Data Control Language (DCL)

Data Control Language commands are used to restrict user access to the database, perform auditing, and control transaction processing. Table 3.3 shows the commonly used DCL commands.

Table 3.3   Commonly Used DCL Commands

Oracle SQL's DCL Command	Usage
Alter rollback segment	Change the characteristics of a rollback segment such as storage parameters or bringing the rollback segment online or offline.
Alter session	Change session characteristics. Modify parameters that affect your connection to the database. These settings remain in effect until you disconnect from the database.
Alter tablespace	Alter an existing tablespace or one or more of its data files.
Alter user	Change the authentication or database resource characteristics of a user.
Audit	Perform an audit.
Commit	Commit a transaction.
Create rollback segment	Create a rollback segment.
Create tablespace	Create a tablespace.

Oracle SQL's DCL Command	Usage
Grant	Grant privileges (system or object) to a user.
Noaudit	Disable auditing.
Revoke	Revoke privileges (system or object) from a user.
Rollback	Roll back a transaction.
Savepoint	Identify a point in a transaction to which you can later roll back.
Set transaction	Establish the current transaction as read-only or read-write, specify its isolation level, or assign it to a particular rollback segment.

Embedded SQL (EMB)

Embedded SQL commands are specific to Oracle and are used to embed DDL, DML, and DCL commands inside a 3GL program. Thus, embedded SQL enables you to get the benefits of both a 3GL language (flexibility) and a 4GL language (efficiency). Table 3.4 shows the commonly used Embedded SQL commands.

Table 3.4   Commonly Used Embedded SQL Commands

Oracle's Embedded SQL Command	Usage
Close <cursor>	Close an open cursor
Connect	Make a database connection
Declare cursor	Declare a cursor
Describe	Obtain a description of a database object
Execute	Execute a statement
Fetch	Fetch values using a cursor
Open <cursor>	Open a cursor
Whenever	Perform a specified statement whenever the specified condition is true

SQL Operators and Built-in Functions

When working with SQL commands you should also become familiar with some commonly used operators that affect the end result that is displayed to the user. Table 3.5 shows some commonly used operators. Please refer to the Oracle SQL Language Reference manual for a full description of these operators.

Table 3.5   Commonly Used SQL Operators

SQL Operator Type	Operator(s)
Arithmetic	()
	+
	-
	*
	/
Character	||
Comparison	()
	=
	!= or ^= or <> (used interchangeably)
	>=
	<=
	IN
	NOT IN
	ANY
	ALL
	BETWEEN…AND
	NOT BETWEEN…AND
	EXISTS
	NOT EXISTS
	LIKE
	NOT LIKE
	IS NULL
	IS NOT NULL
Logical	()
	NOT
	AND
	OR
Set	UNION
	INTERSECT
	MINUS
Miscellaneous	(+)
	<table>.*

SQL Operator Type	Operator(s)
	COUNT
	ALL
	DISTINCT

In addition, Oracle SQL has numerous built-in functions that perform specific tasks and simplify the developer's work. Table 3.6 shows the commonly used built-in functions provided by Oracle. Please refer to the Oracle SQL Language reference guide for a complete description of these built-in functions.

Table 3.6   Oracle's Commonly Used Built-in Functions

Oracle SQL Function Type	Function(s)
Single-row numeric functions	ABS
	CEIL
	FLOOR
	MOD
	POWER
	ROUND
	SIGN
	SQRT
	TRUNC
Single-row character functions	ASCII
	CHR
	INITCAP
	INSTR
	LENGTH
	LOWER
	LPAD
	LTRIM
	NLSSORT
	REPLACE
	RPAD
	RTRIM
	SOUNDEX
	SUBSTR

continues

Table 3.6   Continued

Oracle SQL Function Type	Function(s)
	TRANSLATE
	UPPER
Group functions	AVG
	COUNT
	MAX
	MIN
	STDDEV
	SUM
	VARIANCE
Conversion functions	CHARTOROWID
	CONVERT
	HEXTORAW
	RAWTOHEX
	TO_CHAR
	TO_DATE
	TO_NUMBER
Date functions	ADD_MONTHS
	LAST_DAY
	MONTHS_BETWEEN
	NEW_TIME
	NEXT_DAY
	ROUND
	SYSDATE
	TRUNC
Miscellaneous	DECODE
	GREATEST
	LEAST
	NVL
	UID
	USER
	USERENV
	VSIZE

Querying and Manipulating JavaStop Using SQL

Oracle provides several commands for manipulating data. We will look at the basic commands for data retrieval and manipulation, namely, SELECT, INSERT, UPDATE, and DELETE. Each of these commands is quite a complex syntax when you consider the various options available with them. Please refer to the Oracle SQL Reference guide for the complete set of options available. In this chapter we will look at the basic but most powerful options available with these DML statements.

The INSERT Statement

The INSERT command is used with existing tables or views to add new information to the database. In order to insert data into an existing table or view, you should have the INSERT object privilege for that object or the object should be in your schema. In order to insert rows into the base table of a view, the owner of the schema containing the view must have INSERT privilege on the base table. You will also need INSERT privilege on the view if the view is not in your schema.

> **Note** The INSERT ANY TABLE system privilege allows you to insert rows into any table or any view's base table.

The basic syntax of the INSERT statement is as follows:

```
SYNTAX: INSERT [hint] INTO table_expression [(column_list)]
        [value_list¦sub_query];
```

where

- hint is a comment that passes instructions to the optimizer on choosing an execution plan for the statement
- table_expression specifies the object into which data is to be inserted
- column_list can be optionally specified to indicate if you want to insert values only in certain columns and not the entire row
- value_list specifies a list of values to be inserted
- sub_query specifies that values to be inserted are to be derived using a sub-query

> **Note** When using a subquery, you have to be sure that the source and target have the same number of columns and the rows you select have to match with regard to the datatypes and length of data.

Listing 3.1 shows the use of INSERT statements to populate JavaStop.

```
-- Script: populate.sql
-- Author: Megh Thakkar
-- Populate the database tables

-- Populate the PRODUCTSs table
INSERT INTO PRODUCTS VALUES ( 103120 , 'African Cinnamon');
INSERT INTO PRODUCTS VALUES ( 103121 , 'Island Coconut');
INSERT INTO PRODUCTS VALUES ( 103130 , 'Swiss chocolate');
INSERT INTO PRODUCTS VALUES ( 103131 , 'Chocolate mint');
INSERT INTO PRODUCTS VALUES ( 103140 , 'Irish cream');
INSERT INTO PRODUCTS VALUES ( 103141 , 'Triple treat');
INSERT INTO PRODUCTS VALUES ( 102132 , 'Tropical vanilla');
INSERT INTO PRODUCTS VALUES ( 104350 , 'Almonds only');
INSERT INTO PRODUCTS VALUES ( 104351 , 'Hazelnut');
INSERT INTO PRODUCTS VALUES ( 104352 , 'Brazilian Santos');
INSERT INTO PRODUCTS VALUES ( 104360 , 'Hawaiian delight');
INSERT INTO PRODUCTS VALUES ( 104361 , 'Sumatra manhedling');
INSERT INTO PRODUCTS VALUES ( 104362 , 'Kenya AA');
INSERT INTO PRODUCTS VALUES ( 102134 , 'Zimbabwe 053');
INSERT INTO PRODUCTS VALUES ( 105123 , 'Mocha Java');
INSERT INTO PRODUCTS VALUES ( 105124 , 'Breakfast brew');
INSERT INTO PRODUCTS VALUES ( 105125 , 'Mountain forest');
INSERT INTO PRODUCTS VALUES ( 105126 , 'French roast');
INSERT INTO PRODUCTS VALUES ( 105127 , 'Italian roast');
INSERT INTO PRODUCTS VALUES ( 105128 , 'Jamaican roast');
INSERT INTO PRODUCTS VALUES ( 102136 , 'Vienna roast');

-- Populate the price table
INSERT INTO PRICE VALUES
    (103120,23.2,18.6,TO_DATE(2447528,'J'),TO_DATE(2447892,'J'));
INSERT INTO PRICE VALUES
    (103120,24,19.2,TO_DATE(2447893,'J'),TO_DATE(2448043,'J'));
INSERT INTO PRICE VALUES
    (103120,25,20,TO_DATE(2448044,'J'),NULL);
INSERT INTO PRICE VALUES
    (103121,27.8,22.3,TO_DATE(2447528,'J'),TO_DATE(2447892,'J'));
INSERT INTO PRICE VALUES
    (103121,28.8,23,TO_DATE(2447893,'J'),TO_DATE(2448043,'J'));
INSERT INTO PRICE VALUES
    (103121,30,24,TO_DATE(2448044,'J'),NULL);
INSERT INTO PRICE VALUES
    (103130,4,3.5,TO_DATE(2447528,'J'),TO_DATE(2447892,'J'));
INSERT INTO PRICE VALUES
    (103130,4.2,3.6,TO_DATE(2447893,'J'),NULL);
INSERT INTO PRICE VALUES
    (103131,4.2,3.6,TO_DATE(2447528,'J'),TO_DATE(2447892,'J'));
INSERT INTO PRICE VALUES
    (103131,4.5,3.9,TO_DATE(2447893,'J'),NULL);
```

```
INSERT INTO PRICE VALUES
   (103140,20,15,TO_DATE(2447573,'J'),NULL);
INSERT INTO PRICE VALUES
   (103141,20,15,TO_DATE(2447573,'J'),NULL);
INSERT INTO PRICE VALUES
   (102132,3.4,2.8,TO_DATE(2447757,'J'),NULL);
INSERT INTO PRICE VALUES
   (104350,40,32,TO_DATE(2447528,'J'),TO_DATE(2447892,'J'));
INSERT INTO PRICE VALUES
   (104350,42,33.6,TO_DATE(2447893,'J'),TO_DATE(2448043,'J'));
INSERT INTO PRICE VALUES
   (104350,44,35.3,TO_DATE(2448044,'J'),NULL);
INSERT INTO PRICE VALUES
   (104351,23.6,18.9,TO_DATE(2447528,'J'),TO_DATE(2447892,'J'));
INSERT INTO PRICE VALUES
   (104351,24.8,19.8,TO_DATE(2447893,'J'),TO_DATE(2448043,'J'));
INSERT INTO PRICE VALUES
   (104351,26,20.8,TO_DATE(2448044,'J'),NULL);
INSERT INTO PRICE VALUES
   (104352,50,35,TO_DATE(2447528,'J'),TO_DATE(2447892,'J'));
INSERT INTO PRICE VALUES
   (104352,54,37.8,TO_DATE(2447893,'J'),TO_DATE(2448043,'J'));
INSERT INTO PRICE VALUES
   (104352,58.3,40.8,TO_DATE(2448044,'J'),NULL);
INSERT INTO PRICE VALUES
   (104360,36,29.5,TO_DATE(2447528,'J'),TO_DATE(2447892,'J'));
INSERT INTO PRICE VALUES
   (104360,39,32,TO_DATE(2447893,'J'),NULL);
INSERT INTO PRICE VALUES
   (104361,47,33,TO_DATE(2447528,'J'),TO_DATE(2447892,'J'));
INSERT INTO PRICE VALUES
   (104361,50,35,TO_DATE(2447893,'J'),NULL);
INSERT INTO PRICE VALUES
   (104362,5,4,TO_DATE(2447573,'J'),NULL);
INSERT INTO PRICE VALUES
   (102134,3.4,2.8,TO_DATE(2447757,'J'),NULL);
INSERT INTO PRICE VALUES
   (105123,36.3,29,TO_DATE(2447528,'J'),TO_DATE(2447892,'J'));
INSERT INTO PRICE VALUES
   (105123,37.7,32,TO_DATE(2447893,'J'),TO_DATE(2448043,'J'));
INSERT INTO PRICE VALUES
   (105123,40,34,TO_DATE(2448044,'J'),NULL);
INSERT INTO PRICE VALUES
   (105124,10,7.6,TO_DATE(2447528,'J'),TO_DATE(2447892,'J'));
INSERT INTO PRICE VALUES
   (105124,12,9,TO_DATE(2447893,'J'),TO_DATE(2448043,'J'));
INSERT INTO PRICE VALUES
   (105124,15,10,TO_DATE(2448044,'J'),NULL);
INSERT INTO PRICE VALUES
   (105125,2,1.7,TO_DATE(2447528,'J'),TO_DATE(2447892,'J'));
```

continues

Listing 3.1   Continued

```
INSERT INTO PRICE VALUES
   (105125,3,2.6,TO_DATE(2447893,'J'),NULL);
INSERT INTO PRICE VALUES
   (105126,5,4.3,TO_DATE(2447528,'J'),TO_DATE(2447892,'J'));
INSERT INTO PRICE VALUES
   (105126,6,5,TO_DATE(2447893,'J'),NULL);
INSERT INTO PRICE VALUES
   (105127,6,5,TO_DATE(2448211,'J'),NULL);
INSERT INTO PRICE VALUES
   (105128,10,8,TO_DATE(2448211,'J'),NULL);
INSERT INTO PRICE VALUES
   (102136,3.4,2.8,TO_DATE(2447757,'J'),NULL);

INSERT INTO CUSTOMERS
  (ZIP_CODE, STATE, PHONE_NUMBER,
  NAME,
  CUSTOMER_ID, CITY, AREA_CODE, ADDRESS,
  COMMENTS)
  VALUES ('96711', 'CA', '5986609',
  'JOCKSPORTS',
  '100', 'BELMONT', '415', '345 VIEWRIDGE',
  'Buys a lot of Decaf.');

INSERT INTO CUSTOMERS
  (ZIP_CODE, STATE,  PHONE_NUMBER,
  NAME,
  CUSTOMER_ID,  CITY, AREA_CODE, ADDRESS,
  COMMENTS)
  VALUES ('94061', 'CA', '3681223',
  'TKB SPORT SHOP',
  '101', 'REDWOOD CITY', '415', '490 BOLI RD.',
  '');

INSERT INTO CUSTOMERS
  (ZIP_CODE, STATE,  PHONE_NUMBER,
  NAME,
  CUSTOMER_ID,  CITY, AREA_CODE, ADDRESS,
  COMMENTS)
  VALUES ('95133', 'CA',  '6443341',
  'VOLLYRITE',
  '102', 'BURLINGAME', '415', '9722 HAMILTON',
  '');

INSERT INTO CUSTOMERS
  (ZIP_CODE, STATE,  PHONE_NUMBER,
  NAME,
  CUSTOMER_ID,  CITY, AREA_CODE, ADDRESS,
  COMMENTS)
  VALUES ('97544', 'CA',  '6779312',
  'JUST TENNIS',
  '103', 'BURLINGAME', '415', 'HILLVIEW MALL',
```

```
'');

INSERT INTO CUSTOMERS
  (ZIP_CODE, STATE,  PHONE_NUMBER,
  NAME,
  CUSTOMER_ID,  CITY, AREA_CODE, ADDRESS,
  COMMENTS)
  VALUES ('93301', 'CA',  '9962323',
  'EVERY MOUNTAIN',
  '104',  'CUPERTINO', '408', '574 SURRY RD.',
  'Hyperactive customer.');

INSERT INTO CUSTOMERS
  (ZIP_CODE, STATE,  PHONE_NUMBER,
  NAME,
  CUSTOMER_ID,  CITY, AREA_CODE, ADDRESS,
  COMMENTS)
  VALUES ('91003', 'CA',  '3769966',
  'K + T SPORTS',
  '105',  'SANTA CLARA', '408', '3476 EL PASEO',
  'Tends to order large amounts of roasted coffee.');

INSERT INTO CUSTOMERS
  (ZIP_CODE, STATE,  PHONE_NUMBER,
  NAME,
  CUSTOMER_ID,  CITY, AREA_CODE, ADDRESS,
  COMMENTS)
  VALUES ('94301', 'CA',  '3649777',
  'SHAPE UP',
  '106',  'PALO ALTO', '415', '908 SEQUOIA',
  '');

INSERT INTO CUSTOMERS
  (ZIP_CODE, STATE,  PHONE_NUMBER,
  NAME,
  CUSTOMER_ID,  CITY, AREA_CODE, ADDRESS,
  COMMENTS)
  VALUES ('93301', 'CA',  '9674398',
  'WOMENS SPORTS',
  '107',  'SUNNYVALE', '408', 'VALCO VILLAGE',
  '');

INSERT INTO CUSTOMERS
  (ZIP_CODE, STATE,  PHONE_NUMBER,
  NAME,
  CUSTOMER_ID,  CITY, AREA_CODE, ADDRESS,
  COMMENTS)
  VALUES ('55649', 'MN',  '5669123',
  'NORTH WOODS HEALTH AND FITNESS SUPPLY CENTER',
  '108',  'HIBBING', '612', '98 LONE PINE WAY', '');
```

continues

Listing 3.1   Continued

```
INSERT INTO CUSTOMERS VALUES
  ( 201 , 'STADIUM SPORTS', '47 IRVING PL.',
  'NEW YORK', 'NY', 'USA', '10003',
  '212', '5555335',
  '');
INSERT INTO CUSTOMERS VALUES
  ( 202 , 'HOOPS', '2345 ADAMS AVE.',
  'LEICESTER', 'MA', 'USA', '01524',
  '508', '5557542',
  'Member of the coffee club.');


INSERT INTO CUSTOMERS VALUES
  ( 203 , 'REBOUND SPORTS', '2 E. 14TH ST.',
  'NEW YORK', 'NY', 'USA', '10009',
  '212', '5555989',
  '');

INSERT INTO CUSTOMERS VALUES
  ( 204 , 'THE POWER FORWARD', '1 KNOTS LANDING',
  'DALLAS', 'TX', 'USA', '75248',
  '214', '5550505',
  '');

INSERT INTO CUSTOMERS VALUES
  ( 205 , 'POINT GUARD', '20 THURSTON ST.',
  'YONKERS', 'NY', 'USA', '10956',
  '914', '5554766',
  'Tremendous potential for an exclusive agreement.');
INSERT INTO CUSTOMERS VALUES
  ( 206 , 'THE COLISEUM', '5678 WILBUR PL.',
  'SCARSDALE', 'NY', 'USA', '10583',
  '914', '5550217',
  '');
INSERT INTO CUSTOMERS VALUES
  ( 207 , 'FAST BREAK', '1000 HERBERT LN.',
  'CONCORD', 'MA', 'USA', '01742',
  '508', '5551298',
  '');
INSERT INTO CUSTOMERS VALUES
  ( 208 , 'AL AND BOB''S SPORTS', '260 YORKTOWN CT.',
  'AUSTIN', 'TX', 'USA', '78731',
  '512', '5557631',
  '');
INSERT INTO CUSTOMERS VALUES
  ( 211 , 'AT BAT', '234 BEACHEM ST.',
  'BROOKLINE', 'MA', 'USA', '02146',
  '617', '5557385',
  '');
INSERT INTO CUSTOMERS VALUES
```

```
     ( 212 , 'ALL SPORT', '1000 38TH ST.',
     'BROOKLYN', 'NY', 'USA', '11210',
     '718', '5551739',
     '');
INSERT INTO CUSTOMERS VALUES
     ( 213 , 'GOOD SPORT', '400 46TH ST.',
     'SUNNYSIDE', 'NY', 'USA', '11104',
     '718', '5553771',
     '');

INSERT INTO CUSTOMERS VALUES
     ( 214 , 'AL''S PRO SHOP', '45 SPRUCE ST.',
     'SPRING', 'TX', 'USA', '77388',
     '713', '5555172',
     '');

INSERT INTO CUSTOMERS VALUES
     ( 215 , 'BOB''S FAMILY SPORTS', '400 E. 23RD',
     'HOUSTON', 'TX', 'USA', '77026',
     '713', '5558015',
     '');

INSERT INTO CUSTOMERS VALUES
     ( 216 , 'THE ALL AMERICAN', '547 PRENTICE RD.',
     'CHELSEA', 'MA', 'USA', '02150',
     '617', '5553047',
     '');

INSERT INTO CUSTOMERS VALUES
     ( 217 , 'HIT, THROW, AND RUN', '333 WOOD COURT',
     'GRAPEVINE', 'TX', 'USA', '76051',
     '817', '5552352',
     '');

INSERT INTO CUSTOMERS VALUES
     ( 218 , 'THE OUTFIELD', '346 GARDEN BLVD.',
     'FLUSHING', 'NY', 'USA', '11355',
     '718', '5552131',
     '');

INSERT INTO CUSTOMERS VALUES
     ( 221 , 'WHEELS AND DEALS', '2 MEMORIAL DRIVE',
     'HOUSTON', 'TX', 'USA', '77007',
     '713', '5554139',
     '');

INSERT INTO CUSTOMERS VALUES
     ( 222 , 'JUST BIKES', '4000 PARKRIDGE BLVD.',
     'DALLAS', 'TX', 'USA', '75205',
     '214', '5558735',
     '');
```

continues

Listing 3.1   Continued

```
INSERT INTO CUSTOMERS VALUES
  ( 223 , 'VELO SPORTS', '23 WHITE ST.',
  'MALDEN', 'MA', 'USA', '02148',
  '617', '5554983',
  '');

INSERT INTO CUSTOMERS VALUES
  ( 224 , 'JOE''S BIKE SHOP', '4500 FOX COURT',
  'GRAND PRAIRIE', 'TX', 'USA', '75051',
  '214', '5559834',
  '');

INSERT INTO CUSTOMERS VALUES
  ( 225 , 'BOB''S SWIM, CYCLE, AND RUN', '300 HORSECREEK CIRCLE',
  'IRVING', 'TX', 'USA', '75039',
  '214', '5558388',
  '');

INSERT INTO CUSTOMERS VALUES
  ( 226 , 'CENTURY SHOP', '8 DAGMAR DR.',
  'HUNTINGTON', 'NY', 'USA', '11743',
  '516', '5553006',
  '');

INSERT INTO CUSTOMERS VALUES
  ( 227 , 'THE TOUR', '2500 GARDNER RD.',
  'SOMERVILLE', 'MA', 'USA', '02144',
  '617', '5556673',
  'Customer referred to us by Mocha shop');

INSERT INTO CUSTOMERS VALUES
  ( 228 , 'FITNESS FIRST', '5000 85TH ST.',
  'JACKSON HEIGHTS', 'NY', 'USA', '11372',
  '718', '5558710',
  'Interested in being our sole distributor in Texas.');

-- Populate the orders tables

INSERT INTO orders VALUES
   (610,TO_DATE(2448264,'J'),101,TO_DATE(2448265,'J'),101.4);
INSERT INTO orders VALUES
   (611,TO_DATE(2448268,'J'),102,TO_DATE(2448268,'J'),45);
INSERT INTO orders VALUES
   (612,TO_DATE(2448272,'J'),104,TO_DATE(2448277,'J'),5860);
INSERT INTO orders VALUES
   (601,TO_DATE(2448013,'J'),106,TO_DATE(2448042,'J'),60.8);
INSERT INTO orders VALUES
   (602,TO_DATE(2448048,'J'),102,TO_DATE(2448063,'J'),56);
INSERT INTO orders VALUES
   (600,TO_DATE(2448013,'J'),103,TO_DATE(2448041,'J'),42);
```

```
INSERT INTO orders VALUES
   (604,TO_DATE(2448058,'J'),106,TO_DATE(2448073,'J'),642);
INSERT INTO orders VALUES
   (605,TO_DATE(2448087,'J'),106,TO_DATE(2448103,'J'),8374);
INSERT INTO orders VALUES
   (606,TO_DATE(2448087,'J'),100,TO_DATE(2448103,'J'),3.4);
INSERT INTO orders VALUES
   (609,TO_DATE(2448105,'J'),100,TO_DATE(2448119,'J'),102.5);
INSERT INTO orders VALUES
   (607,TO_DATE(2448091,'J'),104,TO_DATE(2448091,'J'),5.6);
INSERT INTO orders VALUES
   (608,TO_DATE(2448098,'J'),104,TO_DATE(2448098,'J'),35.2);
INSERT INTO orders VALUES
   (603,TO_DATE(2448048,'J'),102,TO_DATE(2448048,'J'),224);
INSERT INTO orders VALUES
   (620,TO_DATE(2448328,'J'),100,TO_DATE(2448328,'J'),4450);
INSERT INTO orders VALUES
   (613,TO_DATE(2448289,'J'),108,TO_DATE(2448289,'J'),6400);
INSERT INTO orders VALUES
   (614,TO_DATE(2448289,'J'),102,TO_DATE(2448293,'J'),23940);
INSERT INTO orders VALUES
   (616,TO_DATE(2448291,'J'),103,TO_DATE(2448298,'J'),764);
INSERT INTO orders VALUES
   (619,TO_DATE(2448310,'J'),104,TO_DATE(2448320,'J'),1260);
INSERT INTO orders VALUES
   (617,TO_DATE(2448293,'J'),105,TO_DATE(2448319,'J'),46370);
INSERT INTO orders VALUES
   (615,TO_DATE(2448289,'J'),107,TO_DATE(2448294,'J'),710);
INSERT INTO orders VALUES
   (618,TO_DATE(2448303,'J'),102,TO_DATE(2448322,'J'),3083);
INSERT INTO orders VALUES
   (621,TO_DATE(2448331,'J'),100,TO_DATE(2448348,'J'),730);
INSERT INTO orders VALUES
   (509,TO_DATE(2447682,'J'),226,TO_DATE(2447688,'J'),1174);


-- Populate the items table
INSERT INTO items VALUES (600,1,103120,42,1,42);
INSERT INTO items VALUES (610,3,103130,58,1,58);
INSERT INTO items VALUES (611,1,103120,45,1,45);
INSERT INTO items VALUES (612,1,103120,30,100,3000);
INSERT INTO items VALUES (601,1,103120,2.4,12,28.8);
INSERT INTO items VALUES (601,2,103121,32,1,32);
INSERT INTO items VALUES (602,1,103120,2.8,20,56);
INSERT INTO items VALUES (604,1,103120,58,3,174);
INSERT INTO items VALUES (604,2,103121,42,2,84);
INSERT INTO items VALUES (604,3,103130,32,12,384);
INSERT INTO items VALUES (603,1,103120,32,7,224);
INSERT INTO items VALUES (610,1,103120,35,1,35);
INSERT INTO items VALUES (610,2,103121,2.8,3,8.4);
INSERT INTO items VALUES (613,4,103131,2.2,200,440);
```

continues

Listing 3.1   Continued

```
INSERT INTO items VALUES (614,1,103120,35,444,15540);
INSERT INTO items VALUES (614,2,103121,2.8,1000,2800);
INSERT INTO items VALUES (612,2,103130,40.5,20,810);
INSERT INTO items VALUES (612,3,103130,10,150,1500);
INSERT INTO items VALUES (620,1,103120,35,10,350);
INSERT INTO items VALUES (620,2,103121,2.4,1000,2400);
INSERT INTO items VALUES (620,3,103130,3.4,500,1700);
INSERT INTO items VALUES (613,1,103120,5.6,100,560);
INSERT INTO items VALUES (613,2,103121,24,200,4800);
INSERT INTO items VALUES (613,3,103130,4,150,600);
INSERT INTO items VALUES (619,3,102136,3.4,100,340);
INSERT INTO items VALUES (617,1,103120,35,50,1750);
INSERT INTO items VALUES (617,2,103121,45,100,4500);
INSERT INTO items VALUES (614,3,103130,5.6,1000,5600);
INSERT INTO items VALUES (616,1,103120,45,10,450);
INSERT INTO items VALUES (616,2,103121,2.8,50,140);
INSERT INTO items VALUES (616,3,103130,58,2,116);
INSERT INTO items VALUES (616,4,102131,3.4,10,34);
INSERT INTO items VALUES (616,5,103140,2.4,10,24);
INSERT INTO items VALUES (619,1,103120,4,100,400);
INSERT INTO items VALUES (619,2,103121,2.4,100,240);
INSERT INTO items VALUES (615,1,103120,45,4,180);
INSERT INTO items VALUES (607,1,103120,5.6,1,5.6);
INSERT INTO items VALUES (615,2,103121,2.8,100,280);
INSERT INTO items VALUES (617,3,103130,2.8,500,1400);
INSERT INTO items VALUES (617,4,103131,5.6,500,2800);
INSERT INTO items VALUES (617,5,103140,58,500,29000);
INSERT INTO items VALUES (617,6,103141,24,100,2400);
INSERT INTO items VALUES (617,7,102131,12.5,200,2500);
INSERT INTO items VALUES (617,8,102136,3.4,100,340);
INSERT INTO items VALUES (617,9,105123,2.4,200,480);
INSERT INTO items VALUES (617,10,105124,4,300,1200);
INSERT INTO items VALUES (609,2,105123,2.5,5,12.5);
INSERT INTO items VALUES (609,3,103120,50,1,50);
COMMIT;
```

Listing 3.2   Create Indexes for JavaStop

```
-- Script: cr_idx.sql
-- Author: Megh Thakkar
-- Create Indexes
CREATE UNIQUE INDEX UI_PRODUCTS ON PRODUCTS (PRODUCT_ID);
CREATE UNIQUE INDEX UI_PRICE ON PRICE (PRODUCT_ID, START_DATE);
CREATE UNIQUE INDEX UI_CUSTOMERS ON CUSTOMERS (CUSTOMER_ID);
CREATE UNIQUE INDEX UI_ORDERS ON ORDERS (ORDER_ID);
CREATE UNIQUE INDEX UI_ITEMS ON ITEMS (ORDER_ID, ITEM_ID);
```

Listing 3.3   Create Constraints for JavaStop

```
-- Script: cr_constr.sql
-- Author: Megh Thakkar
-- Create Constraints
```

```
ALTER TABLE CUSTOMERS ADD
   CHECK (CUSTOMER_ID IS NOT NULL);
ALTER TABLE CUSTOMERS ADD
   CHECK (CUSTOMER_ID > 0);
ALTER TABLE CUSTOMERS ADD
   CHECK (STATE = UPPER(STATE));
ALTER TABLE CUSTOMERS ADD
   CHECK (LENGTH(NVL(ZIP_CODE, '99999')) IN (5, 9));
ALTER TABLE ITEMS ADD
   CHECK (ORDER_ID IS NOT NULL);
ALTER TABLE ITEMS ADD
   CHECK (ITEM_ID IS NOT NULL);
ALTER TABLE PRICE ADD
   CHECK (PRODUCTS_ID IS NOT NULL);
ALTER TABLE PRICE ADD
   CHECK (START_DATE IS NOT NULL);
ALTER TABLE PRICE ADD
   CHECK (LIST_PRICE IS NULL OR MIN_PRICE IS NULL OR MIN_PRICE <= LIST_PRICE);
ALTER TABLE PRICE ADD
   CHECK (END_DATE IS NULL OR START_DATE <= END_DATE);
ALTER TABLE PRODUCTS ADD
   CHECK (PRODUCT_ID IS NOT NULL);
ALTER TABLE ORDERS ADD
   CHECK (ORDER_ID IS NOT NULL);
ALTER TABLE ORDERS ADD
   CHECK (CUSTOMER_ID IS NOT NULL);
ALTER TABLE ORDERS ADD
   CHECK (TOTAL >= 0);
ALTER TABLE CUSTOMERS ADD
   PRIMARY KEY (CUSTOMER_ID);
ALTER TABLE ITEMS ADD
   PRIMARY KEY (ORDER_ID, ITEM_ID);
ALTER TABLE PRICE ADD
   PRIMARY KEY (PRODUCTS_ID, START_DATE);
ALTER TABLE PRODUCTSS ADD
   PRIMARY KEY (PRODUCTS_ID);
ALTER TABLE ORDERS ADD
   PRIMARY KEY (ORDER_ID);
ALTER TABLE ITEMS ADD
   FOREIGN KEY (ORDER_ID) REFERENCES ORDERS;
ALTER TABLE ITEMS ADD
   FOREIGN KEY (PRODUCTS_ID) REFERENCES PRODUCTSS;
ALTER TABLE PRICE ADD
   FOREIGN KEY (PRODUCTS_ID) REFERENCES PRODUCTSS;
ALTER TABLE ORDERS ADD
   FOREIGN KEY (CUSTOMER_ID) REFERENCES CUSTOMERS;


--Commit your changes to the database
COMMIT;
```

The UPDATE Statement

The UPDATE statement is used to modify values in the columns of existing rows. In order to update values in a table, the following must be true:

- The table must be in your own schema or
- You must have UPDATE privilege on the table.

In order to update values in the base table of a view, the following must be true:

- You must have UPDATE privilege on the view, and
- The owner of the schema containing the view must have UPDATE privilege on the base table.

 Note The UPDATE ANY TABLE system privilege allows you to update values in any table or any view's base table.

The basic syntax of the UPDATE statement is as follows:

```
SYNTAX: UPDATE [hint] table_expression
        Set_clause [where_clause] [returning_clause]
```

where

- hint is a comment that passes instructions to the optimizer on choosing an execution plan for the statement
- table_expression specifies the object whose data is to be updated
- set_clause specifies the column(s) of the table or view that is to be updated
- where_clause restricts the update to rows for which the specified condition is true
- returning_clause retrieves the rows affected by the update

 Note If the SQL92_SECURITY initialization parameter is set to TRUE, for an UPDATE to be successful, you must have SELECT privilege on the table whose column values you are referencing.

Let us consider some examples of using the UPDATE statement

- Update the description of Swiss chocolate to Swiss Almond chocolate. This product has the product_id of 103130.

```
SQL> update products
  2     set description = 'Swiss Almond chocolate'
  3     where product_id = 103130;
```

- Change the address of the customer WOMENS SPORTS.

```
SQL> update customers
  2     set address = '101 Disney drive',
  3     city = 'Orlando',
  4     state = 'FL',
  5     zip_code = 92610,
  6     area_code = '407',
  7     phone_number = '5551000'
  8     where name = 'WOMENS SPORTS';
```

The DELETE Statement

The DELETE statement is used to delete one or more rows from a table or view. In order to delete rows from a table, the following must be true:

- The table must be in your own schema, or
- You must have DELETE privilege on the table.

In order to delete rows from the base table of a view, the following must be true:

- You must have DELETE privilege on the view, and
- The owner of the schema containing the view must have DELETE privilege on the base table.

 Note   The DELETE ANY TABLE system privilege allows you to delete rows from any table or table partition, or any view's base table.

The basic syntax of the DELETE statement is as follows:

```
SYNTAX: DELETE [hint] FROM table_expression
        [where_clause] [returning_clause]
```

where

- hint is a comment that passes instructions to the optimizer on choosing an execution plan for the statement
- table_expression specifies the object whose data is to be deleted
- where_clause restricts the delete operation to rows for which the specified condition is true
- returning_clause retrieves the rows affected by the delete

> **Note**
> If the SQL92_SECURITY initialization parameter is set to TRUE then for a DELETE statement to be successful you must have SELECT privilege on the table whose column values you are referencing.

Let us consider an example of using the DELETE statement:

- JavaStop is no longer selling Almonds only.

```
SQL> delete products
2    where product_id = 104350;
```

Because the price table has the price for all products, we should be sure that we have some way of deleting the child record in the price table when the parent record is deleted from the products table. This can be done by using a trigger that fires for a delete on the products table and performs the following SQL:

```
SQL> delete price where product_id = 104350;
```

The SELECT Statement

The SELECT statement is used for retrieving information from the database. In order to select rows from a table, the following must be true:

- The table must be in your own schema, or
- You must have SELECT privilege on the table.

In order to select rows from the base table of a view, the following must be true:

- You must have SELECT privilege on the view, and
- The owner of the schema containing the view must have SELECT privilege on the base table.

> **Note**
> The SELECT ANY TABLE system privilege allows you to select rows from any table or table partition, or any view's base table.

The basic syntax of the SELECT statement is as follows:

```
SYNTAX: SELECT [hint] [ALL¦UNIQUE¦DISTINCT] [column_list¦*]
   FROM table_expression
       [where_clause] [hierarchical_query¦group_by_clause]
       [[MINUS¦INTERSECT¦UNION[ALL]] (subquery)]
   [order_by_clause]
```

where

- `hint` is a comment that passes instructions to the optimizer on choosing an execution plan for the statement
- `UNIQUE` and `DISTINCT` are synonymous and are used to retrieve only one copy of duplicate rows
- `ALL` is the default choice and is used to retrieve all the rows (even the duplicate rows)
- `column_list` specifies the columns that are to be retrieved
- `*` specifies that you want to select all the columns from all the tables, views, and snapshots specified in the `FROM` clause
- `table_expression` specifies the object whose data is to be selected
- `where_clause` restricts the select operation to rows for which the specified condition is true
- `hierarchical_query` clause allows you to specify the selected rows in a hierarchical order
- `group_by_clause` groups selected rows and returns a single row of summary information for each group

 **Note** If the `group_by_clause` contains `CUBE` or `ROLLUP` extensions, it produces super-aggregate grouping in addition to regular groupings.

- UNION, UNION ALL, MINUS, and INTERSECT are set operators that combine the results from multiple `SELECT` statements into one result.
- `order_by_clause` is used to order rows returned by the `SELECT` statement.

Let us consider some examples of `SELECT` statements:

- Find a list of all products sold by JavaStop

```
SQL> select product_id , description
2    from products;
```

The output of this statement could be

PRODUCT_ID	DESCRIPTION
103120	African Cinnamon
103121	Island Coconut
103130	Swiss chocolate

continues

PRODUCT_ID	DESCRIPTION
103131	Chocolate mint
103140	Irish cream
103141	Triple treat
102132	Tropical vanilla
104350	Almonds only
104351	Hazelnut
104352	Brazilian Santos
104360	Hawaiian delight
104361	Sumatra manhedling
104362	Kenya AA
102134	Zimbabwe 053
105123	Mocha Java
105124	Breakfast brew
105125	Mountain forest
105126	French roast
105127	Italian roast
105128	Jamaican roast
102136	Vienna roast

- Find the names of all customers who live in California

```
SQL> select name
2     from customers
3     where state = 'CA';
```

The output of this can be as follows:

NAME
JOCKSPORTS
TKB SPORT SHOP
VOLLYRITE
JUST TENNIS
EVERY MOUNTAIN
SHAPE UP
K + T SPORTS
WOMENS SPORTS

- Find the total dollar value of all the orders placed by VOLLYRITE

```
SQL> select sum(orders.total)
  2    from customers, orders
  3    where customers.customer_id = orders.customer_id
  4    and customers.name = 'VOLLYRITE';
```

The preceding example makes use of a join operation to join information from the customers and the orders tables.

> A join operation is used to join information from two or more tables by using the column(s) that are common in both the tables.

Procedural SQL Programming

PL/SQL is essentially an application development language. It adds a number of procedural non-SQL statements to the built-in SQL. PL/SQL can be used to create transactions; in other words, it can be used to group SQL statements, operators, and functions into a block that can be sent to the database as a single unit of work. As a result, PL/SQL reduces network traffic by sending all the statements at once. However, PL/SQL doesn't support the DDL statements and also doesn't support the DCL statements CONNECT, REVOKE, and GRANT. You have to enter these commands directly through a utility (server manager) that doesn't process the commands before sending them to the database server. Table 3.7 shows the most commonly used PL/SQL commands. Please refer to the Oracle PL/SQL User's guide and reference manual for a complete description of these commands.

> Native dynamic SQL can be used to execute DDL and DCL statements from within PL/SQL.

Table 3.7   Commonly Used PL/SQL Commands

PL/SQL Command	Usage
Begin	Begin a PL/SQL block.
Close	Close a cursor. This disables the result set.
Commit	Commit a transaction.
Declare	Declare a cursor.
Delete	Remove data.

continues

Table 3.7   Continued

PL/SQL Command	Usage
End	End a PL/SQL block.
Exception	Define exceptions (warning or error messages).
Exit	Force a loop to complete unconditionally.
Fetch	Retrieve information from a cursor.
Goto	Branch to a label unconditionally.
IF...THEN...ELSEIF...ELSE	Conditional statement execution.
Insert	Insert data.
Lock table	Lock an entire table in the desired lock mode.
Loop	Execute statements iteratively.
Null	Explicitly specify inaction.
Open	Open a cursor.
Raise	Raise an exception.
Rollback	Roll back a transaction.
Savepoint	Specify a point to which you can later roll back a transaction.
Select...into	Retrieve values and place them in the specified variables.
Set transaction	egin a read-only or read-write transaction, specify an isolation level, or assign a transaction to a specific rollback segment.
Update	Modify data.

PL/SQL and Java are complementary. PL/SQL is more appealing to SQL programmers, while Java (via SQLJ) is more attractive to Java programmers who need high-performance access to the database.

Note   SQL, PL/SQL, and Java call each other seamlessly. PL/SQL stored procedures can be extended with Java and SQL will see the Java stored procedures just as it sees PL/SQL.

A PL/SQL block consists of the following sections:

- **An optional declaration section**—All variables and constants that are referenced in the PL/SQL statements must be declared. A declarations section is used by beginning the PL/SQL block with the word DECLARE. Each variable or constant declaration consists of its name, its datatype, and an optional default value. Each declaration is terminated with a semicolon. In addition to the normal Oracle SQL datatypes, PL/SQL enables you to declare variables with additional datatypes described in Table 3.8.

- **An execution section**—The executable section of a PL/SQL block starts with the word BEGIN. Each PL/SQL statement is terminated with a semicolon. PL/SQL statements can be categorized as follows:

  Assignment statements

  Control-of-flow statements

  Cursor statements

  SQL statements

- **An optional exceptions section**—The exception section contains the exception handlers for predefined and user-defined exceptions that occur during the execution of the PL/SQL block. Each exception handler basically consists of one or more PL/SQL statements that indicate what to do when the error condition occurs.

 **Note** An anonymous PL/SQL block is an unnamed PL/SQL block that takes no arguments and also does not return any value.

Table 3.8   Additional Datatypes Provided by PL/SQL

Datatype	Description
BOOLEAN	Can be assigned the predefined constants TRUE, FALSE, or NULL
BINARY_INTEGER	Can be used to manipulate signed integers in the range of -2,147,483,647 to 2,147,483,647
NATURAL	Allows a set of integers from 0 to 2,147,483,647
POSITIVE	Allows a set of integers from 1 to 2,147,483,647
%TYPE	Allows the declaration of a variable's datatype as being equivalent to the specified column's datatype
%ROWTYPE	Allows you to declare a composite variable that is equivalent to a row in the specified table. This is very useful with cursors

The following example shows how PL/SQL can be used to insert additional products in the products table:

```
SQL> declare
2     max_records constant int:= 10;
3     I int:= 1;
4     Prod_desc varchar2(20);
```

```
5    Begin
6       For I in 1..max_records loop
7       Prod_desc:= 'Coffee#' ¦¦ I;
8         Insert into products
9         Values (I, prod_desc);
10     End loop;
11     Commit;
12     End;
/
```

The preceding PL/SQL procedure will add 10 new products.

Next Steps

In this chapter we have seen how to make use of the various SQL commands and their Oracle extensions to manipulate JavaStop. In the next chapter we will learn some Java basics and understand how object-oriented concepts are applied using Java. The basic knowledge of Java that we will gain in the next chapter will lay the foundation for helping us understand the Java code that we will be using in the rest of the book.

Chapter 4

Java Basics for Developing JavaStop

Introduction

So far in this book we have seen how to use Oracle8i for creating and populating the JavaStop database that will be used to store the data. For developing our e-commerce application, we will use Java as the programming language. This chapter introduces you to the fundamentals of Java and can serve as a quick review for those already familiar with Java.

Java is known as an interpreted language. In reality, however, it can be viewed as both interpreted and compiled because about 20 percent of the Java code is interpreted by the browser and the rest is compiled locally. In other words, the Java programmer first compiles the Java program into bytecodes, which is platform-independent. These bytecodes are then interpreted by the Java runtime environment (such as a browser) for a specific platform. This interpretation has the advantage that the Java programmers don't have to worry about which platform the Java code is going to run on. However, the disadvantage of interpretation is that the performance is not as good as compiled code because the browser has to do some work on the class files before they can be run. As a result, Java programs would run 1/2 to 1/6 the speed of their counterparts such as C++ programs (that are compiled). The drawback of using interpreters is minimized by the use of Just-In-Time (JIT) compilers that are built into the browsers. These JIT compilers convert Java methods into native code for the platform you are using.

Java is an object-oriented language and therefore defines data as objects. Actions that can occur on the objects are defined by the methods. We will discuss some of the object-oriented features of Java, but for more details on object-oriented programming please refer to the references mentioned in Chapter 15, "Enhancing JavaStop."

 Note   Unlike C++, Java doesn't support multiple inheritance.

Java enables you to create interfaces, which are classes that don't implement any of their methods and leave the implementation of the methods to the subclasses. Interfaces enable you to define methods that can be shared by different classes, with each class providing its own implementation of the methods.

Java Datatypes

Java has several types of data with which it can deal. They are placed into two categories: Primitive types and reference types.

Primitive Java Types

Java provides eight primitive data types that can be used to store data. These types are boolean, byte, short, int, long, char, float, and double.

Boolean

Boolean data types are the simplest form of datatypes. Variables of this type can store two possible values: true or false. Boolean variables are generally used to store information that is binary. For example, a product can be available or not available.

```
boolean coffee_available = true;
```

The previous example sets a boolean variable to `true`.

Integer

Integer data can be stored in several types based on the value you are attempting to store. Table 4.1 shows the various integer types available.

Table 4.1   Integer Types and Their Limits

Integer Type	Range of Values
byte	−128 to 127
short	−32768 to 32767
int	−2,147,483,648 to 2,147,483,647
long	-2^{63} to $2^{63}-1$
char	0 to 65535 or Unicode character

It is not advisable to use the long data type for all numeric data because you will be wasting space, even though it can store huge numbers.

For example

```
byte byte_data=100;
short short_data=100;
int int_data=100;
long long_data=100;
char char_data='m';
```

Table 4.2 shows the various operations that can be applied to integer datatypes.

Table 4.2   Integer Operations

Operation	Description
=, +=, -=, *=, /=	Assignment
==, !=	Equality and inequality
<, <=, >, >=	Comparison
+, -	Unary sign
+, -, *, /, %	Binary operators (addition, subtraction, multiplication, division, and modulus)
++, --	Increment and decrement
<<, >>, >>>, <<=, >>=, >>>	Bitwise operators
~	Bitwise logical negation
&, ¦, ^, &=, ¦=, ^=	Bitwise AND, OR, XOR, and assign operators

Floating-Point

Numeric data that can have a decimal point in it is stored in floating-point variables. Two primitive data types are used in Java for floating-point data:

float	(from 1.40239846e–45f to 3.40282347e+38f)
double	(from 4.94065645841246544e–324d to 1.7976931348623157e+308d)

In addition, floating-point numbers can have four unique states:

Positive infinity

Negative infinity

Zero

Not a number

Operations that can be performed on floating-point variables are shown in Table 4.3.

Table 4.3   Floating-Point Operations

Operation	Description
=, +=, -=, *=, /=	Assignment
==, !=	Equality and inequality
<, <=, >, >=	Comparison
+, -	Unary sign
+, -, *, /	Binary operators (addition, subtraction, multiplication, division, and modulus)
++, --	Increment and decrement

Reference Variables

Java supports three types of reference variables: classes, interfaces, and arrays.

We discussed interfaces earlier. Classes will be discussed in more detail later. For now, let us understand the use of arrays in Java.

An array enables you to have multiple objects in a row. Each element in the array is identified by an index using the [ ] notation. For example

```
Int price[] = {4,10,31,2};

    Int x = price[2];
```

The value of variable x is 31.

 Java arrays start with an index value of 0.

 Java enables whitespace to be declared anywhere in the source code without influencing the meaning of the code.

The Java Vector Class and Arrays

A Java Vector is similar to an array in that it can store multiple objects that are retrieved using an index value. The main difference between an array and a Vector is that the array is fixed in size (it can hold a predetermined maximum number of objects) but the Vector can grow in size as needed. Also, a Vector provides additional methods for manipulating the elements, such as inserting a new element between two existing elements and so on. When creating a Vector, you can optionally specify the initial size of the Vector and the amount of increment using one of the following:

- `Public Vector()`—Creates an empty Vector that grows as needed
- `public Vector(int initSize)`—Creates a Vector that is initially capable of holding `initSize` elements
- `public Vector(int initSize, int incrAmount)`—Creates a Vector that is initially capable of holding `initSize` elements and then grows by `incrAmount` increments as needed

 Note   If `incrAmount` is not specified, the vector doubles its size when it grows.

4

Several important methods associated with the Vector include

- `public final synchronized void addElement(Object newElement)`—Adds the new element to the end of the Vector.
- `NoSuchElementException public final synchronized void insertElementAt(Object newElement, int index) throws ArrayIndexOutOfBoundsException`—Inserts a new element at the specified index. If the specified index is out of bounds, the `ArrayIndexOutOfBoundsException` exception is thrown.
- `public final synchronized Object elementAt(int index) throws ArrayIndexOutOfBoundsException`—This method is used to access elements of the vector. Unlike an array, the `[]` (square brackets) notation can't be used to access elements of a vector. If the specified index is out of bounds, the `ArrayIndexOutOfBoundsException` exception is thrown.
- `public final synchronized Object firstElement() throws`—It returns the first element in the vector and throws the `NoSuchElementException` exception if the vector is empty.
- `public final synchronized Object lastElement() throws`—It returns the last element in the vector and throws the `NoSuchElementException` exception if the vector is empty.
- `public final boolean isEmpty()`—It tests whether the vector is empty or not.
- `public final int size()`—It returns the number of objects in the vector.

Java Type Conversions

Java is a strongly typed language because at compile time the type of every variable is known. Type conversion refers to the problem of how the different types interrelate with each other—for example, adding a byte variable to a long variable. There are two kinds of type conversions:

- Explicit type conversion—This is done using the `cast` operator. For example

  ```
  float a = 1.9;

  float b = 3.2;

  float c = 4.7;

  a = (int)(a/b*c)
  ```

  The preceding casts the result into an int.

- Implicit type conversion—This is done automatically by the language as needed.

 Note   In Java, an implicit conversion between numeric data types is performed only if it doesn't result in loss of precision or magnitude. Attempts to covert data types that would cause a loss of precision or magnitude result in compiler errors unless an explicit conversion by cast is specified.

 Note   Java uses the + operator to concatenate strings. For example

```
string s;
    s = "Jack"+"and"+"Jill";
```

The value of s is Jack and Jill.

Comments

Comments enable you to place information about the program within the program. These can be useful to programmers when they are revisiting the code because it helps them understand what is happening in the source code. Java supports three types of comments:

- **Traditional C-style comments**—Traditional C-style comments are placed between `/*` and `*/`. For example,

  ```
  /**
   *  The Constructor is used to instantiate the User Interface.
  ```

```
 *  This is a traditional C-style comment.
 **/
 public JdbcDml(){
    m_JdbcGui = new JdbcDmlGui(this);
    m_JdbcGui.setVisible(true);
 }
```

- **C++ style comments**—C++ style comments begin with // and end with the current line of source code. Such comments are useful for quickly commenting on the current line of code. For example

```
// Delete a record from the customers table

public void deleteRecord(String p_custid) {
   try {
       //Prepare a SQL statement to delete a record
       PreparedStatement l_pst = m_connection.prepareStatement(
               " Delete from customers where customer_id=?");

      // Assign positional arguments
       l_pst.setString(1,p_custid);


       l_pst.executeUpdate();

      //close the preparedStatement
       l_pst.close();

       m_JdbcGui.deleteFromJTable();

       m_JdbcGui.putStatus("Record deleted successfully");
   } catch(Exception ex){
      m_JdbcGui.putStatus("Error in deleting record.... "
                          +'\n'+ex.toString());
   }
 }

 }
```

- **Javadoc comments**—Javadoc comments are used by the javadoc tool to generate documentation. These comments open with /** and close with */. For example

```
/** This program shows how to connect to a database
  * using JDBC.
 * Make sure that the CLASSPATH variable is set
 * properly.*/
```

Control of Flow Functions

Control of flow statements enable you to control the flow of execution in a program. Control of flow statements enable programmers to break the sequential flow of programs. Several types of control flow statements are supported in Java:

- `if` statements—The syntax of the `if` statement is as follows:

```
If (expression)
    Statement;
```

  The `if` statement checks the expression value (which returns a boolean) and if the value is true, it executes the statement block. On the other hand, if the expression value is false, the statement block is skipped and execution proceeds.

- `if-else` statement—The syntax of the `if-else` statement is as follows:

```
If (expression)
    Statement1;
Else
    Statement2;
```

  The expression is checked and if it returns `true`, `statement1` is executed; otherwise, `statement2` is executed.

- `while`—while is an example of an iteration statement. The syntax of the `while` statement is as follows:

```
While (expression)
    Statement;
```

  The expression is checked, and if it is true, the statement is executed repeatedly until the expression becomes false.

- `do`—The do statement is an example of an iteration statement. The syntax of the `do` statement is as follows:

```
Do
    Statement;
    While (expression)
```

  The statement is executed, the expression is checked, and the statement is repeatedly executed while the expression is true.

 Note

Unlike a `while` statement block that might never be executed, a do statement block is executed at least once.

- for—The `for` loop is an example of an iteration statement. It is executed a predetermined number of times. The syntax of the `for` loop is as follows:

```
for (initialization, expression, step)
statement;
```

The initialization code is executed first, and then the expression is evaluated. If it returns `true`, the statement is executed, the step is performed, and the expression is reevaluated until is becomes false.

 Note

The equivalent `while` statement for a `for` loop is as follows:

```
Initialization;
While (expression){
    Statement;
    Step;
}
```

- switch—A `switch` statement is like a multiple `if` statement. It passes control to one of the many statements within its block, depending on the value of the expression in the statement. Control is passed to the first statement following a case label that matches the value of its expression. If there is no match then control is passed to the default label. The syntax of the `switch` statement is as follows:

```
Switch (expression){
Case V1: statement1;
Break;
Case V2: statement2;
Break;
Case V3: statement3;
Break;
Default: statementd;
}
```

- break—The `break` statement is used to pass control to another part of the program. An unlabeled `break` statement in an iteration passes control to the next line after the current iteration.

 Note

If a `finally` clause is used in a `try` statement and a `break` is also used, the control is passed to the `finally` clause before it is passed on (as specified by the `break`).

- continue—A continue statement is only allowed in the substatement block of an iteration statement. The effect of the continue statement is to skip the remainder of the block for the current iteration and go on to the next pass of the iteration.

- return—A return statement is used to pass control to the caller. If a finally clause is used in a try statement and a break is also used, the control is passed to the finally clause before it is passed on (as specified by the return).

Java Classes

Classes are an essential part of any Java application or applet. Java is made up of a number of classes that are made available for general use with the help of the Java Development Kit (JDK). Objects are created as instances of a class, and these objects can include all the code of the class. In other words, you can consider a class as a template, and individual objects are created using that template.

Each Java class consists of two parts:

- **Declaration**—Java class declarations have the form

  ```
  [AccessSpecifier] class  NameOfNewClass [extends NameOfSuperClass]
  [implements NameOfInterface];
  ```

  where AccessSpecifier determines how the class can be used in development. Several access specifiers are allowed:

  Public/Protected—Public specifies that this class will be accessible by all objects. The default is Protected, which specifies that the class can be extended and used by other classes but that it can be used only by objects within the same package.

  final—final specifies that this class can't have any subclasses.

  abstract—abstract specifies that this class has at least one method that has not been implemented. Abstract classes can be extended and the methods implemented by its subclasses.

  NameOfNewClass specifies the name of the new class you are creating.

  NameOfSuperClass specifies the name of the superclass that the new class extends.

  NameOfInterface specifies the name of the interface that the new class implements.

Abstract classes have methods without implementation, and therefore you can't have instances of abstract classes.

- **Body**—Contains the Java code that implements the methods of the class.

Superclass

Java, like other object-oriented languages, enables you to reuse code by extending existing classes and building bigger and more complex classes. Classes are extended in the declaration section of the new class. The class that is being extended is called the *superclass* while the class that extends a superclass is called its *subclass*. After extending a superclass, if you leave the subclass as is, you will have a new class that is identical to the superclass—with the same methods and fields. Subclasses give you an opportunity to extend the superclass.

Java, unlike C++, doesn't allow multiple inheritance. Therefore, each Java class can extend only one class.

Every Java class is considered to be an object, so even if it doesn't extend any other class, it still extends `java.lang.Object`.

Constructors

Constructors of a class are unique methods that perform a special task. Constructors are automatically executed when a new instance of a class is created. Constructors have the same name as the class. Constructors don't have a return argument because they are not called as a regular method but are invoked when a new instance is created. Generally, constructors are used to initialize the class's fields and perform initialization tasks, such as connecting to the database. The following code listing shows the use of a constructor to initialize the GUI and make it visible.

Listing 4.1   Using a Constructor to Initialize the GUI

```
public class JdbcConnection {
  //Create a connection object
  Connection  m_connection = null;
```

continues

Listing 4.1   Continued

```
//The User Interface for this application is handled by JdbcConnectionGui
JdbcConnectionGui  m_GUI;

/**
*  Instantiate the GUI frame.
*  This is the constructor for the JdbcConnection class
**/
public JdbcConnection(){
   m_GUI = new JdbcConnectionGui(this);
   m_GUI.setVisible(true);
}

/**
*  Make a database connection to JSTP
**/
public static void main(String args[]){

  JdbcConnection JdbcCon = new JdbcConnection();
  JdbcCon.dbConnection();
}
```

 Note   Overriding methods inherited from a superclass enables you to modify the implementation to suit your particular needs and also implement a technique that provides optimal performance.

Instantiating a Class

Instantiating a class refers to the process of creating a new object of the type of the class. In this manner, a class can be treated as a data type because it enables you to have new items based on a specified template. Any class (except abstract classes) can be instantiated. Instantiating a class is accomplished by using the new operator. For example,

```
JdbcConnection JdbcCon = new JdbcConnection();
```

creates a new object JdbcCon of the class JdbcConnection.

It is not necessary to instantiate a class to use it. Instantiation is required only if you are planning to call class methods or variables that are not static. However, it should be understood that static methods can refer only to static class variables. For example, you can use the println method of the System class without any instantiation as shown in Listing 4.2.

Listing 4.2   Referencing Static Class Variables

```java
// Connecting to the database
 public void dbConnection(){
    try {
        System.out.println("Connecting to the Database....please wait.....");

        //Register the JDBC driver
        DriverManager.registerDriver(new oracle.jdbc.driver.OracleDriver());

        // The connection parameters specified in ConnectionSpecs.java are used
        String l_dbConnectString =
            "(DESCRIPTION=(ADDRESS=(HOST="+ConnectionSpecs.s_hostName+")"+
            "(PROTOCOL=tcp)(PORT="+ConnectionSpecs.s_portNumber+"))"+
            "(CONNECT_DATA=(SID="+ConnectionSpecs.s_databaseSID+")))";


        m_connection = DriverManager.getConnection(
                    "jdbc:oracle:thin:@"+l_dbConnectString,
                    ConnectionSpecs.s_userName,ConnectionSpecs.s_password);

        /*
         * Setting autocommit to false will prevent actual changes
         * to the database
         */
        m_connection.setAutoCommit(false);


        System.out.println("Successfully connected as user " +
                    ConnectionSpecs.s_userName +" to database "
                    +ConnectionSpecs.s_databaseSID );
    } catch(Exception ex){
      System.out.println ("Unable to connect....."
                    +ex.toString());

    }
 }
```

The Java Virtual Machine plays an important role in creating the first class for your application or applet. In the case of an application, when you run the application by typing java MyAppClass, the Virtual Machine will call the static main() method in MyAppClass. The main() method is static, so it can be called without any instantiation. Generally, you will write the code to instantiate your class in the main() method. However, in the case of an applet, when a browser encounters the <APPLET> tag, such as <APPLET CODE="MyAppClass">, it creates an instance of the class MyAppClass and calls the init() method. For example, the following main() method creates an instance of the class JdbcConnection:

```java
/**
 *  Make a database connection to JSTP
 **/
```

```
public static void main(String args[]){

  JdbcConnection JdbcCon = new JdbcConnection();
  JdbcCon.dbConnection();
}
```

Referencing Class Components

Java uses the standard dot notation used in other object-oriented programming languages to reference components (such as fields and methods) belonging to a class. In other words, the following notation is used:

```
InstanceOfClass.MethodOrVariable
```

For an example, see Listing 4.3.

Listing 4.3   Using the Dot Notation to Reference Components

```
/* Delete a record from the customers table using SQL DELETE statement*/
public void deleteRecord(String p_custid) {
  try {
      //Prepare a SQL statement to delete a record
      PreparedStatement l_pst = m_connection.prepareStatement(
              " Delete from customers where customer_id=?");


      l_pst.setString(1,p_custid);


      l_pst.executeUpdate();


      l_pst.close();

      m_JdbcGui.deleteFromJTable();

      m_JdbcGui.putStatus("Record deleted successfully");
  } catch(Exception ex){
    m_JdbcGui.putStatus("Error in deleting record.... "
                      +'\n'+ex.toString());
  }
 }

}
```

In the previous listing, l_pst is an instance of the PreparedStatement class. setString, executeUpdate, and close are methods defined in the PreparedStatement class (or its superclass).

The Variable `this`

We already have seen several examples of how a class can refer to instances of other classes. The special variable `this` is used by a class to refer to itself. The `this` variable might be needed in several situations:

- You are using two variables with the same name in your class—one variable belongs to the class and the other to a method in the class. The `this` variable can help you in identifying the class variable.

- A class needs to pass itself as an argument to one of its methods.

Listing 4.4 contains code from JdbcDml.java and JdbdDmlGui.java and will help you understand the use of the `this` operator.

Listing 4.4   Using the `this` Operator

```java
/**
 *  The Constructor is used to instantiate the User Interface
 **/
public JdbcDml(){
    m_JdbcGui = new JdbcDmlGui(this);
    m_JdbcGui.setVisible(true);
}
/**
 * The constructor is used to set up the listeners for the events
 **/
public JdbcDmlGui(JdbcDml p_parent) {
  try {
      m_parent = p_parent;

      // Initialize JTable
      jtableInit();
      jbInit();

      //Set up the listeners for the various events
      setupListeners();
  } catch (Exception ex) {
      m_statusField.setText("Error occurred during initialization..."
                              +'\n'+ex.toString());
  }
}
// INSERT button listener
  m_insertButton.addActionListener(new java.awt.event.ActionListener(){
    public void actionPerformed(ActionEvent evt){
      if(evt.getActionCommand() == "INSERT") {
        // Pass the event to the parent
        m_parent.dispatchEvent("INSERT");
      }
```

continues

Listing 4.4   Continued

```
    }
  });

  //UPDATE button listener
  m_updateButton.addActionListener(new java.awt.event.ActionListener(){
    public void actionPerformed(ActionEvent evt) {
      if(evt.getActionCommand() =="UPDATE"){
        // Pass the event to the parent
        m_parent.dispatchEvent("UPDATE");
      }
    }
  });
```

 The previous constructor for `JdbcDml` is used to pass itself to `JdbcDmlGui` (where the user interface is implemented).

 The previous constructor for `JdbcDmlGui` takes the `JdbcDml` instance and initializes `m_parent` so that events can be dispatched back to it.

 Events are dispatched back to the calling class using the `m_parent.dispatchEvent()` method.

 Similar to the `this` variable, the special variable `super` enables you to access a class's superclass.

Java API

The Java API is a set of classes developed by Sun for use with the Java Programming language. The Java API helps you build applications and applets. As mentioned earlier, reusing code by extending a superclass is very beneficial. You can quickly write applications by extending the Java API classes. The Java API classes are grouped into packages, which are a way of organizing your classes so that they can be easily used. The Java core API that ships with Java 1.1 comes with a number of built-in packages, shown in Table 4.4.

Table 4.4 Important Java Core Packages with Java 1.1

Package	Contents
java.applet	Classes that help in creating Java applets that run under Netscape 2.0 (or higher) or other Java-compatible browsers.
java.awt	Classes that help in creating platform-independent GUI—for example, GridBagLayout, Button, TextField, and so on.
java.awt.datatransfer	Classes that help you in data transfer.
java.awt.event	Classes that enable you to use events.
java.awt.image	Tools to manipulate images.
java.awt.peer	Interfaces between your code and the computer.
java.io	Classes for performing I/O—for example, the String class.
Java.lang	Classes that provide the Java core functionality. It is implicitly imported. Important classes belonging to this package include • Basic data types—Character, Integer, and so on • Error handling—Throwable and Error classes • Runtime system control—SecurityManager, System, and so on
Java.lang.reflect	Tools that enable you to reflect objects and inspect a runtime object for its methods and fields.
java.net	Classes that help in making network connections.
java.rmi, java.rmi. registry, and java. rmi.server	Tools that enable you to perform remote method invocation (RMI). RMI is a technique that enables you to create objects on a remote computer and use them locally.
java.security, java.security.acl, and java.security	Tools to enable encryption in Java programs and secure data transfer between client and server interfaces.
java.sql	Java Database Connectivity (JDBC) that enables you to access relational databases such as Oracle.
java.util	Tools that provide data structures such as vectors, stacks, and so on.

4

Note   Every meaningful application or applet you write will use at least one class from the Java Core API.

In addition to the previously listed packages, the Java Core API has the following less important packages:

- `java.bean`
- `java.util.zip`
- `java.text`

JDK 1.2 provides additional packages:

- **Java Commerce API**—Enables secure purchasing and finance management. For example, JavaWallet implements a client-side framework for credit card and debit card transactions.
- **Java Enterprise API**—Supports connectivity to enterprise databases enabling you to run distributed client/server applets and Java applications that run on any OS or hardware platform.
- **Java Management API**—Provides Java objects and methods for building applets that can manage enterprise networks over the intranet and Internet.
- **Java Media API**—Consists of several packages that support multimedia such as telephony, animation, and so on.
- **Java Security API**—Provides security functionality in applets and applications. Functionality includes encryption, authentication, and cryptography.
- **Java Server API**—Enables you to quickly develop Java servlets.

 Note Servlets are executable programs that can be uploaded to run on networks or servers. They are similar to applets except that applets are downloaded on the client and execute on the client.

JDK Tools

The JDK provides a variety of tools:

- Java Interpreter
- AppletViewer
- Java Compiler
- Java Disassembler
- javah
- Java Documentation Generator
- Java Debugger

The Java Interpreter

Compiled Java applications are run by using the Java interpreter *java*. The syntax for the Java interpreter is

```
java [options] nameofclassonly
```

where

- *nameofclassonly* specifies the class name (the extension .class is not required).
- *options* specifies various options that can be used with the Java interpreter. These options are shown in Table 4.5.

Table 4.5   Java Interpreter Options

Option	Description
-help	Shows all the available options.
-version	Displays the JDK version in use.
-v or -verbose	Displays classes as they are loaded.
-cs or –checksource	Checks whether the source code is newer than its class file and compiles it if that is the case.
-debug	Generates a password that will be used with the password option of the jdb (Java debugger) tool.
-prof	Places profiling information in the file \Java.prof.
-classpath <dirs>	Specifies the directories where class files need to be searched.
-noaynscgc	Turns off asynchronous garbage collection. By default, asynchronous garbage collection is used.
-verbosegc	Prints a message each time garbage collection occurs.
-noclassgc	Disables garbage collection for classes.
-verify	Verifies loaded classes.
-verifyremote	Verifies imported or inherited classes.
-noverify	Disables class verification.
-mx value	Sets the maximum Java heap size to the specified value. The default value is 16MB.
-ms value	Sets the initial Java heap size. The default value is 1MB.
-ss value	Sets the stack size of a C process to the specified value.
-oss value	Sets the stack size of a Java process to the specified value.

AppletViewer

Applets are Java programs that can run embedded in an HTML document. Under normal conditions, an applet can't run on its own. An *AppletViewer* is a tool that enables you to run applets without the overhead of using browsers.

The AppletViewer is used with the following syntax:

```
appletViewer [options] URLs
```

where

- *URLs* are the uniform resource locators to HTML files that contain applet tags
- *options* can be -debug, enabling you to run the AppletViewer in the debug mode

The Java Compiler

.java files can be compiled into class files by using the Java compiler, *javac*. The class files can then be run by the Java interpreter. The options available with the Java compiler are listed in Table 4.6.

Table 4.6   Java Compiler Options

Option	Description
-O	Turns optimization on. It places all static, final, and private methods inline—making the class files larger but the overall performance better.
-classpath	Overrides the default CLASSPATH.
-d	Specifies where the resulting class files are to be placed.
-g	Is used with jdb for debugging class files.
-nowarn	Turns off compiler warnings.
-verbose	Displays the source files that are being compiled and loaded.
-depend	Enables compiling of dependent class files as well as specified class files.
-Jjavaoption	Enables a single argument to be passed to the Java interpreter running the compiler, such as changing the allocated amount of heap memory.

The Java Disassembler

The Java disassembler *javap* is a tool that is used to disassemble compiled Java byte-code and print information about the member variables and methods.

The Java disassembler has the following syntax:

```
javap [options] NamesOfClasses
```

where

- *NamesOfClasses* is the name of the classes (separated by spaces) that are to be disassembled.
- *options* specifies the available options (shown in Table 4.7).

Table 4.7   Java Disassembler Options

Option	Description
-version	Displays the JDK version in use
-c	Disassembles the source file and displays the bytecodes produced
-l	Displays the local variables
-public	Displays public classes and members only
-protected	Displays protected and public classes and members
-private	Displays all classes and members
-package	Displays private, protected, and public member variables and members
-verbose	Displays stacks, local variables, and member methods as the disassembly occurs
-s	Displays internal type signatures
-classpath	Overrides the default CLASSPATH
-verify	Verifies the classes being loaded

C-header and Stub File Creation

C-header and stub files needed to extend Java code with the C language can be created with the javah tool.

javah has the following syntax:

```
javah [options] NameOfClass
```

where

- *NameOfClass* is the name of the Java class
- *options* specifies the available options (shown in Table 4.8)

Table 4.8   Options Available with javah

Option	Description
-version	Displays the build version
-help	Displays the available options
-jni	Creates a header file that can be used with JNI
-td	Specifies the temporary directory to use
-trace	Adds trace information to stub files
-d	Specifies the directory where header and stub files are to be created
-v	Displays the status of header and stub creation
-classpath	Overrides the default CLASSPATH
-stubs	Creates stub files instead of header files
-o	Specifies the file in which the stub and header files are placed

The Java Documentation Generator

The Java documentation generator, *javadoc*, can be used to create an HTML file by using the tags (or comments) placed in the Java source files. The options available with javadoc are shown in Table 4.9.

Table 4.9   Options Available with javadoc

Option	Description
-classpath	Overrides the default CLASSPATH
-d	Specifies the directory in which the HTML files generated are to be placed
-sourcefile	Specifies the directories (separated by colons) in which the source files are located
-doctype	Specifies the type of output file, such as HTML (default), MIF, and so on
-verbose	Displays information about files being documented
-nodepreciated	Ignores @depreciated paragraphs
-author	Uses the @author paragraphs
-noindex	Doesn't create an index file
-notree	Doesn't create a tree file
-J<flag>	Specifies flags that can be passed to the Java runtime

The Java Debugger

The Java debugger, *jdb*, is a command-line–driven debugging tool for the Java environment. jdb can be used to debug files on the local machine as well as those on the remote machines (using the `-host` and `-password` options). The various options available with jdb are

- `-host`—Specifies the name of the remote computer on which the Java program resides

- `-password`—Specifies the password for the remote Java file. This password is generated by the Java interpreter using the `-debug` option.

> **Note**
>
> CLASSPATH is the one important environment variable used by all the JDK tools. It specifies the directories (separated by colons for UNIX and semicolons for DOS) where all the classes reside.
>
> For example, for UNIX the syntax is
>
> `setenv CLASSPATH .:/users/megh/java:/usr/jdk1.2/classes`
>
> For DOS the syntax is
>
> `Set CLASSPATH=.;c:\users\megh\java;c:\tools\jdk1.2\classes`

Organizing Components

The basic interface widgets that you find in a GUI environment are implemented by the AWT components. The AWT components are organized using containers and layout managers.

> **Note**
>
> To display an AWT component, you must place it in a container.

A *layout manager* is a set of instructions to the container about how and where to place the new component. Every time a new component is added to the container, the container consults the layout manager for its placement details.

> **Note**
>
> Containers are themselves components and therefore can be placed in other containers.

Several containers are defined in the AWT including

- **Panels**—Used only for organizing components.
- **Frames**—Can be used to create separate windows for your application and even to build stand-alone graphical applications.
- **Dialogs**—Pop-up windows. They can be modal as well as non-modal. Modal dialogs prevent focus from shifting away from them and therefore prevent input to other windows while they are being displayed.

The layout managers in the AWT are

- **FlowLayout**—Arranges components from left to right until no other component can fit on that row. After the row is full, it starts on the next row.
- **GridLayout**—Works similarly to the FlowLayout except that each component is assigned an equal size.
- **BorderLayout**—Components are assigned a location as specified by the compass location: NORTH, SOUTH, EAST, WEST, or CENTER. The exact position is based on the relative size of the components.
- **CardLayout**—Components are stacked and treated as a stack of cards. At any time only one component is visible.
- **GridBagLayout**—This is the most flexible component layout. The container is treated as a grid of cells similar to GridLayout except that a component can occupy more than one cell as specified by its `GridBagConstraints`. The `GridBagConstraints` class has a number of variables that specify component placement:
  - `gridx` and `gridy`—These represent the co-ordinates of the cell where the component is to be placed. If the component is going to occupy more than one cell, it represents the upper-left cell of the component. The default values for `gridx` and `gridy` are both `GridBagConstraints.RELATIVE`. For `gridx` this means the cell just to the right of the component that was last added, and for `gridy` it means the cell just to the bottom of the component that was last added.
  - `gridwidth` and `gridheight`—This specifies how many cells wide and tall a component will be. The default value for both is `1`.
  - `fill`—This specifies what to do in case the component is smaller than its specified display area. Several values can be used.
  - `GridBagConstraints.NONE`—This specifies that you want to leave the component as is.

- GridBagConstraints.HORIZONTAL—This specifies that the component should be stretched horizontally as needed to fill the display area allocated to it.

- GridBagConstraints.VERTICAL—This specifies that the component should be stretched vertically as needed to fill the display area allocated to it.

- GridBagConstraints.BOTH—This specifies that the component should be stretched horizontally and vertically as needed to fill the display area allocated to it.

- ipadx and ipady—This specifies how many pixels to add to the component size in the x and y direction. For each direction, it is added to both the sides of the component. The default value for both is 0.

- insets—An instance of the Insets class. The inset specifies how much space to leave between the component borders and its display area. The inset has its own set of top, bottom, left, and right specifications.

- anchor—If the component is smaller than its display area, the anchor is used to specify where it is anchored. The default is GridBagConstraints.CENTER. Other possible values are

  ```
  -GridBagConstraints.NORTH
  -GridBagConstraints.NORTHEAST
  -GridBagConstraints.EAST
  -GridBagConstraints.SOUTHEAST
  -GridBagConstraints.SOUTH
  -GridBagConstraints.SOUTHWEST
  -GridBagConstraints.WEST
  -GridBagConstraints.NORTHWEST
  ```

- weightx and weighty—This is used to set the relative size of components. For example, components with the weightx of 3.0 are three times the size (in the horizontal direction) of a component with a weightx of 1.0.

For an example, see Listing 4.5.

Listing 4.5   Code Snippet Demonstrating How to Lay Out a GUI Component

```
// Intialize all the GUI components
public void jbInit() throws Exception {
   this.getContentPane().setLayout(m_gridBagLayout);
   this.setSize(new Dimension(856, 629));
```

continues

Listing 4.5   Continued

```
this.addWindowListener(new java.awt.event.WindowAdapter() {
  public void windowClosing(WindowEvent e) {
    m_parent.dispatchEvent("CLOSE");
  }
});
this.setTitle("Using SQLJ to perform DML in JavaStop");
m_jtable.setRowHeight(20);
m_jtable.setToolTipText("Table displays the rows");
m_clearButton.setMaximumSize(new Dimension(97, 29));
m_clearButton.setText("CLEAR");
m_clearButton.setPreferredSize(new Dimension(97, 29));
m_clearButton.setFont(new Font("Dialog", 1, 16));
m_clearButton.setToolTipText("Press to clear the text fields");
m_clearButton.setMinimumSize(new Dimension(97, 29));
m_statusField.setFont(new Font("Dialog", 0, 14));
m_statusField.setToolTipText("Status bar");
m_statusField.setEditable(false);
m_statusField.setBackground(Color.lightGray);
m_custidLabel.setText("Customer ID");
m_custidLabel.setFont(new Font("Dialog", 1, 14));
m_nameLabel.setText("Name");
m_nameLabel.setFont(new Font("Dialog", 1, 14));
m_custidTextfield.setToolTipText("Enter the Customer ID");
m_nameTextfield.setToolTipText("Enter the Customer Name");
m_addressTextfield.setToolTipText("Enter the Customer Address");
m_addressLabel.setText("Customer Address");
m_addressLabel.setFont(new Font("Dialog", 1, 14));
m_insertButton.setMaximumSize(new Dimension(97, 29));
m_insertButton.setText("INSERT");
m_insertButton.setPreferredSize(new Dimension(97, 29));
m_insertButton.setFont(new Font("Dialog", 1, 16));
m_insertButton.setToolTipText("Press to insert the record");
m_insertButton.setMinimumSize(new Dimension(97, 29));
m_selectButton.setMaximumSize(new Dimension(127, 29));
m_selectButton.setText("SELECT");
m_selectButton.setPreferredSize(new Dimension(127, 29));
m_selectButton.setFont(new Font("Dialog", 1, 16));
m_selectButton.setToolTipText("Press to select records");
m_selectButton.setMinimumSize(new Dimension(127, 29));
m_updateButton.setMaximumSize(new Dimension(97, 29));
m_updateButton.setText("UPDATE");
m_updateButton.setPreferredSize(new Dimension(97, 29));
m_updateButton.setFont(new Font("Dialog", 1, 16));
m_updateButton.setToolTipText("Press to update the record");
m_updateButton.setMinimumSize(new Dimension(97, 29));
m_delButton.setText("DELETE");
m_delButton.setFont(new Font("Dialog", 1, 16));
m_delButton.setToolTipText("Press to delete the record");
m_closeButton.setMaximumSize(new Dimension(147, 29));
m_closeButton.setText("CLOSE");
m_closeButton.setPreferredSize(new Dimension(147, 29));
```

```
    m_closeButton.setFont(new Font("Dialog", 1, 16));
    m_closeButton.setToolTipText("Press to exit the application");
    m_closeButton.setMinimumSize(new Dimension(147, 29));
    this.getContentPane().add(m_jScrollPane1, new GridBagConstraintsJstp
➥(0, 0, 12, 1, 1.0, 1.0
    ,GridBagConstraints.CENTER, GridBagConstraints.BOTH, new Insets
➥(19, 2, 0, 0), 291, -67));
    m_jScrollPane1.getViewport().add(m_jtable, null);
    this.getContentPane().add(m_custidLabel, new GridBagConstraintsJstp
➥(0, 1, 1, 1, 0.0, 0.0
    ,GridBagConstraints.WEST, GridBagConstraints.NONE, new Insets(20, 2, 0, 0),
➥ 4, 19));
    this.getContentPane().add(m_custidTextfield, new GridBagConstraintsJstp
➥(1, 1, 1, 1, 1.0, 0.0
    ,GridBagConstraints.WEST, GridBagConstraints.HORIZONTAL, new Insets
➥(25, 0, 0, 0), 143, 11));
    this.getContentPane().add(m_nameLabel, new GridBagConstraintsJstp
➥(2, 1, 2, 1, 0.0, 0.0
    ,GridBagConstraints.WEST, GridBagConstraints.NONE, new Insets(24, 9, 0, 0),
➥ 14, 14));
    this.getContentPane().add(m_nameTextfield, new GridBagConstraintsJstp
➥(4, 1, 4, 1, 1.0, 0.0
    ,GridBagConstraints.WEST, GridBagConstraints.HORIZONTAL, new Insets
➥(25, 0, 0, 0), 309, 10));
    this.getContentPane().add(m_addressLabel, new GridBagConstraintsJstp
➥(8, 1, 1, 1, 0.0, 0.0
    ,GridBagConstraints.WEST, GridBagConstraints.NONE, new Insets(25, 27, 0, 0),
➥ 4, 14));
    this.getContentPane().add(m_addressTextfield, new GridBagConstraintsJstp
➥(9, 1, 2, 1, 1.0, 0.0
    ,GridBagConstraints.WEST, GridBagConstraints.BOTH, new Insets(26, 0, 0, 0),
➥ 68, 9));
    this.getContentPane().add(m_selectButton, new GridBagConstraintsJstp
➥(1, 2, 2, 1, 0.0, 0.0
    ,GridBagConstraints.CENTER, GridBagConstraints.NONE, new Insets
➥(51, 44, 0, 0), 9, 18));
    this.getContentPane().add(m_updateButton, new GridBagConstraintsJstp
➥(5, 2, 1, 1, 0.0, 0.0
    ,GridBagConstraints.CENTER, GridBagConstraints.NONE, new Insets
➥(51, 0, 0, 0), 18, 18));
    this.getContentPane().add(m_delButton, new GridBagConstraintsJstp
➥(6, 2, 1, 1, 0.0, 0.0
    ,GridBagConstraints.CENTER, GridBagConstraints.NONE, new Insets
➥(52, 14, 0, 0), 8, 16));
    this.getContentPane().add(m_closeButton, new GridBagConstraintsJstp
➥(9, 2, 3, 1, 0.0, 0.0
    ,GridBagConstraints.WEST, GridBagConstraints.BOTH, new Insets
➥(51, -1, 0, 15), -14, 17));
    this.getContentPane().add(m_statusField, new GridBagConstraintsJstp
➥(0, 3, 12, 1, 1.0, 0.0
```

continues

Listing 4.5   Continued

```
    ,GridBagConstraints.WEST, GridBagConstraints.HORIZONTAL, new Insets
➥(9, 2, 4, 0), 747, 43));
    this.getContentPane().add(m_insertButton, new GridBagConstraintsJstp
➥(3, 2, 2, 1, 0.0, 0.0
    ,GridBagConstraints.CENTER, GridBagConstraints.NONE, new Insets
➥(51, 0, 0, 13), 3, 18));
    this.getContentPane().add(m_clearButton, new GridBagConstraintsJstp
➥(8, 2, 2, 1, 0.0, 0.0
    ,GridBagConstraints.WEST, GridBagConstraints.NONE, new Insets(52, 10, 0, 14),
➥0, 17));
  }
}
```

The Java Virtual Machine

The Java Virtual Machine (JVM) is the heart of Java. The JVM is a virtual computer that resides in memory and enables a Java program to be executed on a variety of platforms. Oracle JServer provides the Aurora JVM, which resides in Oracle8i. The Oracle JVM is discussed in Chapter 1, "Introduction to the Internet Capabilities of Oracle 8i."

 Note   The Java Virtual Machine makes Java portable because it takes care of all the platform-specific interactions.

Addresses in JVM are 32-bit size and can address up to 4GB of memory. The stack, garbage-collection heap, and method area reside in this 4GB of addressable memory. The following registers are used to manage the system stack:

- **Program counter**—It keeps track of the current execution location in the program.
- **optop**—It points to the top of the operand stack.
- **Frame**—It points to the current execution environment.
- **Vars**—It points to the first variable of the current execution environment.

The garbage collection heap is a collection of memory from which new instances of a class are allocated. The runtime environment keeps track of each object reference in the heap and automatically frees the memory when the object is no longer referenced. This garbage collection automatically runs as a thread in the background.

Two more memory areas are used by the JVM:

- Method area stores the methods.
- Constant pool stores the constants.

Next Steps

This chapter provided you with a basic understanding of Java as well as some object-oriented programming concepts. The knowledge gained in this chapter will help you understand the Java code that we will be using in the rest of the book.

The next chapter shows you how to use JDBC to interact with JavaStop.

4

Chapter 5

Using JDBC to Connect to JavaStop

Understanding JDBC

After you have stored the data in the JSTP database, you need some way to access it over the Web. Oracle8i provides two different client-side programmatic interfaces for Java developers: JDBC and SQLJ (enabling SQL to be embedded in Java). In this chapter we will discuss JDBC connectivity. Chapter 6, "Using JDBC to Access the Data in JavaStop,") discusses how to manipulate JavaStop data using JDBC and Chapter 7, "Implementing Efficient JavaStop Code Using SQLJ," discusses how SQLJ can be used to write efficient programs.

Working with Java Database Connectivity

Java Database Connectivity (JDBC) is a standard API that enables application developers to access and manipulate relational databases from within Java programs. The JDBC standard was defined by Sun Microsystems. It enables individual providers to implement and extend the standard with their own JDBC drivers. JDBC is based on the X/Open SQL Call Level Interface (CLI) and complies with the SQL92 Entry Level standard, which provides a DBMS-independent interface that enables access to the database from Java. The JDBC framework includes a JDBC driver manager and the JDBC drivers. The driver manager can support multiple drivers connecting to different databases. The JDBC drivers can either be entirely written in Java so that they can be downloaded as part of an applet, or they can be implemented using native methods to bridge to existing database access libraries.

> **Note**   JDBC has become the de facto industry standard for accessing databases from Java applications.

If you are familiar with the Oracle Call Interface (OCI) layer of client-side C code, you will recognize that JDBC provides the power and flexibility for Java programs similar to that provided by OCI to C and C++ programs. JDBC enables you to perform dynamic SQL. *Dynamic SQL* refers to the performing of query and DML activities against a database when, for example, the number or types of columns are not known until runtime.

The JDBC API defines Java classes to represent database connections, SQL statements, result sets, database metadata, and so on. Java programs can issue SQL statement against the database and process the results.

Oracle JDBC Drivers

Oracle provides three types of JDBC drivers, which you can use for different types of applications:

- **Oracle Thin JDBC driver**—This driver is written completely in Java and is only 900KB (compressed), making it ideal for Java applets that can be used with a browser. When you download an applet from an HTML page, the thin JDBC driver is downloaded with it. A direct Net8 connection is established between the applet and database. Scalability is provided with the use of the Net8 connection manager.

- **Oracle JDBC/OCI driver**—This driver uses Oracle client libraries such as OCILIB, CORE, and Net8 to provide OCI calls to access the database. You have to perform client installation of the JDBC/OCI driver because it is not downloadable. It can be used for client/server Java applications, as well as middle-tier Java applications running in a Java application server. However, these JDBC/OCI drivers can't be used with applets.

- **Oracle JDBC Server driver**—The JDBC Server Driver (also referred to as KPRB driver) enables Java programs to use the Oracle8i Java Virtual Machine. The Server Driver runs inside the database to communicate with the SQLEngine. No network round trips are involved because the Server Driver and the SQLEngine both run in the same address space. This driver is for server-side use only and provides server-side JDBC support for any Java program used in the database, Java stored procedure, and Enterprise Java Beans (EJB). In addition, it enables communication with SQL and PL/SQL programs.

 Regardless of which driver you use, the Java code you write to access Oracle is the same. The particular driver used affects only the connect string.

The JDBC drivers provided by Oracle have several important features, and they all provide the same functionality:

- JDBC 1.22-compliant
- Support most of the JDBC 2.0 features
- Have the same syntax and APIs
- Provide the same Oracle extensions
- Support Oracle7 and Oracle8 object-relational data types
- Support manipulation of LOB data
- Provide performance enhancement features such as array interface, prefetching, and batch SQL statement execution
- Can access PL/SQL and Java stored procedures
- Support all Oracle character sets
- Provide full support for multithreaded applications

The only differences between the Oracle JDBC drivers are how they connect to the database and how they transfer data.

 The Oracle JDBC Drivers support the JDBC 2.0 standard.

 The JDBC-ODBC bridge driver is the result of a joint effort by JavaSoft and Intersolv. It translates JDBC method calls into ODBC function calls. Using the JDBC-ODBC bridge driver you can use ODBC from Java.

Choosing the Appropriate Driver

We already have seen that all the Oracle JDBC drivers have the same functionality and differ only in the way they connect to the database and how they transfer data. There are, however, some factors that you should consider when choosing between the various drivers for your application or applet (see Table 5.2, which compares the JDBC thin driver and the JDBC OCI driver):

- If you are writing an applet, you must use the JDBC thin driver because the JDBC OCI-based driver classes cannot be downloaded to a Web browser.
- If you need to connect to your Oracle8i data server by using an application or an applet, you should choose the JDBC thin driver.
- If you desire maximum performance from your application, you should use the JDBC OCI driver.
- If your Java program is running in the Oracle database server using at least the Oracle 8.1.5 Java VM, you should choose the JDBC Server driver.

Table 5.1 shows the compatibilties between the different Oracle database versions and the JDBC drivers.

Table 5.1   Compatibility Between JDBC Drivers and Oracle Databases

Oracle Version	JDBC Thin Driver	JDBC OCI Driver	JDBC Server Driver
8.1.5	Yes	Yes	Yes
8.1.4	Yes	Yes	Yes
8.0.x	Yes	Yes	No
7.x	Yes	Yes	No

Notes:

- When run against an 8.1.5 database, both client- and server-side drivers offer full object support.
- When run against an 8.1.4 database, both client- and server-side drivers offer full object support.
- When run against an 8.0.x database, the JDBC thin and OCI drivers do not support objects.
- When run against an 7.x database, the JDBC thin and OCI drivers do not support objects. Also, the JDBC OCI driver does not support LOBs.

The JDBC OCI drivers work with Java VMs that are based on JavaSoft's Virtual Machine code. These include:

- Netscape
- Borland
- Oracle JDeveloper
- Symantec

> **Note**
>
> The JDBC OCI driver doesn't work with Microsoft's VM because the native method interface is different. However, the Oracle 8.1.6 and above JDBC OCI drivers don't have this restriction because they have been ported to the JNI 1.1 specification.

Table 5.2   JDBC OCI and JDBC Thin Drivers Comparison

Feature	JDBC/OCI Driver	JDBC Thin Driver
Applet support	No.	Yes.
Oracle-specific datatype support	Yes.	Yes.
National language support	Yes.	Yes.
Firewall support	Works with any SQL*Net certified firewall.	Works with any SQL*Net certified firewall.
Support for SQL*Net	Supports all SQL*Net adapters, including IPC, Named Pipes, and TCP/IP.	Only TCP/IP is supported.
Net8 connection manager support	Yes.	Yes. Used for applets that try to connect to database servers that reside on a different machine from the Web server.
Encryption	Yes, by using the Advanced Networking Option of Net8.	Not supported.
Driver type	Type 2 driver: implements JDBC interfaces that use OCI to interact with the Oracle database.	Type 4 driver: Java sockets are used to connect directly to the Oracle database.

Steps to Use JDBC

There are several steps that you need to perform when using JDBC. In order to connect to and query JSTP from the client, you must provide code to perform several tasks:

1. Import packages
2. Register JDBC drivers
3. Open a connection to JSTP
4. Create a statement object
5. Execute a Query and return a resultset object
6. Process the resultset
7. Close the resultset and statement objects
8. Close the connection

For the first three tasks, you need to provide Oracle driver-specific information so that you can use the JDBC API to access the JSTP database. Standard JDBC Java code can be used for the other tasks.

Setting Up PATH and CLASSPATH Environment Variables

If you are using the thin driver or the JDBC OCI driver and you don't set up the PATH and CLASSPATH environment variables correctly, your Java program might get a SQLException error with the value java.lang.NoClassDefFoundError.

The Oracle installer installs the JDBC drivers in the $ORACLE_HOME/jdbc directory. Table 5.3 shows the settings that should be made based on the operating system and JDK version in use.

 **Note**

Do not attempt to have multiple versions of the JDBC drivers in your CLASSPATH; otherwise, you will receive unpredictable results.

Table 5.3   Environment Settings Based on JDK Versions

	JDK 1.1.1	JDK 1.0.2
Win95/Win98/NT	•Add [ORACLE_HOME]\ jdbc\lib\ classes111.zip and [ORACLE_HOME]\ jdbc\lib\nls_ chaset11.zip to your CLASSPATH •Add [ORACLE _HOME]\jdbc\lib to your PATH	•Add [ORACLE_HOME] \jdbc\lib\ classes102.zip and [ORACLE_HOME]\ jdbc\lib\nls_ chaset10.zip to your CLASSPATH •Add [ORACLE_HOME]\ jdbc\lib to your PATH

	JDK 1.1.1	**JDK 1.0.2**
Solaris	•Add [ORACLE_HOME]/ jdbc/lib/ classes111.zip and [ORACLE_HOME]/ jdbc/lib/nls_ chaset11.zip to your CLASSPATH •Add [ORACLE_ HOME]/jdbc/lib to your LD_ LIBRARY_PATH	•Add [ORACLE_HOME]/ jdbc/lib/classes 102.zip and [ORACLE_HOME]/ jdbc/lib/nls_ chaset10.zip to your CLASSPATH •Add [ORACLE_HOME]/ jdbc/lib to your LD_LIBRARY_PATH

Import Packages

Regardless of which Oracle JDBC driver you are using for your application, the following import statements must be included at the beginning of your program:

- `import java.sql.*`—This enables JDBC packages to be used by your Java program.

- `import java.math.*`—This enables the use of Java math packages, such as the `BigDecimal` classes.

- `import oracle.jdbc.driver.*` and `import oracle.sql.*`—These enable you to use the extended functionality provided by the Oracle drivers.

Register JDBC Drivers

The installed driver must be registered with your program. You can do this by using the `registerDriver()` method of the JDBC `DriverManager` class. For example,

```
DriverManager.registerDriver(new oracle.jdbc.driver.OracleDriver());
```

Alternatively, the `forName()` method of the `java.lang.Class` class can be used to load the JDBC drivers directly. However, it is valid only for JDK-compliant Java Virtual Machines. For example,

```
Class.forName("oracle.jdbc.driver.OracleDriver");
```

Open a Connection to a Database

The static `getConnection()` method of the JDBC `DriverManager` class can be used to open a connection to the database. This method returns an object of the JDBC `Connection` class. The `Connection` object requires the following input:

- userid
- password
- connection string that identifies the JDBC driver to use, and the name of the database to which you want to connect

While connecting to the database, you must specify Oracle JDBC driver-specific information in the `getConnection()` method.

The `getConnection()` method is an overloaded method that can be used to specify the connection string using a variety of forms:

- Specifying a database URL, userid, and password

```
getConnection(String URL, String user, String password);
```

where the URL is of the form

```
jdbc:oracle:<drivertype>:@<database>
```

For example

```
Connection conn=DriverManager.getConnection
("jdbc:oracle:thin:@myhost:1521:jstp","scott","tiger");
```

The previous example opens a connection to the JSTP database using a thin driver and port 1521 of host `myhost`. The user `scott` with password `tiger` is used for making the connection.

Note

The default connection for an OCI driver can be used as follows:

```
Connection conn=DriverManager.getConnection
("jdbc:oracle:oci8:@","scott","tiger");
```

- Specifying a database URL that includes a userid and password

```
getConnection(String URL);
```

where the URL is of the form:

```
jdbc:oracle:<drivertype>:<user>/<password>@<database>
```

For example

```
Connection conn=
DriverManager.getConnection("jdbc:oracle:oci8:scott/tiger@myhost");
```

The previous example opens a connection to the JSTP database using an OCI driver and port 1521 of host `myhost`. The user `scott` with password `tiger` is used for making the connection.

- Specifying a database URL and `Properties` object

```
getConnection(String URL, Properties info);
```

Where the URL is of the form:

```
jdbc:oracle:<drivertype>:@<database>
```

and `info` is an object of the standard Java properties class.

For example

```
Java.util.Properties info = new java.util.Properties();
Info.put ("user", "scott");
Info.put ("password", "tiger");
Connection conn=getConnection ("jdbc:oracle:oci8:@",info);
```

When opening a connection for the JDBC OCI driver you can specify the database with a TNSNAMES entry. However, when using the thin driver you cannot use a TNSNAMES entry to identify the database to which you want to connect. Instead, you have to list the database's host name, TCP/IP port, and Oracle SID.

> **Note**
>
> The TNSNAMES entries are listed in a file called `tnsnames.ora` on the client computer. On Windows NT this file is located in `$ORACLE_HOME\network\admin` and on UNIX systems, it is found in `/var/opt/oracle`.

For the JDBC server-side driver (also known as JDBC KPRB), you don't need to pass information about the database because you can connect only to the database you are executing in. For example,

```
Connection conn = DriverManager.getConnection("jdbc:oracle:kprb:");
```

Note that in the previous example, the trailing : is necessary.

The steps for manipulating data will be discussed in Chapter 6.

Close the Connection

After you are finished accessing and manipulating the database, the connection to the database also should be closed:

```
Conn.close();
```

Listing 5.1 shows a simple code listing that demonstrates all the previous steps.

Listing 5.1   The JdbcConnect Application

```
import java.sql.*;
import java.math.*;
import java.io.*;
import java.awt.*;

class JdbcConnect {

public static void main (String args []) throws SQLException {

DriverManager.registerDriver (new
      oracle.jdbc.driver.OracleDriver());

    Connection conn =
DriverManager.getConnection ("jdbc:oracle:oci8:@mthakkar","scott","tiger");

    Statement stmt = conn.createStatement ();
    ResultSet rset = stmt.executeQuery ("select description from products");

While (rset.next())

System.out.println (rset.getString(1));

rset.close();
stmt.close();
conn.close();

}
    }
```

The `Oracle8i JDBC Developer's Guide and Reference` shows that JDBC, Java Native, and Oracle datatypes are matches (see Table 5.4). In Table 5.4

- The Standard JDBC datatypes column lists the datatypes supported by the JDBC 1.22 standard. These datatypes are defined in the `java.sql.Types` class.
- The Java Native datatypes column lists the datatypes defined by the Java language.
- The SQL datatypes column lists the SQL datatypes that exist in the database.
- Oracle extensions are the Java classes that represent SQL datatypes.

Table 5.4   Mapping JDBC, Java Native, and Oracle Datatypes

Standard JDBC Datatypes	Java Native Datatypes	SQL Datatypes	Oracle Extensions
java.sql.Types.CHAR	java.lang.String	CHAR	oracle.sql.CHAR
java.sql.Types.VARCHAR	java.lang.String	VARCHAR2	oracle.sql.CHAR
java.sql.Types.LONGVARCHAR	java.lang.String	LONG	oracle.sql.CHAR

Standard JDBC Datatypes	Java Native Datatypes	SQL Datatypes	Oracle Extensions
java.sql.Types.NUMERIC	java.math.BigDecimal	NUMBER	oracle.sql.NUMBER
java.sql.Types.DECIMAL	java.math.BigDecimal	NUMBER	oracle.sql.NUMBER
java.sql.Types.BIT	boolean	NUMBER	oracle.sql.NUMBER
java.sql.Types.TINYINT	byte	NUMBER	oracle.sql.NUMBER
java.sql.Types.SMALLINT	short	NUMBER	oracle.sql.NUMBER
java.sql.Types.SMALLINT	int	NUMBER	oracle.sql.NUMBER
java.sql.Types.SMALLINT	long	NUMBER	oracle.sql.NUMBER
java.sql.Types.SMALLINT	float	NUMBER	oracle.sql.NUMBER
java.sql.Types.SMALLINT	double	NUMBER	oracle.sql.NUMBER
java.sql.Types.SMALLINT	double	NUMBER	oracle.sql.NUMBER
java.sql.Types.SMALLINT	byte[]	NUMBER	oracle.sql.NUMBER
java.sql.Types.SMALLINT	byte[]	RAW	oracle.sql.RAW
java.sql.Types.SMALLINT	byte[]	LONGRAW	oracle.sql.NUMBER
java.sql.Types.SMALLINT	java.sql.Date	DATE	oracle.sql.DATE
java.sql.Types.SMALLINT	java.sql.Time	DATE	oracle.sql.DATE
java.sql.Types.SMALLINT	java.sql.Timestamp	DATE	oracle.sql.DATE

Applications Versus Applets

In order to connect to the database, you can write your Java program as an application or applet. Applications can use either the Oracle JDBC thin driver or Oracle JDBC OCI driver. If you use a JDBC OCI driver in an application, the application will require the installation of Net8 and client libraries. Applications can achieve encryption by using the Net8 advanced networking option.

 **Note**   Applications that can run on the client using the JDBC OCI driver can run on the server using the JDBC server driver.

An applet can use only the JDBC thin driver that gets downloaded with it. An applet can open only network connections to the host machine from which it was downloaded. Therefore it can directly connect only to databases on the originating machine. Applets can't use data encryption but can connect to a database through a firewall.

Connecting to JavaStop Using JDBC

The application JdbcConnection demonstrates how to connect to JSTP using a JDBC thin driver. It should be noted that if you intend to use the JDBC OCI driver, the code is the same except for the database URL syntax.

The application has the following features:

- After the application is launched, it shows the connection status and any errors.
- When the user presses the Disconnect button, the application closes the connection and exits.

The JdbcConnection.jar file contains the following files:

- JdbcConnection.java—This is the source file for the application.
- JdbcConnectionGui.java—This is the source file for the user interface used by the application.
- JdbcConnection.jws—This is the JDeveloper workspace file.
- JdbcConnection.jpr—This is the JDeveloper project file.
- GridBagConstraintsJstp.java—This is the source file for the GridBagConstraintsJstp class that uses the java.awt.GridBagconstraints.
- ConnectionSpecs.java—This file contains the parameters that specify how to connect to JSTP.

To use the application you need the following software:

- Calling program:

  JDK 1.1.5 or above

  JFC Swing 1.0.2 or above

  Oracle JDBC drivers for Oracle v7.3.2 and above

  You can download the Oracle JDBC drivers from the Oracle Web site at www.oracle.com.

The following steps can be used to run the JdbcConnection application:

1. Unjar JdbcConnection.jar using Winzip, or by using the following command:

   ```
   > jar xvf JdbcConnection.jar
   ```

 Note   jar.exe can be found in JDEVELOPER_HOME\java\bin, where JDEVELOPER_HOME is the root directory of the JDeveloper installation.

2. Edit the `ConnectionSpecs.java` file to specify the hostname, port, username, and password for your system.

3. Import the appropriate version of swing by editing the `JdbcConnectionGui.java` file. By default, swing 1.1 is used.

   ```
   * If swing 1.0.2, the import statements should be:
               import com.sun.java.swing.*;

   * If swing 1.1, the import statements should be:
               import  javax.swing.*;
   ```

4. Using the JDeveloper File/Open option, select the `JdbcConnection.jws` file.

5. From the Project menu, select Make Project JdbcConnection.jpr.

6. Run the application by selecting Run JdbcConnection from the Run menu or pressing the F9 key.

Listing 5.2   The JdbcConnection Application

```java
/* Listing for file ConnectionSpecs.java */

/**
 * @author  Megh Thakkar
 * @version 1.0
 *
 * Development Environment      :  JDeveloper 3.0
 * Name of the Application      :  ConnectionSpecs.java
 *
 * Application Notes:
 * This application contains static variables that specify the connection
 * parameters used to connect to JSTP. You should edit these parameters
 * to suit your environment
 */

public class ConnectionSpecs {

    // The machine on which the database JSTP resides
    public final static String s_hostName    = "mthakkar";

    // The TNS listener port for JavaStop
    public final static String s_portNumber  = "1521";

    // Name of the database
    public final static String s_databaseSID = "JSTP";

    // Userid
    public final static String s_userName    = "scott";

    // Password
    public final static String s_password    = "tiger";
```

continues

Listing 5.2   Continued

```
    }

/* Listing for file GridBagConstraintsJstp.java */

/**
 * @author  Megh Thakkar
 * @version 1.0
 *
 * Development Environment      :  JDeveloper 3.0
 * Name of the Application      :  GridBagConstraintsJstp.java
 * Application Notes:
 *
 * This is an easier way to use java.awt.GridBagConstraints
 */
import java.awt.*;

public class GridBagConstraintsJstp extends GridBagConstraints {
 /**
 * This Constructor initializes the GridBagConstraints variables.
 *
 **/
  public GridBagConstraintsJstp(int p_gx, int p_gy, int p_gw, int p_gh,double
➡p_wx,
          double p_wy, int p_anc, int p_fil, Insets p_ins,int p_ix, int p_iy)
➡ {

     gridx = p_gx;
      gridy = p_gy;

     gridwidth = p_gw;
     gridheight = p_gh;

   weightx = p_wx;
     weighty = p_wy;

     anchor = p_anc;
     fill = p_fil;

     insets = p_ins;
     ipadx = p_ix;
     ipady = p_iy;
   }
}

/* Listing for file JdbcConnectionGui.java */

/**
 * @author  Megh Thakkar
 * @version 1.0
 *
```

```
 * Development Environment      :  JDeveloper 3.0
 * Name of the Application      :  JdbcConnectionGui.java
 * Application Notes:
 *
 * The User Interface for the JdbcConnection application is handled here.
 *
 */

import java.awt.*;
import java.awt.event.*;

/** Import statements for SWING version 1.0.2 **/
//import com.sun.java.swing.*;

/** Import statements for SWING version 1.1. This is the default **/
import javax.swing.*;

public class JdbcConnectionGui extends JFrame {
  //This frame is used by the JdbcConnection class
  JdbcConnection m_parent;

  //Elements that comprise the User Interface
  JButton      m_disconnectButton = new JButton();    //Disconnect Button
  TextArea     m_statusbar  = new TextArea();  //Statusbar
  JTextField   m_results    = new JTextField();//Results area

  //Layout manager object
  GridBagLayout m_gridBagLayout = new GridBagLayout();

/**
 *   The GUI components are initialized by this constructor
 **/
  public JdbcConnectionGui(JdbcConnection p_parent) {
    try{
      m_parent = p_parent;
      jbInit();   //initialize the GUI components
      setupListeners(); //Set up listeners for the GUI components
    } catch(Exception ex){
      putStatus(ex.toString());
    }
  }

/**
 *   Set up listener for the Exit button so that the application can be closed.
 **/
  public void setupListeners() {
    m_disconnectButton.addActionListener(new java.awt.event.ActionListener(){
      public void actionPerformed(ActionEvent evt){
        if(evt.getActionCommand() =="Disconnect")
          //The event is passed to the m_parent for handling
          m_parent.dispatchEvent("Disconnect");
```

continues

Listing 5.2   Continued

```
      }
    });
  }

  /**
  *   Display the connection status
  **/
  public void putStatus(String p_status) {
    m_statusbar.setText(p_status);
  }

  /**
  * Append p_status to the current status displayed
  **/
  public void appendStatus(String p_status) {
    String l_status = m_statusbar.getText();
    m_statusbar.setText(l_status+"\n"+p_status);
  }


  /**
  *   Display p_text in the Text Area
  **/
  public void putResults(String p_text) {
    m_results.setText(p_text);
  }

  /**
  * Append p_text to the current message in the Text Area
  **/
  public void appendResults(String p_text) {
    String l_results = m_results.getText();
    m_results.setText(l_results+"\n"+"\n"+p_text);
  }

  /**
  *   Initialize all the GUI components
  **/
  public void jbInit() throws Exception {
    this.getContentPane().setLayout(m_gridBagLayout);
    this.setTitle("Connecting to JSTP using JDBC");
    this.setSize(new Dimension(533, 249));
    this.addWindowListener(new java.awt.event.WindowAdapter() {
      public void windowClosing(WindowEvent e) {
          m_parent.dispatchEvent("Disconnect");
      }
    });
    m_disconnectButton.setText("Disconnect");
    m_disconnectButton.setFont(new Font("Dialog", 1, 16));
    m_disconnectButton.setToolTipText("Press to Disconnect");
```

```
      m_statusbar.setFont(new Font("Dialog", 0, 14));
      m_statusbar.setEditable(false);
      m_statusbar.setBackground(Color.lightGray);
      m_results.setFont(new Font("Dialog", 0, 14));
      m_results.setDisabledTextColor(Color.white);
      m_results.setToolTipText("Displays the connection status");
      m_results.setEditable(false);
      this.getContentPane().add(m_disconnectButton, new GridBagConstraintsJstp(0,
➥1, 1, 1, 0.0, 0.0
      ,GridBagConstraints.CENTER, GridBagConstraints.NONE, new Insets(9, 400, 0,
0),
➥42, 10));
      this.getContentPane().add(m_statusbar, new GridBagConstraintsJstp(0, 2, 2, 1,
➥1.0, 1.0
      ,GridBagConstraints.CENTER, GridBagConstraints.BOTH, new Insets(14, 1, 0, 2),
➥0, 0));
      this.getContentPane().add(m_results, new GridBagConstraintsJstp(0, 0, 1, 1,
➥1.0, 0.0
      ,GridBagConstraints.WEST, GridBagConstraints.HORIZONTAL, new Insets(2, 1,
➥0, 0), 505, 46));
   }
}

/* Listing for file JdbcConnection.java */

/**
 * @author   Megh Thakkar
 * @version 1.0
 *
 * Development Environment        : JDeveloper 3.0
 * Name of the Application        : JdbcConnection.java
 * Application Notes :
 *
 * This application demonstrates how to connect to JSTP using
 * a JDBC thin driver.
 *
 */
// Import the packages for the JDBC classes
import java.sql.*;

public class JdbcConnection {
  //Create a connection object
  Connection  m_connection = null;

  //The User Interface for this application is handled by JdbcConnectionGui
  JdbcConnectionGui  m_GUI;

 /**
  *  Instantiate the GUI frame
  **/
  public JdbcConnection(){
```

continues

Listing 5.2   Continued

```
    m_GUI = new JdbcConnectionGui(this);
    m_GUI.setVisible(true);
}

/**
*  Make a database connection to JSTP
**/
public static void main(String args[]){

  JdbcConnection JdbcCon = new JdbcConnection();
  JdbcCon.dbConnection();
}

/**
*  This method is invoked by the listeners set up in the
*  JdbcConnectionGui class. When the user clicks the "Disconnect" button,
*  it is handled here.
**/
public void dispatchEvent(String p_eventName) {
  if(p_eventName.equals("Disconnect"))
     exitApplication();

}

// Connecting to the database
public void dbConnection(){
  try {
      m_GUI.putStatus("Connecting to the Database....please wait.....");

      //Register the JDBC driver
      DriverManager.registerDriver(new oracle.jdbc.driver.OracleDriver());

      // The connection parameters specified in ConnectionSpecs.java are used
      String l_dbConnectString =
          "(DESCRIPTION=(ADDRESS=(HOST="+ConnectionSpecs.s_hostName+")"+
          "(PROTOCOL=tcp)(PORT="+ConnectionSpecs.s_portNumber+"))"+
          "(CONNECT_DATA=(SID="+ConnectionSpecs.s_databaseSID+")))";


      m_connection = DriverManager.getConnection(
                    "jdbc:oracle:thin:@"+l_dbConnectString,
                    ConnectionSpecs.s_userName,ConnectionSpecs.s_password);

      /*
      * Setting autocommit to false will prevent actual changes
      * to the database
      */
      m_connection.setAutoCommit(false);

      m_GUI.putStatus("");
```

```
            m_GUI.putResults("Successfully connected as user " +
                        ConnectionSpecs.s_userName +" to database "
                        +ConnectionSpecs.s_databaseSID );
    } catch(Exception ex){
        m_GUI.appendStatus("Unable to connect....."
                        +ex.toString());

    }
}

/**
 *  Close the connection to JSTP and exit the application
 **/
public void exitApplication() {
    try {
        m_GUI.putStatus("Disconnecting from JSTP.......");
        if(m_connection != null)
            // close the connection
            m_connection.close();
    } catch(SQLException ex){
        // Trap any errors
        m_GUI.putStatus(ex.toString());
    }
    //Exit the application
    System.exit(0);
}
}
```

5

Next Steps

The JDBC API enables you to access Oracle databases from Java. This chapter discussed the various JDBC drivers available and how to connect to JavaStop from Java applications. The next chapter will show you how to use JDBC to access and manipulate the data in JavaStop.

Chapter 6

Using JDBC to Perform Data Manipulation in JavaStop

Accessing JavaStop Using JDBC

In the previous chapter we looked at the connection aspects of JDBC and the various JDBC drivers and their features. In this chapter we will look at how the data in JavaStop can be accessed using JDBC.

Revisiting the Steps to Use JDBC

Let's review the steps required to use JDBC, which we discussed in the previous chapter:

1. Import packages
2. Register JDBC drivers
3. Open a connection to JSTP
4. Create a statement object
5. Execute a query and return a Resultset object
6. Process the Resultset
7. Close the Resultset and statement objects
8. Close the connection

Steps 1, 2, 3, and 8 were discussed in the previous chapter. Let's look at the other steps.

Create a `Statement` Object

Once a connection to an Oracle database has been made, the next step is to create a `Statement` object using standard JDBC syntax. The `createStatement()` method of the JDBC `Connection` object returns an object of the JDBC `Statement` class. For example,

```
Statement stmt = conn.createStatement();
```

Execute a Query and Return a `ResultSet` Object

The `Statement` object can be used to query and manipulate the database. The database can be queried by using the `executeQuery()` method of the `Statement` object. The `executeQuery` method takes an SQL statement as input and returns an object of the JDBC class `ResultSet`. For example,

```
ResultSet rset = stmt.executeQuery ("select name from products");
```

The previous example shows how you can query the JSTP database to obtain the names of all the products.

Process the Resultset

As seen from the previous step, `executeQuery` returns the results of executing the query in a `ResultSet` object. The `next()` method of the `ResultSet` object can be used to iterate through the resultset row by row until the end of the records is reached. While iterating through the resultset, you can pull the desired values out of the resultset by using the various `getXXX()` methods of the `ResultSet` object, where `XXX` corresponds to a Java datatype.

For example, the following code prints the names of all the products retrieved by the previous resultset:

```
While (rset.next())

System.out.println (rset.getString(1));
```

When the end of the resultset is reached, the `next()` method returns `false`.

Close the `ResultSet` and `Statement` Objects

After you are done with the `ResultSet` and `Statement` objects, you should explicitly close them using the `close()` method. Otherwise, there is potential for memory leaks and running out of cursors in the database. For example,

```
Rset.close();

Stmt.close();
```

Accessing JavaStop

The application JdbcDml demonstrates how to perform DML operations such as SELECT, INSERT, UPDATE, and DELETE in JavaStop using a JDBC thin driver. It should be noted that if you intend to use the JDBC OCI driver, the code is the same except for the database URL syntax.

Some of the features of this application include

- After the application is launched, it shows the connection status and any errors.
- When the user presses the CLOSE button, the application closes the connection and exits.
- When the user presses the SELECT button, it retrieves all the records from the customers table unless a customer ID is specified, in which case it will retrieve only that record.
- When the user presses the CLEAR button, it clears the text in the text fields.
- When the user presses the INSERT button, it inserts a new record in the customers table using the values in the text fields.
- When the user presses the UPDATE button, it updates the selected record.
- When the user presses the DELETE button, it deletes the selected record.

 Java archive files—Zipped files with the extension JAR. JAR files can be un-jarred before use or can be stored in the database as is.

The JdbcDml.jar file contains the following files:

- JdbcDml.java—This is the source file for the application.
- JdbcDmlGui.java—This is the source file for the user interface used by the application.
- JdbcDml.jws—This is the JDeveloper workspace file.
- JdbcDml.jpr—This is the JDeveloper project file.
- GridBagConstraintsJstp.java—This is the source file for the `GridBagConstraintsJstp` class that makes use of the `java.awt.GridBagconstraints`. This is identical to the file used earlier.
- ConnectionSpecs.java—This file contains the parameters that specify how to connect to JSTP. This is identical to the file used earlier.
- genTableModel.java—This class is provided by Oracle Corporation and maintains the data for a JTable. Any application using JTables can use this class as a table model.

To use the application, you need the following software:

- Calling program:

  JDK 1.1.5 or above

  JFC Swing 1.0.2 or above

  Oracle JDBC drivers for Oracle v7.3.2 and above

  SQLJ Translator for Oracle v7.3.2 and above

The following steps can be used to run the JdbcDml application:

1. Unjar JdbcDml.jar using WinZip, or using the following command:

   ```
   > jar xvf JdbcDml.jar
   ```

 Note   jar.exe can be found in `JDEVELOPER_HOME\java\bin`, where `JDEVELOPER_HOME` is the root directory of the JDeveloper installation.

2. Edit the ConnectionSpecs.java file to specify the hostname, port, username, and password for your system.

3. Import the appropriate version of swing by editing the JdbcDmlGui.java file. By default, swing 1.1 is used.

   ```
   * If swing 1.0.2, the import statements should be:
             import com.sun.java.swing.*;

   * If swing 1.1, the import statements should be:
             import  javax.swing.*;
   ```

4. Using the JDeveloper File/Open option, select the JdbcDml.jws file.

5. From the Project menu, select Make Project "JdbcDml.jpr".

6. Run the application by selecting Run JdbcDml from the Run menu or pressing the F9 key.

The code for several important files is shown in Listing 6.1 for quick analysis.

Listing 6.1   The JdbcDml Application

```
/* Listing for file genTableModel.java */

/**
 *
 * Development Environment      :  JDeveloper 3.0
 * Name of the Application      :  genTableModel.java
 *
 * Application Notes :
```

```
**This class is provided by Oracle Corporation and is used to maintain
➡the data for a JTable
* Any application using JTables can make use of this class as a table model
*
* The constructor takes an array of columnNames, number of rows to be created
* initially. Also it takes an array of default value object (which may be
* heterogeneous). This helps in deciding the column type.
*
*
*/

import java.awt.*;
import java.sql.*;
import java.awt.event.*;
import java.util.*;


/** Import statements for SWING version 1.0.2**/
//import com.sun.java.swing.*;
//import com.sun.java.swing.table.*;
//import com.sun.java.swing.event.*;

/** Import statements for SWING version 1.1**/
import javax.swing.*;
import javax.swing.table.*;
import javax.swing.event.*;

public class genTableModel extends AbstractTableModel {

  // The data is held in a vector for efficient processing
  Vector m_data;

  // The column names are held in an array
  String[] m_columnNames;

  /*
  * The constructor is used to initialize the table structure with the
  * specified number of columns, the default value, and the rows
  */
  public genTableModel(String p_columns[], Object p_defaultv[], int p_rows) {

    // Initialize number of columns and column headings
    m_columnNames = new String[p_columns.length];
    for (int i=0; i<p_columns.length; i++)
      m_columnNames[i] = new String(p_columns[i]);

    // The vector is filled with the default values
    m_data = new Vector();
    for (int i=0; i<p_rows; i++) {
      Vector l_cols = new Vector();
```

continues

Listing 6.1 Continued

```java
      for (int j=0; j<p_columns.length; j++)
        l_cols.addElement(p_defaultv[j]);
      m_data.addElement(l_cols);
      }
}


/**
 * Overrides AbstractTableModel method.
 * Returns the value at the specified cell
 **/
public Object getValueAt(int p_row, int p_col) {
  Vector l_colvector = (Vector) m_data.elementAt(p_row);
  return l_colvector.elementAt(p_col);
}

/**
 * Overrides AbstractTableModel method. Returns the number of rows in table
 **/
public int getRowCount() {
  return m_data.size();
}

/**
 *  Overrides AbstractTableModel method.
 * Returns the number of columns in table
 **/
public int getColumnCount() {
  return m_columnNames.length;
}


/**
 * Overrides AbstractTableModel method. Sets the value at the specified cell
 * to p_obj
 **/
public void setValueAt( Object p_obj, int p_row, int p_col) {
  Vector l_colvector = (Vector) m_data.elementAt(p_row);
  l_colvector.setElementAt(p_obj, p_col);
}

/**
 * Adds a new row to the table
 **/
public void insertRow(Vector p_newrow) {
  m_data.addElement(p_newrow);
  super.fireTableDataChanged();
}

/**
```

```
 * Deletes the specified row from the table
 **/
public void deleteRow(int p_row) {
  m_data.removeElementAt(p_row);
  super.fireTableDataChanged();
}


/**
 * Returns the values at the specified row as a vector
 **/
public Vector getRow(int p_row) {
  return (Vector) m_data.elementAt(p_row);
}


/**
 * Updates the specified row. It replaces the row vector at the specified
 * row with the new vector.
 **/
public void updateRow(Vector p_updatedRow, int p_row) {
  m_data.setElementAt(p_updatedRow,p_row);
  super.fireTableDataChanged();
}


/**
 * Repopulates the table data. The table is populated with the rows returned
 * by the ResultSet
 **/
public void populateFromResultSet(ResultSet p_rset) {

  // Create a new instance of data vector.
  m_data = new Vector();


  try {
  // Iterate through the result set, and fill up the rows from the table
  // into the data vector
    while (p_rset.next()) {
      Vector l_cols = new Vector();
      // Go through each column for the current row, and store the column
      // values in a row vector.
      for (int i=0; i<m_columnNames.length; i++)
        l_cols.addElement(p_rset.getObject(i+1));
      m_data.addElement(l_cols);
      }
      p_rset.close();
    } catch (SQLException ex) {
      ex.printStackTrace();
    }
  super.fireTableDataChanged();
}
```

6

Listing 6.1   Continued

```java
/**
 * Overrides AbstractTableModel method. Returns the column name for the
 * specified column
 **/
public String getColumnName(int p_col){
  return m_columnNames[p_col];
}

/**
 * Overrides AbstractTableModel method. Returns the class for the
 * specified column
 **/
public Class getColumnClass(int p_col) {
  return getValueAt(0,p_col).getClass();
}


/**
 * Clears the table data
 **/
public void clearTable() {
  m_data = new Vector();
  super.fireTableDataChanged();
}
}


/* Listing for file JdbcDmlGui.java */

/**
 * @author   Megh Thakkar
 * @version 1.0
 *
 * Development Environment        :  JDeveloper 3.0
 * Name of the Application        :  JdbcDmlGui.java
 * Application Notes :
 *
 * The User Interface for the JdbcDml application is handled here
 *
 */
import java.awt.*;
import java.awt.event.*;
import java.util.*;

/** Import statements for SWING version 1.0.2 **/
//import com.sun.java.swing.*;
//import com.sun.java.swing.event.*;
//import com.sun.java.swing.table.*;
```

```
/** Import statements for SWING version 1.1 **/
import javax.swing.*;
import javax.swing.event.*;
import javax.swing.table.*;

public class JdbcDmlGui extends JFrame {
   //The main application class which uses this User Interface
   JdbcDml m_parent;

   //Labels for the textfields in the UI
   JLabel m_custidLabel   = new JLabel();
   JLabel m_addressLabel = new JLabel();
   JLabel m_nameLabel     = new JLabel();

   //These textfields are used for displaying and entering records
   JTextField m_custidTextfield   = new JTextField();
   JTextField m_nameTextfield     = new JTextField();
   JTextField m_addressTextfield = new JTextField();

   //This textfield is used to display messages
   JTextField m_statusField = new JTextField();

   //These buttons are used for specifying the DML operations to be performed

   JButton m_selectButton = new JButton();
   JButton m_insertButton = new JButton();
   JButton m_updateButton = new JButton();
   JButton m_delButton    = new JButton();
   JButton m_closeButton   = new JButton();
   JButton m_clearButton  = new JButton();

   //This scroll pane is used for holding m_jtable
   JScrollPane m_jScrollPane1 = new JScrollPane();

   // The database rows are displayed in this table
   JTable m_jtable;

   // The JTable model is specified by genTableModel
   genTableModel m_tmodel;

   //Layout Manager object
   GridBagLayout m_gridBagLayout = new GridBagLayout();

/**
* The constructor is used to set up the listeners for the events
**/
public JdbcDmlGui(JdbcDml p_parent) {
  try {
      m_parent = p_parent;

      // Initialize JTable
      jtableInit();
```

continues

Listing 6.1   Continued

```
      jbInit();

      //Setup the listeners for the various events
      setupListeners();
  } catch (Exception ex) {
    m_statusField.setText("Error occurred during initialization..."
                         +'\n'+ex.toString());
  }
}

/**
 *  The following methods are used for manipulating the JTable
 **/

// Insert the specified row in the JTable
public void insertJTable(String p_custid,String p_name,String p_address) {
  Vector l_newrow = new Vector();

  //Fill the vector with the new elements
  l_newrow.addElement(p_custid);
  l_newrow.addElement(p_name);
  l_newrow.addElement(p_address);

  //Add the row to the JTable
  m_tmodel.insertRow(l_newrow);
  m_jScrollPane1.repaint();

  // Clear the textfields
  cleartxt();
}

// Update an existing row in the JTable
public void updateJTable(String p_custid,String p_name,String p_address) {

  // Retrieve the index of the specified row.
  // This index will be used to update the appropriate row
  int l_selectedIndex = m_jtable.getSelectedRow();

  Vector l_newrow = new Vector();

  //The column values are added to the Vector
  l_newrow.addElement(p_custid);
  l_newrow.addElement(p_name);
  l_newrow.addElement(p_address);

  // Using the retrieved index, update the row in the JTable
  m_tmodel.updateRow(l_newrow, l_selectedIndex);
  m_jScrollPane1.repaint();

  //Clear the textfields.
  cleartxt();
}
```

```java
// Delete the specified row from the JTable
public void deleteFromJTable() {

  // Retrieve the index for the specified row
  int l_selectedIndex = m_jtable.getSelectedRow();

  //Using the retrieved index, delete from the JTable
  m_tmodel.deleteRow(l_selectedIndex);
  m_jScrollPane1.repaint();

  //Clear the textfields.
  cleartxt();
}

// Display the selected row in the textfields
public void displaySel(JTable p_table,int p_selectedRow) {
  //Retrieve the values for the selected row
  TableModel l_model = p_table.getModel();
  String l_custid   = (String) l_model.getValueAt(p_selectedRow,0);
  String l_name     = (String) l_model.getValueAt(p_selectedRow,1);
  String l_address  = (String) l_model.getValueAt(p_selectedRow,2);

  //Display the selected row
  m_custidTextfield.setText(l_custid);
  m_nameTextfield.setText(l_name);
  m_addressTextfield.setText(l_address);

  m_statusField.setText("The selected row is displayed");

  // The insert button can now be enabled
  // since we are simply displaying the selected row
  m_insertButton.setEnabled(false);
}

// Initialize the JTable with the column name and the table model
public void jtableInit() {
  String[] l_cols = {"Customer ID", "Name", "Customer Address"};
  Object[] l_defaultv = {"", "", ""};

  m_tmodel = new genTableModel(l_cols,l_defaultv, 0);
  m_jtable = new JTable(m_tmodel);
}

// Set up the listeners for the various events
public void setupListeners() {
 // Allow single rows to be selected from the JTable
 m_jtable.setSelectionMode(ListSelectionModel.SINGLE_SELECTION);

 m_jtable.getSelectionModel().addListSelectionListener
➥(new ListSelectionListener(){
    public void valueChanged(ListSelectionEvent e) {
      ListSelectionModel l_lsm = (ListSelectionModel)e.getSource();
```

continues

Listing 6.1　Continued

```
            if(!l_lsm.isSelectionEmpty()){
              // Display the selected row
              int l_selectedRow = l_lsm.getMinSelectionIndex();
              displaySel(m_jtable,l_selectedRow);
            }
          }
        });

        //SELECT button listener
        m_selectButton.addActionListener(new java.awt.event.ActionListener(){
          public void actionPerformed(ActionEvent evt){
            if(evt.getActionCommand() =="SELECT") {
            // Pass the event to the parent
            m_parent.dispatchEvent("SELECT");
          }
          }
        });

        // INSERT button listener
        m_insertButton.addActionListener(new java.awt.event.ActionListener(){
          public void actionPerformed(ActionEvent evt){
            if(evt.getActionCommand() == "INSERT") {
              // Pass the event to the parent
              m_parent.dispatchEvent("INSERT");
            }
          }
        });

        //UPDATE button listener
        m_updateButton.addActionListener(new java.awt.event.ActionListener(){
          public void actionPerformed(ActionEvent evt) {
            if(evt.getActionCommand() =="UPDATE"){
              // Pass the event to the parent
              m_parent.dispatchEvent("UPDATE");
            }
          }
        });

        //DELETE button listener
        m_delButton.addActionListener(new java.awt.event.ActionListener(){
          public void actionPerformed(ActionEvent evt){
            if(evt.getActionCommand() =="DELETE") {
              // Pass the event to the parent
              m_parent.dispatchEvent("DELETE");
            }
          }
        });

        //CLEAR button listener
        m_clearButton.addActionListener(new java.awt.event.ActionListener(){
          public void actionPerformed(ActionEvent evt){
```

```
      if(evt.getActionCommand() =="CLEAR") {
        // Clear the textfields and enable the INSERT button
        cleartxt();
        m_insertButton.setEnabled(true);
      }
    }
  });

 //CLOSE button listener
 m_closeButton.addActionListener(new java.awt.event.ActionListener(){
   public void actionPerformed(ActionEvent evt) {
     if(evt.getActionCommand() =="CLOSE")
       // Pass the event to the parent
       m_parent.dispatchEvent("CLOSE");
   }
 });
}

// Clear the textfields
public void cleartxt() {
  m_custidTextfield.setText("");
  m_nameTextfield.setText("");
  m_addressTextfield.setText("");
}

/* The following functions handle the status messages */

// This function clears the status field
public void clearStatus() {
  m_statusField.setText("");
  m_statusField.setScrollOffset(0);
}

// This function places the p_status value in the status field
public void putStatus(String l_status) {
  m_statusField.setText(l_status);
  m_statusField.setScrollOffset(0);
}

// This function appends the p_status value to the status field
public void appendStatus(String p_status) {
  String l_status = m_statusField.getText();
  m_statusField.setText(l_status+"\n"+p_status);
  m_statusField.setScrollOffset(0);
}

// Initialize all the GUI components

public void jbInit() throws Exception {
  this.getContentPane().setLayout(m_gridBagLayout);
  this.setSize(new Dimension(856, 629));
  this.addWindowListener(new java.awt.event.WindowAdapter() {
```

6

continues

Listing 6.1   Continued

```
        public void windowClosing(WindowEvent e) {
          m_parent.dispatchEvent("CLOSE");
        }
    });
this.setTitle("Using JDBC to perform DML in JavaStop");
m_jtable.setRowHeight(20);
m_jtable.setToolTipText("Table displays the rows");
m_clearButton.setMaximumSize(new Dimension(97, 29));
m_clearButton.setText("CLEAR");
m_clearButton.setPreferredSize(new Dimension(97, 29));
m_clearButton.setFont(new Font("Dialog", 1, 16));
m_clearButton.setToolTipText("Press to clear the text fields");
m_clearButton.setMinimumSize(new Dimension(97, 29));
m_statusField.setFont(new Font("Dialog", 0, 14));
m_statusField.setToolTipText("Status bar");
m_statusField.setEditable(false);
m_statusField.setBackground(Color.lightGray);
m_custidLabel.setText("Customer ID");
m_custidLabel.setFont(new Font("Dialog", 1, 14));
m_nameLabel.setText("Name");
m_nameLabel.setFont(new Font("Dialog", 1, 14));
m_custidTextfield.setToolTipText("Enter the Customer ID");
m_nameTextfield.setToolTipText("Enter the Customer Name");
m_addressTextfield.setToolTipText("Enter the Customer Address");
m_addressLabel.setText("Customer Address");
m_addressLabel.setFont(new Font("Dialog", 1, 14));
m_insertButton.setMaximumSize(new Dimension(97, 29));
m_insertButton.setText("INSERT");
m_insertButton.setPreferredSize(new Dimension(97, 29));
m_insertButton.setFont(new Font("Dialog", 1, 16));
m_insertButton.setToolTipText("Press to insert the record");
m_insertButton.setMinimumSize(new Dimension(97, 29));
m_selectButton.setMaximumSize(new Dimension(127, 29));
m_selectButton.setText("SELECT");
m_selectButton.setPreferredSize(new Dimension(127, 29));
m_selectButton.setFont(new Font("Dialog", 1, 16));
m_selectButton.setToolTipText("Press to select records");
m_selectButton.setMinimumSize(new Dimension(127, 29));
m_updateButton.setMaximumSize(new Dimension(97, 29));
m_updateButton.setText("UPDATE");
m_updateButton.setPreferredSize(new Dimension(97, 29));
m_updateButton.setFont(new Font("Dialog", 1, 16));
m_updateButton.setToolTipText("Press to update the record");
m_updateButton.setMinimumSize(new Dimension(97, 29));
m_delButton.setText("DELETE");
m_delButton.setFont(new Font("Dialog", 1, 16));
m_delButton.setToolTipText("Press to delete the record");
m_closeButton.setMaximumSize(new Dimension(147, 29));
m_closeButton.setText("CLOSE");
m_closeButton.setPreferredSize(new Dimension(147, 29));
m_closeButton.setFont(new Font("Dialog", 1, 16));
m_closeButton.setToolTipText("Press to exit the application");
```

```
    m_closeButton.setMinimumSize(new Dimension(147, 29));
    this.getContentPane().add(m_jScrollPane1,
➥new GridBagConstraintsJstp(0, 0, 12, 1, 1.0, 1.0
    ,GridBagConstraints.CENTER, GridBagConstraints.BOTH,
➥new Insets(19, 2, 0, 0), 291, -67));
    m_jScrollPane1.getViewport().add(m_jtable, null);
    this.getContentPane().add(m_custidLabel,
➥new GridBagConstraintsJstp(0, 1, 1, 1, 0.0, 0.0
    ,GridBagConstraints.WEST, GridBagConstraints.NONE,
➥new Insets(20, 2, 0, 0), 4, 19));
    this.getContentPane().add(m_custidTextfield,
➥new GridBagConstraintsJstp(1, 1, 1, 1, 1.0, 0.0
    ,GridBagConstraints.WEST, GridBagConstraints.HORIZONTAL,
➥new Insets(25, 0, 0, 0), 143, 11));
    this.getContentPane().add(m_nameLabel,
➥new GridBagConstraintsJstp(2, 1, 2, 1, 0.0, 0.0
    ,GridBagConstraints.WEST, GridBagConstraints.NONE,
➥new Insets(24, 9, 0, 0), 14, 14));
    this.getContentPane().add(m_nameTextfield,
➥new GridBagConstraintsJstp(4, 1, 4, 1, 1.0, 0.0
    ,GridBagConstraints.WEST, GridBagConstraints.HORIZONTAL,
➥new Insets(25, 0, 0, 0), 309, 10));
    this.getContentPane().add(m_addressLabel,
➥new GridBagConstraintsJstp(8, 1, 1, 1, 0.0, 0.0
    ,GridBagConstraints.WEST, GridBagConstraints.NONE,
➥new Insets(25, 27, 0, 0), 4, 14));
    this.getContentPane().add(m_addressTextfield,
➥new GridBagConstraintsJstp(9, 1, 2, 1, 1.0, 0.0
    ,GridBagConstraints.WEST, GridBagConstraints.BOTH,
➥new Insets(26, 0, 0, 0), 68, 9));
    this.getContentPane().add(m_selectButton,
➥new GridBagConstraintsJstp(1, 2, 2, 1, 0.0, 0.0
    ,GridBagConstraints.CENTER, GridBagConstraints.NONE,
➥new Insets(51, 44, 0, 0), 9, 18));
    this.getContentPane().add(m_updateButton,
➥new GridBagConstraintsJstp(5, 2, 1, 1, 0.0, 0.0
    ,GridBagConstraints.CENTER, GridBagConstraints.NONE,
➥new Insets(51, 0, 0, 0), 18, 18));
    this.getContentPane().add(m_delButton,
➥new GridBagConstraintsJstp(6, 2, 1, 1, 0.0, 0.0
    ,GridBagConstraints.CENTER, GridBagConstraints.NONE,
➥new Insets(52, 14, 0, 0), 8, 16));
    this.getContentPane().add(m_closeButton,
➥new GridBagConstraintsJstp(9, 2, 3, 1, 0.0, 0.0
    ,GridBagConstraints.WEST, GridBagConstraints.BOTH,
➥new Insets(51, -1, 0, 15), -14, 17));
    this.getContentPane().add(m_statusField,
➥new GridBagConstraintsJstp(0, 3, 12, 1, 1.0, 0.0
    ,GridBagConstraints.WEST, GridBagConstraints.HORIZONTAL,
➥new Insets(9, 2, 4, 0), 747, 43));
    this.getContentPane().add(m_insertButton,
```

6

continues

Listing 6.1   Continued

```
➥new GridBagConstraintsJstp(3, 2, 2, 1, 0.0, 0.0
  ,GridBagConstraints.CENTER, GridBagConstraints.NONE,
➥new Insets(51, 0, 0, 13), 3, 18));
   this.getContentPane().add(m_clearButton,
➥new GridBagConstraintsJstp(8, 2, 2, 1, 0.0, 0.0
  ,GridBagConstraints.WEST, GridBagConstraints.NONE,
➥new Insets(52, 10, 0, 14), 0, 17));
 }
}

/* Listing for file JdbcDml.java */

/**
 * @author  Megh Thakkar
 * @version 1.0
 *
 * Development Environment        : JDeveloper 3.0
 * Name of the Application        : JdbcDml.java
 * Application Notes :
 *
 * This application demonstrates how to perform DML in JSTP using
 * a JDBC thin driver.
 *
 */
// Import the packages for the JDBC classes
import java.sql.*;

public class JdbcDml {
  //Create a connection object
  Connection  m_connection = null;

  //The User Interface for this application is handled by JdbcDmlGui
  JdbcDmlGui  m_JdbcGui;

  /**
   *  The Constructor is used to instantiate the User Interface
   **/
  public JdbcDml(){
    m_JdbcGui = new JdbcDmlGui(this);
    m_JdbcGui.setVisible(true);
  }

  /**
   *  This is the main entry point that makes a database connection to JSTP
   **/
  public static void main(String args[]){

    JdbcDml JDml = new JdbcDml();
    JDml.dbConnection();

  }
```

```
/**
*  The various events that can occur are handled in this class
**/
public void dispatchEvent(String p_eventName) {
  // Store the values input by the user
  String l_custid = m_JdbcGui.m_custidTextfield.getText();
  String l_name = m_JdbcGui.m_nameTextfield.getText();
  String l_address = m_JdbcGui.m_addressTextfield.getText();

  // Handle the various events
  if(p_eventName.equals("CLOSE"))
     exitApplication();
  else if (p_eventName.equals("SELECT"))
      selectRecords(l_custid, l_name, l_address);
  else if (p_eventName.equals("INSERT"))
      insertRecord(l_custid, l_name, l_address);
  else if (p_eventName.equals("UPDATE"))
      updateRecord(l_custid, l_name, l_address);
  else if (p_eventName.equals("DELETE"))
      deleteRecord(l_custid);

}

 public void dbConnection() {
 try {
     m_JdbcGui.putStatus("Connecting to the Database....please wait.....");

     //Register the JDBC driver
     DriverManager.registerDriver(new oracle.jdbc.driver.OracleDriver());

     m_connection = DriverManager.getConnection(
                     "jdbc:oracle:thin:@"+
                     ConnectionSpecs.s_hostName+":"+
                     ConnectionSpecs.s_portNumber+":"+
                     ConnectionSpecs.s_databaseSID,
                     ConnectionSpecs.s_userName,ConnectionSpecs.s_password);

     /*
     * Setting autocommit to false will prevent actual changes
     * to the database
     */
     m_connection.setAutoCommit(false);

     m_JdbcGui.putStatus("Successful Connection to " +
                     ConnectionSpecs.s_databaseSID+ " as "
                     +ConnectionSpecs.s_userName);


   } catch(Exception ex){
       m_JdbcGui.appendStatus("Error during connection....."
                     +ex.toString());
```

6

continues

Listing 6.1   Continued

```
        }
    }

    /**
    *  Close the connection to JSTP and exit the application
    **/
    public void exitApplication() {
      try {
          m_JdbcGui.putStatus("Disconnecting from JSTP.......");
          if(m_connection != null)
              // close the connection
              m_connection.close();
      } catch(SQLException ex){
          m_JdbcGui.putStatus("Error during disconnection....."
                              +ex.toString());
      }
      //Exit the application
      System.exit(0);
    }

    /* Retrieve records from the customer table using SQL SELECT statement*/
    public void selectRecords(String p_custid,String p_name,String p_address) {
      // Build the SQL statement to select records from the customer table
      String l_query = "select customer_id, name, address from customers "
          +"where customer_id like ? AND name like ? AND address like ?";
      try {
          // If no condition is specified then we will retrieve all the records
          if(p_custid.equals(""))
              p_custid = "%";
          if(p_name.equals(""))
              p_name = "%";
          if(p_address.equals(""))
              p_address = "%";

          // Create a preparedStatement using the above query
          PreparedStatement l_pst = m_connection.prepareStatement(l_query);


          //Bind the prepared statement with the specified conditions
          l_pst.setString(1,p_custid);
          l_pst.setString(2,p_name);
          l_pst.setString(3,p_address);

          //Execute the prepared statement and store the result set
          ResultSet l_resultSet = l_pst.executeQuery();

          //Clear the Jtable and then populate it using the retrieved records

          m_JdbcGui.m_tmodel.clearTable();

          while (l_resultSet.next()) {
              String l_custid = l_resultSet.getString(1);
```

```
            String l_name = l_resultSet.getString(2);
            String l_address = l_resultSet.getString(3);

            m_JdbcGui.insertJTable(l_custid, l_name, l_address);
        }

        //Close the PreparedStatement object
        l_pst.close();

    } catch (SQLException ex) {
        m_JdbcGui.putStatus("Error occurred during selecting from JavaStop... "
                            +ex.toString());
    }
}

/* Insert a new record into the customer table using SQL INSERT statement*/
public void insertRecord(String p_custid,String p_name,String p_address) {
  try {
        // Prepare a SQL statement for inserting a new record
        PreparedStatement l_pst = m_connection.prepareStatement(
            "insert into customers(customer_id, name, address) values (?,?,?)");

        // Bind the variables
        l_pst.setString(1,p_custid);
        l_pst.setString(2,p_name);
        l_pst.setString(3,p_address);

        l_pst.execute();

        l_pst.close();

        // Update the JTable to reflect the new record
        m_JdbcGui.insertJTable(p_custid, p_name, p_address);
        m_JdbcGui.putStatus("The Record is successfully inserted");
    } catch (SQLException ex) {
        m_JdbcGui.putStatus("Unable to insert new record... "
                            +'\n'+ex.toString());
    }
}


/* Update a record from the customer table using SQL UPDATE statement*/
public void updateRecord(String p_custid,String p_name,String p_address) {
  try {
        //Prepare a SQL statement for updating a record
        PreparedStatement l_pst = m_connection.prepareStatement(
        "update customers set name = ?, address = ? where customer_id = ?");

        // Bind the variables
        l_pst.setString(1,p_name);
        l_pst.setString(2,p_address);
        l_pst.setString(3,p_custid);
```

continues

Listing 6.1   Continued

```
        l_pst.executeUpdate();

        //Close the PreparedStatement object
        l_pst.close();

        m_JdbcGui.updateJTable(p_custid, p_name, p_address);

        m_JdbcGui.putStatus("Record updated successfully ");
    } catch (SQLException ex) {
      m_JdbcGui.putStatus("Error in updating record..."
                          + '\n'+ex.toString());
    }
  }

  /* Delete a record from the customers table using SQL DELETE statement*/
  public void deleteRecord(String p_custid) {
    try {
        //Prepare a SQL statement to delete a record
        PreparedStatement l_pst = m_connection.prepareStatement(
                " Delete from customers where customer_id=?");


        l_pst.setString(1,p_custid);


        l_pst.executeUpdate();


        l_pst.close();

        m_JdbcGui.deleteFromJTable();

        m_JdbcGui.putStatus("Record deleted successfully");
    } catch(Exception ex){
      m_JdbcGui.putStatus("Error in deleting record.... "
                          +'\n'+ex.toString());
    }
  }

}
```

Oracle JDBC Limitations

The current implementation of Oracle JDBC has several limitations:

- CursorName is not supported. Oracle JDBC drivers do not support the
  getCursorName() and setCursorName() methods because there is no easy way
  to map them to equivalent Oracle constructs. The workaround for this limitation is to use the Oracle ROWID.

- SQL92 Outer join escapes are not supported. The workaround is to use the Oracle SQL syntax with (+).

- Calling arguments or return values of the PL/SQL TABLE, BOOLEAN, or RECORD types is not supported.

- The arithmetic for the Oracle NUMBER type does not comply with the IEEE 754 standard for floating-point arithmetic, and therefore the results of computations performed by Oracle and the same computations performed by Java might have small mismatches.

- Read-only connections are not supported.

- SQLWarning class is not supported. Usually this class can be used to obtain information on a database access warning.

- Bind by name is not supported.

The following is not supported in Oracle JDBC drivers:

```
    PreparedStatement p = conn.prepareStatement
➡("select name from products where prod_id = :prdid");
    p.setInt(1, 10210);
```

6

Tip

The version of the JDBC driver in use can be obtained by using the `getDriverVersion()` method of the `OracleDatabaseMetaData` class as shown in the following code:

```
import java.sql.*;
import oracle.jdbc.driver.*;

class JDBCgetversion
{
    public static void main (String args [])
        throws SQLException
    {
        DriverManager.registerDriver(new
➡oracle.jdbc.driver.OracleDriver());

Connection conn = DriverManager.getConnection
➡("jdbc:oracle:thin:@myhost:1521:jstp","scott""tiger");

        // Create an Oracle DatabaseMetaData object
        DatabaseMetaData md = conn.getMetaData ();

        System.out.println("JDBC driver version used is " +
➡md.getDriverVersion());

    }
}
```

JDBC Scalability

Java native threads are fully preemptive and provide good scalability on multi-processor machines. There is another implementation of Java threads that is not pre-emptive—Java Green Threads. On Windows NT, the default is native OS thread, whereas on Solaris the default is the Green thread. JDBC drivers do not have any scalability restrictions by themselves but the number of connections might be restricted by the number of processes specified in the init.ora file on the database server. It should be further noted that if the Green threads, which are non-preemptive, are used, the number of connections might be much lower than that indicated by the processes parameter.

Next Steps

I have mentioned earlier that Oracle8i provides two client-side alternatives for accessing Oracle databases from Java—JDBC and SQLJ. The previous chapter showed us the connection aspects of JDBC while this chapter demonstrated how to access the data in JavaStop using JDBC client-side drivers.

The next chapter will demonstrate the use of SQLJ for accessing JavaStop data. We will also learn how SQLJ helps in writing efficient code.

Implementing Clean and Compact Code Using SQLJ

Introduction

Oracle8i provides two techniques that can be used to communicate with the database from within Java code: JDBC and SQLJ. Prior to this chapter, we have been focusing on the use of JDBC for implementing JavaStop. In this chapter, we will focus on the use of SQLJ as an alternative technique of implementing JavaStop. Using SQLJ instead of JDBC will result in code that is very compact and easy to understand.

Embedding SQL Statements Within Java Using SQLJ

SQLJ enables developers to write efficient and compact programs. SQLJ is built on top of JDBC and enables application developers to embed SQL statements within Java programs. A preprocessor is used to translate SQLJ syntax to Java code that makes JDBC calls to the database. Oracle's JDeveloper, which is a standard Java development tool, can be used to develop and debug SQLJ programs. Use of SQLJ improves the productivity and manageability of Java code for several reasons:

- It provides code that's significantly compact compared to JDBC.
- Typed cursors enable the use of strong-typed queries.
- SQL statements are checked at compile time, enabling early detection of errors.

Using JDBC, a calling program can perform dynamic SQL by constructing SQL statements at runtime. No analysis or checking of the SQL statements is performed and any errors made in the SQL code raise runtime errors. However, if you have applications that use static SQL, where the SQL statements are fixed or static, SQLJ can be used to improve efficiency and trap SQL errors at compile time. Several important tasks are performed by the precompile step of a SQLJ program:

- Syntax checking of the embedded SQL
- Type checking against the database to ensure that the data exchanged between Java and SQL have compatible types and proper type conversions
- Schema checking

The result of the precompilation is Java source code with SQL runtime code. The generated Java code compiles and runs like any other Java program.

 **Note**   SQLJ also can inter-operate with dynamic SQL through JDBC.

Advantages of SQLJ over JDBC for Static SQL

JDBC provides a complete dynamic SQL interface to access databases from Java programs. Although static SQL statements can be used in your JDBC programs, they are more conveniently represented in SQLJ. Using SQLJ instead of JDBC for static SQL provides several advantages:

- SQLJ provides a shorter syntax compared to JDBC, making the programs more compact.
- JDBC is a dynamic API and therefore doesn't perform any type checking until runtime. SQLJ, on the other hand, can trap errors earlier.
- SQLJ enables Java bind expressions to be embedded directly within SQL statements.
- SQLJ simplifies the calling of SQL stored procedures and functions.

The biggest disadvantage of using SQLJ is the extra steps that result from the use of a preprocessor, which can sometimes result in programs that are slower than pure JDBC programs. However, the difference in performance is generally insignificant. Another thing to note is that if you have a mixed environment that uses dynamic and static SQL, it is usually better to use only JDBC because SQLJ doesn't provide significant advantages and could potentially make the program harder to read.

General Guidelines for Using JDBC and SQLJ

We have discussed different pros and cons of using JDBC versus SQLJ. Table 7.1 summarizes some of these uses.

Table 7.1   Guidelines for Using JDBC Versus SQLJ

Characteristic	Use SQLJ?	Use JDBC?
You want to be able to check your program for SQL errors at translation time	Yes	No
You want to write the application so that it can be deployed to another database	Yes	No
You want to use Static SQL extensively	Yes	No
You want to use Dynamic SQL extensively	No	Yes
You do not want to have a SQLJ layer during deployment or development	No	Yes
You want to minimize the download time for the applet	No	Yes
You want to be able to compile SQL statements	Yes	No

Interacting with the Database Using SQLJ

SQLJ provides a standard way in which SQL statements can be embedded in Java programs. When writing a SQLJ program, a user writes a Java program and embeds SQL statements in it. The SQL statements are embedded following certain standard syntactic rules that govern how SQL statements can be embedded in Java programs. A SQLJ translator is then used to convert the SQLJ program to a standard Java program by replacing the embedded SQL statements with calls to the SQLJ runtime. Then, any Java compiler can be used to compile the generated Java program and run it against the database.

The SQLJ runtime environment consists of a thin SQLJ runtime library that calls a JDBC driver targeting the appropriate database.

Using SQLJ to Manipulate Oracle Databases

Several steps are required to use SQLJ in your program. The main steps are as follows:

1. Import required packages. Import any JDBC or SQLJ packages you will use. Some of the classes you might need are

    - `java.sql.*`—This package contains important classes such as `java.sql.SQLException`, `java.sql.Date`, and others.

    - `oracle.sqlj.runtime.*`—This package contains the Oracle class that can be used to instantiate the `DefaultContext` object and establish a default connection.

    - `sqlj.runtime.*` and `sqlj.runtime.ref.*`

2. Register JDBC classes and set the default connection.

3. Create a `main()` that calls the constructor for the program and use a try/catch block in the `main()` to trap any runtime SQL errors.

4. Create a method that does all the work, including

    - Setting up host variables

    - Preparing and executing SQLJ clauses

    - Processing the results (using iterators)

    - Throwing any SQL exceptions to the `main()` for processing

Connecting to JavaStop Using SQLJ

The application SqljConnection (see Listing 7.1) demonstrates how to connect to JSTP using a JDBC-thin driver and SQLJ. It should be noted that if you intend to use the JDBC-OCI driver then the code is the same except for the database URL syntax.

The following are the application's features:

- After the application is launched, it shows the connection status and any errors.

- When the user clicks the Disconnect button, the application closes the connection and exits.

The SqljConnection.jar file contains the following files:

- SqljConnection.sqlj—This is the source file for the application.

- SqljConnectionGui.java—This is the source file for the user interface used by the application.

- SqljConnection.jws—This is the JDeveloper workspace file.

- SqljConnection.jpr—This is the JDeveloper project file.
- GridBagConstraintsJstp.java—This is the source file for the
  `GridBagConstraintsJstp` class that uses the `java.awt.GridBagconstraints`.
- ConnectionSpecs.java—This file contains the parameters that specify how to
  connect to JSTP.

To use the application, you need the following software:

- Calling program:

  JDK 1.1.5 or above

  JFC Swing 1.0.2 or above

  Oracle JDBC drivers for Oracle v7.3.2 or above

  SQLJ Translator for Oracle v7.3.2 or above

The following steps can be used to run the SqljConnection application:

1. Unjar SqljConnection.jar using Winzip, or using the following command:

   ```
   > jar xvf SqljConnection.jar
   ```

 Note　jar.exe can be found in `JDEVELOPER_HOME\java\bin`.

In the previous code, `JDEVELOPER_HOME` is the root directory of the JDeveloper installation.

2. Edit the ConnectionSpecs.java file to specify the hostname, port, username, and password for your system.
3. Import the appropriate version of Swing by editing the SqljConnectionGui.java file. By default, Swing 1.1 is used.

   ```
   * If swing 1.0.2, the import statements should be:
             import com.sun.java.swing.*;

   * If swing 1.1, the import statements should be:
             import  javax.swing.*;
   ```

4. Using the JDeveloper File/Open option, select the SqljConnection.jws file.
5. From the Project menu, select Make Project SqljConnection.jpr.
6. Run the application by selecting Run SqljConnection from the Run menu or by pressing the F9 key.

The code for several files is similar to the corresponding files used with
JdbcConnection and are listed here so you can quickly review them.

7

Listing 7.1   The SQLjConnection Application

```java
/* Listing for file ConnectionSpecs.java */


/**
 * @author  Megh Thakkar
 * @version 1.0
 *
 * Development Environment      :  JDeveloper 3.0
 * Name of the Application      :  ConnectionSpecs.java
 *
 * Application Notes:
 * This application contains static variables that specify the connection
 * parameters used to connect to JSTP. You should edit these parameters
 * to suit your environment
 */

public class ConnectionSpecs {

    // The machine on which the database JSTP resides
    public final static String s_hostName   = "mthakkar";

    // The TNS listener port for JavaStop
    public final static String s_portNumber = "1521";

    // Name of the database
    public final static String s_databaseSID = "JSTP";

    // Userid
    public final static String s_userName   = "scott";

    // Password
    public final static String s_password   = "tiger";
}


/* Listing for file GridBagConstraintsJstp.java */


/**
 * @author  Megh Thakkar
 * @version 1.0
 *
 * Development Environment      :  JDeveloper 3.0
 * Name of the Application      :  gridBagConstraintsJstp.java
 * Application Notes:
 *
 * This is an easier way to use java.awt.GridBagConstraints
 */
import java.awt.*;

public class GridBagConstraintsJstp extends GridBagConstraints {
    /**
     * This Constructor initializes the GridBagConstraints variables.
```

```
   *
  **/
   public GridBagConstraintsJstp(int p_gx, int p_gy, int p_gw, int p_gh,double
➥p_wx,
          double p_wy, int p_anc, int p_fil, Insets p_ins,int p_ix, int p_iy) {

      gridx = p_gx;
       gridy = p_gy;

      gridwidth = p_gw;
      gridheight = p_gh;

    weightx = p_wx;
      weighty = p_wy;

      anchor = p_anc;
      fill = p_fil;

      insets = p_ins;
      ipadx = p_ix;
      ipady = p_iy;
   }
}

/* Listing for file SqljConnectionGui.java */

/**
 * @author  Megh Thakkar
 * @version 1.0
 *
 * Development Environment      :  JDeveloper 3.0
 * Name of the Application      :  SqljConnectionGui.java
 * Application Notes:
 *
 * The User Interface for the SqljConnection application is handled here.
 *
 */

import java.awt.*;
import java.awt.event.*;

/** Import statements for SWING version 1.0.2 **/
//import com.sun.java.swing.*;

/** Import statements for SWING version 1.1. This is the default **/
import javax.swing.*;

public class SqljConnectionGui extends JFrame {
   //This frame is used by the SqljConnection class
   SqljConnection m_parent;

   //Elements that comprise the User Interface
```

continues

Listing 7.1   Continued

```
JButton      m_disconnectButton = new JButton();   //Disconnect Button
TextArea     m_statusbar  = new TextArea();  //Statusbar
JTextField   m_results    = new JTextField();//Results area

//Layout manager object
GridBagLayout m_gridBagLayout = new GridBagLayout();

/**
*   The GUI components are initialized by this constructor
**/
public SqljConnectionGui(SqljConnection p_parent) {
  try{
     m_parent = p_parent;
     jbInit();  //initialize the GUI components
     setupListeners(); //Set up listeners for the GUI components
  } catch(Exception ex){
     putStatus(ex.toString());
  }
}

/**
*  Set up listener for the Exit button so that the application can be closed.
**/
public void setupListeners() {
  m_disconnectButton.addActionListener(new java.awt.event.ActionListener(){
    public void actionPerformed(ActionEvent evt){
      if(evt.getActionCommand() =="Disconnect")
         //The event is passed to the m_parent for handling
         m_parent.dispatchEvent("Disconnect");
    }
  });
}

/**
*  Display the connection status
**/
public void putStatus(String p_status) {
  m_statusbar.setText(p_status);
}

/**
* Append p_status to the current status displayed
**/
public void appendStatus(String p_status) {
  String l_status = m_statusbar.getText();
  m_statusbar.setText(l_status+"\n"+p_status);
}


/**
```

```
 *   Display p_text in the Text Area
 **/
public void putResults(String p_text) {
  m_results.setText(p_text);
}

/**
 * Append p_text to the current message in the Text Area
 **/
public void appendResults(String p_text) {
  String l_results = m_results.getText();
  m_results.setText(l_results+"\n"+"\n"+p_text);
}

/**
 *   Initialize all the GUI components
 **/
public void jbInit() throws Exception {
  this.getContentPane().setLayout(m_gridBagLayout);
  this.setTitle("Connecting to JSTP using SQLJ");
  this.setSize(new Dimension(533, 249));
  this.addWindowListener(new java.awt.event.WindowAdapter() {
    public void windowClosing(WindowEvent e) {
        m_parent.dispatchEvent("Disconnect");
    }
  });
  m_disconnectButton.setText("Disconnect");
  m_disconnectButton.setFont(new Font("Dialog", 1, 16));
  m_disconnectButton.setToolTipText("Press to Disconnect");
  m_statusbar.setFont(new Font("Dialog", 0, 14));
  m_statusbar.setEditable(false);
  m_statusbar.setBackground(Color.lightGray);
  m_results.setFont(new Font("Dialog", 0, 14));
  m_results.setDisabledTextColor(Color.white);
  m_results.setToolTipText("Displays the connection status");
  m_results.setEditable(false);
  this.getContentPane().add(m_disconnectButton, new GridBagConstraintsJstp
➥(0, 1, 1, 1, 0.0, 0.0
  ,GridBagConstraints.CENTER, GridBagConstraints.NONE, new Insets
➥(9, 400, 0, 0), 42, 10));
  this.getContentPane().add(m_statusbar, new GridBagConstraintsJstp
➥(0, 2, 2, 1, 1.0, 1.0
  ,GridBagConstraints.CENTER, GridBagConstraints.BOTH, new Insets
➥(14, 1, 0, 2), 0, 0));
  this.getContentPane().add(m_results, new GridBagConstraintsJstp
➥(0, 0, 1, 1, 1.0, 0.0
  ,GridBagConstraints.WEST, GridBagConstraints.HORIZONTAL, new Insets
➥(2, 1, 0, 0), 505, 46));
 }
}

/**
```

continues

Listing 7.1   Continued

```
 * @author  Megh Thakkar
 * @version 1.0
 *
 * Development Environment    :  JDeveloper 3.0
 * Name of the Application    :  SqljConnection.sqlj
 * Application notes:
 *
 * This application connects to the JSTP database using JDBC thin-driver
 * and SQLJ
 *
 */

// Import the SQLJ runtime classes
import sqlj.runtime.*;
import sqlj.runtime.ref.*;

// Import the JDBC classes
import java.sql.*;

public class SqljConnection{

  // Create a connection context object
  DefaultContext  m_connContext = null;

  // The User Interface for this application is handled by SqljConnectionGui
  SqljConnectionGui  m_GUI;

  /**
   *  Instantiate the User Interface in the constructor
   **/
   public SqljConnection(){
      m_GUI = new SqljConnectionGui(this);
      m_GUI.setVisible(true);
   }

  /**
   *  Main entry point that will make the database connection
   **/
   public static void main(String args[]){

     SqljConnection sqljcon = new SqljConnection();
     sqljcon.dbConnection();
   }

  /**
   *  This method is invoked by the listeners set up in the
   *  SqljConnectionGui class. When the user clicks the "Disconnect" button,
   *  it is handled here.
   **/
   public void dispatchEvent(String p_eventName) {
     if(p_eventName.equals("Disconnect")){
```

```
        exitApplication();
    }
}


// Connecting to the database
public void dbConnection(){
    try {

        m_GUI.putStatus("Connecting to the Database....please wait.....");

        //Register the JDBC driver
        DriverManager.registerDriver(new oracle.jdbc.driver.OracleDriver());

        // The connection parameters specified in ConnectionSpecs.java are used
        String l_dbConnectString =
            "(DESCRIPTION=(ADDRESS=(HOST="+ConnectionSpecs.s_hostName+")"+
            "(PROTOCOL=tcp)(PORT="+ConnectionSpecs.s_portNumber+"))"+
            "(CONNECT_DATA=(SID="+ConnectionSpecs.s_databaseSID+")))";

        m_connContext = new DefaultContext(
                "jdbc:oracle:thin:@"+l_dbConnectString,
            ConnectionSpecs.s_userName,ConnectionSpecs.s_password,false);

        // The above connection context is set as the default context
        DefaultContext.setDefaultContext(m_connContext);

        m_GUI.putStatus("");

        m_GUI.putResults("Successfully connected as user " +
                        ConnectionSpecs.s_userName +" to database "
                         +ConnectionSpecs.s_databaseSID );
    } catch(Exception ex){
        m_GUI.appendStatus("Unable to connect....."
                          +ex.toString());

    }
}


/**
*   Close the connection to JSTP and exit the application
**/
public void exitApplication() {
    try {
        m_GUI.putStatus("Closing the connection....please wait.....");
        if(m_connContext != null)
            m_connContext.close(); //Closing the m_connContext object.
    } catch(SQLException ex){ //Trap SQLException
        m_GUI.putStatus(ex.toString());
    }
        System.exit(0);
}
}
```

7

SQLJ Basic Language Constructs

SQLJ statements always begin with a `#sql` token and can be broken into two categories:

- **Declarations**—These can be used to create Java classes for iterators (for processing results similar to result sets of JDBC) or connection contexts (used to establish database connections).
- **Executable statements**—These can be used to execute embedded SQL statements.

SQLJ Declarations

As mentioned earlier, SQLJ declarations can be either iterator declarations or connection context declarations. An *iterator* is defined as an instance of a iterator class and is used (similar to JDBC result sets) to process queries that can return multiple rows. Similarly, each database connection is implemented in SQLJ as an instance of a connection context class. Typically, different connection context classes are used for connections to different types of database schemas.

 Note   SQLJ declarations are allowed in the top-level scope, a class scope, or a nested-class scope but not inside method blocks.

Basic iterator declarations have the following syntax:

```
#sql <modifiers> iterator iterator_classname (type declarations);
```

where

- Modifiers are optional and can be any standard Java class modifiers such as public, static, and so on.
- Type declarations can be used to specify a named iterator or a positional iterator. For named iterators you specify the column names and types, but for positional iterators you specify the types only. For example,

```
#sql public iterator niterator (String name, String address);
```

The previous statement creates a named iterator `niterator` with two string attributes `name` and `address`. The same effect can be obtained by using a positional iterator as follows:

```
#sql public iterator niterator (String, String);
```

Note Any public class should be declared in a separate source file, and the base name of the file should be the same as the class name. For example, a class named SqljDml would be stored in a source file named SqljDml.sqlj.

Basic connection context declarations have the following syntax:

```
#sql <modifiers> context context_classname;
```

where

- Modifiers are optional and can be any standard Java class modifiers such as public, static, and so on.

For example

```
#sql public context test_context;
```

The previous SQLJ statement creates a public `test_context` class. Your SQLJ code can then use instances of this class to create database connections to a schema of a given type.

SQLJ Executable Statements

A SQLJ executable statement consists of a `#sqlj` token followed by a SQLJ clause that can be used to embed SQL statements in Java code. The embedded SQL operation can be any SQL operation supported by the JDBC driver, including

- DML
- DDL
- Transaction control

The following rules must be followed by SQLJ executable statements:

- It is permitted inside method definitions, static initialization blocks, and anywhere in Java code that Java block statements are permitted.
- The embedded SQL must be enclosed in curly brackets { }.

It should be noted that everything inside the curly brackets of a SQL execution statement is treated as a SQL syntax and must follow standard SQL rules, except Java host variables.

 Note The SQLJ translator can parse only DML operations and check them for syntax and semantics. DDL operations and transactional control statements can't be checked.

The basic syntax of SQLJ executable statements is as follows:

- `#sql { SQL operation returning no output };`

  (The previous line is referred to as a SQLJ statement clause.)

  or

- `#sql result = { SQL operation returning output };`

  (The previous line is referred to as a SQLJ assignment clause.)

Table 7.2 shows the supported SQLJ statement clauses, and Table 7.3 shows the supported SQLJ assignment clauses.

Table 7.2   Supported SQLJ Statement Clauses

SQLJ Statement Clause	Use
SELECT INTO	Selects data into Java host expressions
FETCH	Fetches data from a positional iterator
COMMIT	Commits changes to the database
ROLLBACK	Discards changes
Set transaction	Advanced transaction control to specify transaction isolation levels
Procedure	Calls a stored procedure
Assignment	Assigns values to Java host expressions
SQL	SELECT, INSERT, UPDATE, and DELETE operations

Table 7.3   Supported SQLJ Assignment Clauses

SQLJ Assignment Clause	Use
Query	Selects data into an SQLJ iterator
Function	Calls a stored function
Iterator conversion	Converts a JDBC result set into an SQLJ iterator

 **Note**   PL/SQL blocks can be used in the curly brackets of the SQLJ statements just as SQL statements.

Java Expressions in SQLJ Code

Three categories of Java expressions are used in SQLJ code: host expressions, context expressions, and result expressions.

Host Expressions

Java *host expressions* are used to pass arguments between your Java code and SQL operations. The most basic kind of Java host expression consists of a Java identifier called a *host variable*. Java identifiers used as host variables or in a host expression can represent any of the following:

> local variables
>
> declared parameters
>
> class fields
>
> static or instance method calls

Let's consider some examples.

Suppose that you want to use three input host variables to update the name and address of the customer specified by the customer_id. The following code could be used:

```
String custid="11111";
String name="New Horizons";
String address="36 Dreamland Road, Orlando, FL 32815";

#sql { UPDATE customers SET name = :IN name, address = :IN address WHERE
➥customer_id = :IN custid };
```

Context Expressions

A *context expression* specifies a connection context instance or an execution context instance that will be used with a SQLJ statement. The following can be used as a context expression:

> local variables
>
> declared parameters
>
> class fields
>
> array elements

Result Expressions

A *result expression* specifies output variables for query results or function returns. The following can be used as a result expression:

> local variables
>
> declared parameters
>
> class fields
>
> array elements

Evaluation of Java Expressions at Runtime

The syntax of a SQLJ executable statement using all the Java expressions can be as follows:

```
#sql [connctxt_exp, execctxt_exp] res_exp = { SQL with host expression };
```

The Java expressions used in the previous line are evaluated by Java and not by the SQL engine. This results in a side effect in the order of their evaluation. The following ordering is used for the evaluation of Java expressions and statements:

1. Connection context expressions are evaluated before anything else.

2. Execution context expressions are evaluated after connection context expressions but before any result expressions.

3. Execution context expressions are evaluated after connection context expressions but before any host expressions.

4. After the evaluation of connection, execution, and result expressions, host expressions are evaluated left to right as they are encountered in the SQL.

5. IN and INOUT parameters are passed to SQL, and the SQL operation is executed.

6. After the SQL operation is executed, Java OUT and INOUT host expressions are assigned values from left to right as they appear in the SQL operation.

7. Result expressions, if any, are assigned output last.

Note

Do not use in, out, or inout as identifiers in host expressions unless they are enclosed in parentheses. For example, an output host variable called out can be used as follows:

```
:(out) or :OUT (out)
```

Using SQLJ to Perform DML Operations in JavaStop

The application SqljDML (see Listing 7.2) demonstrates how to perform DML operations such as SELECT, INSERT, UPDATE, and DELETE in JavaStop using a JDBC-thin driver and SQLJ. It should be noted that if you intend to use the JDBC-OCI driver, the code is the same except for the database URL syntax.

The application features are as follows:

- After the application is launched, it shows the connection status and any errors.
- When the user clicks the CLOSE button, the application closes the connection and exits.

- When the user clicks the SELECT button, it retrieves all the records from the customers table unless a specified customer ID is specified, in which case it will retrieve only that record.
- When the user clicks the CLEAR button, it clears the text in the text fields.
- When the user clicks the INSERT button, it inserts a new record in the customers table using the values in the text fields.
- When the user clicks the UPDATE button, it updates the selected record.
- When the user clicks the DELETE button, it deletes the selected record.

The SqljDml.jar file contains the following files:

- SqljDml.sqlj—This is the source file for the application.
- SqljDmlGui.java—This is the source file for the user interface used by the application.
- SqljDml.jws—This is the JDeveloper workspace file.
- SqljDml.jpr—This is the JDeveloper project file.
- GridBagConstraintsJstp.java—This is the source file for the `GridBagConstraintsJstp` class that uses the `java.awt.GridBagconstraints`. This is identical to the file used earlier.
- ConnectionSpecs.java—This file contains the parameters that specify how to connect to JSTP. This is identical to the file used earlier.
- genTableModel.java—This class is provided by Oracle Corporation and is used to maintain the data for a JTable. Any application using JTables can use this class as a table model.

To use the application, you need the following software:

- Calling program:

  JDK 1.1.5 or above

  JFC Swing 1.0.2 or above

  Oracle JDBC drivers for Oracle v7.3.2 or above

  SQLJ Translator for Oracle v7.3.2 or above

The following steps can be used to run the SqljDml application:

1. Unjar SqljDml.jar using Winzip, or by using the following command:

   ```
   > jar xvf SqljDml.jar
   ```

2. Edit the ConnectionSpecs.java file to specify the hostname, port, username, and password for your system.

Note   jar.exe can be found in `JDEVELOPER_HOME\java\bin`, where `JDEVELOPER_HOME` is the root directory of the JDeveloper installation.

3. Import the appropriate version of Swing by editing the SqljDmlGui.java file. By default, Swing 1.1 is used.

```
* If swing 1.0.2, the import statements should be:
        import com.sun.java.swing.*;

* If swing 1.1, the import statements should be:
        import javax.swing.*;
```

4. Using the JDeveloper File/Open option, select the SqljDml.jws file.

5. From the Project menu, select Make Project SqljDml.jpr.

6. Run the application by selecting Run SqljDml from the Run menu or pressing the F9 key.

The code for several important files is listed here for quick analysis.

Listing 7.2   The SqljDML Application

```
/* Listing for file sqljDMLGui.java */

/**
 * @author  Megh Thakkar
 * @version 1.0
 *
 * Development Environment       :  JDeveloper 3.0
 * Name of the Application       :  sqljDMLGui.java
 * Application Notes       :
 *
 * The User Interface for the sqljDML is handled here
 *
 */
import java.awt.*;
import java.awt.event.*;
import java.util.*;

/** Import statements for SWING version 1.0.2 **/
//import com.sun.java.swing.*;
//import com.sun.java.swing.event.*;
//import com.sun.java.swing.table.*;

/** Import statements for SWING version 1.1 **/
import javax.swing.*;
import javax.swing.event.*;
import javax.swing.table.*;
```

```
public class sqljDMLGui extends JFrame {
  //The main application class which uses this User Interface
  sqljDML m_parent;

  //Labels for the textfields in the UI
  JLabel m_custidLabel   = new JLabel();
  JLabel m_addressLabel = new JLabel();
  JLabel m_nameLabel     = new JLabel();

  //These textfields are used for displaying and entering records
  JTextField m_custidTextfield    = new JTextField();
  JTextField m_nameTextfield      = new JTextField();
  JTextField m_addressTextfield = new JTextField();

  //This textfield is used to display messages
  JTextField m_statusField = new JTextField();

  //These buttons are used for specifying the DML operations to be performed

  JButton m_selectButton = new JButton();
  JButton m_insertButton = new JButton();
  JButton m_updateButton = new JButton();
  JButton m_delButton    = new JButton();
  JButton m_closeButton   = new JButton();
  JButton m_clearButton  = new JButton();

  //This scroll pane is used for holding m_jtable
  JScrollPane   m_jScrollPane1 = new JScrollPane();

  // The database rows are displayed in this table
  JTable m_jtable;

  // The JTable model is specified by genTableModel
  genTableModel m_tmodel;

  //Layout Manager object
  GridBagLayout m_gridBagLayout  = new GridBagLayout();

  /**
  * The constructor is used to setup the listeners for the events
  **/
  public sqljDMLGui(sqljDML p_parent) {
    try {
        m_parent = p_parent;

        // Intialize JTable
        jtableInit();
        jbInit();

        //Setup the listeners for the various events
        setupListeners();
    } catch (Exception ex) {
```

continues

Listing 7.2   Continued

```
        m_statusField.setText("Error occurred during initialization..."
                            +'\n'+ex.toString());
    }
}

/**
 *  The following methods are used for manipulating the JTable
 **/

// Insert the specified row in the JTable
public void insertJTable(String p_custid,String p_name,String p_address) {
    Vector l_newrow = new Vector();

    //Fill the vector with the new elements
    l_newrow.addElement(p_custid);
    l_newrow.addElement(p_name);
    l_newrow.addElement(p_address);

    //Add the row to the JTable
    m_tmodel.insertRow(l_newrow);
    m_jScrollPane1.repaint();

    // Clear the textfields
    cleartxt();
}

// Update an existing row in the JTable
public void updateJTable(String p_custid,String p_name,String p_address) {

    // Retrieve the index of the specified row.
    // This index will be used to update the appropriate row
    int l_selectedIndex = m_jtable.getSelectedRow();

    Vector l_newrow = new Vector();

    //The column values are added to the Vector
    l_newrow.addElement(p_custid);
    l_newrow.addElement(p_name);
    l_newrow.addElement(p_address);

    // Using the retrieved index, update the row in the JTable
    m_tmodel.updateRow(l_newrow, l_selectedIndex);
    m_jScrollPane1.repaint();

    //Clear the textfields.
    cleartxt();
}

// Delete the specified row from the JTable
public void deleteFromJTable() {
```

```
    // Retrieve the index for the specified row
    int l_selectedIndex = m_jtable.getSelectedRow();

    //Using the retrieved index, delete from the JTable
    m_tmodel.deleteRow(l_selectedIndex);
    m_jScrollPane1.repaint();

    //Clear the textfields.
    cleartxt();
  }

  // Display the selected row in the textfields
  public void displaySel(JTable p_table,int p_selectedRow) {
    //Retrieve the values for the selected row
    TableModel l_model = p_table.getModel();
    String l_custid  = (String) l_model.getValueAt(p_selectedRow,0);
    String l_name    = (String) l_model.getValueAt(p_selectedRow,1);
    String l_address = (String) l_model.getValueAt(p_selectedRow,2);

    //Display the selected row
    m_custidTextfield.setText(l_custid);
    m_nameTextfield.setText(l_name);
    m_addressTextfield.setText(l_address);

    m_statusField.setText("The selected row is displayed");

    // The insert button can now be enabled since we are simply displaying
➥the selected row
    m_insertButton.setEnabled(false);
  }

  // Initialize the JTable with the column name and the table model
  public void jtableInit() {
    String[] l_cols = {"Customer ID", "Name", "Customer Address"};
    Object[] l_defaultv = {"", "", ""};

    m_tmodel = new genTableModel(l_cols,l_defaultv, 0);
    m_jtable = new JTable(m_tmodel);
  }

  // Set up the listeners for the various events
  public void setupListeners() {
   // Allow single rows to be selected from the JTable
   m_jtable.setSelectionMode(ListSelectionModel.SINGLE_SELECTION);

   m_jtable.getSelectionModel().addListSelectionListener(new
➥ListSelectionListener(){
      public void valueChanged(ListSelectionEvent e) {
        ListSelectionModel l_lsm = (ListSelectionModel)e.getSource();
        if(!l_lsm.isSelectionEmpty()){
          // Display the selected row
          int l_selectedRow = l_lsm.getMinSelectionIndex();
```

continues

Listing 7.2   Continued

```
            displaySel(m_jtable,l_selectedRow);
        }
    }
});

//SELECT button listener
m_selectButton.addActionListener(new java.awt.event.ActionListener(){
  public void actionPerformed(ActionEvent evt){
    if(evt.getActionCommand() =="SELECT") {
    // Pass the event to the parent
    m_parent.dispatchEvent("SELECT");
  }
  }
});

// INSERT button listener
m_insertButton.addActionListener(new java.awt.event.ActionListener(){
  public void actionPerformed(ActionEvent evt){
    if(evt.getActionCommand() == "INSERT") {
      // Pass the event to the parent
      m_parent.dispatchEvent("INSERT");
    }
  }
});

//UPDATE button listener
m_updateButton.addActionListener(new java.awt.event.ActionListener(){
  public void actionPerformed(ActionEvent evt) {
    if(evt.getActionCommand() =="UPDATE"){
      // Pass the event to the parent
      m_parent.dispatchEvent("UPDATE");
    }
  }
});

//DELETE button listener
m_delButton.addActionListener(new java.awt.event.ActionListener(){
  public void actionPerformed(ActionEvent evt){
    if(evt.getActionCommand() =="DELETE") {
      // Pass the event to the parent
      m_parent.dispatchEvent("DELETE");
    }
  }
});

//CLEAR button listener
m_clearButton.addActionListener(new java.awt.event.ActionListener(){
  public void actionPerformed(ActionEvent evt){
    if(evt.getActionCommand() =="CLEAR") {
      // Clear the textfields and enable the INSERT button
      cleartxt();
```

```
          m_insertButton.setEnabled(true);
      }
    }
  });

  //CLOSE button listener
  m_closeButton.addActionListener(new java.awt.event.ActionListener(){
    public void actionPerformed(ActionEvent evt) {
      if(evt.getActionCommand() =="CLOSE")
        // Pass the event to the parent
        m_parent.dispatchEvent("CLOSE");
    }
  });
}

// Clear the textfields
public void cleartxt() {
  m_custidTextfield.setText("");
  m_nameTextfield.setText("");
  m_addressTextfield.setText("");
}

/* The following functions handle the status messages */

// This function clears the status field
public void clearStatus() {
  m_statusField.setText("");
  m_statusField.setScrollOffset(0);
}

// This function places the p_status value in the status field
public void putStatus(String l_status) {
  m_statusField.setText(l_status);
  m_statusField.setScrollOffset(0);
}

// This function appends the p_status value to the status field
public void appendStatus(String p_status) {
  String l_status = m_statusField.getText();
  m_statusField.setText(l_status+"\n"+p_status);
  m_statusField.setScrollOffset(0);
}

// Intialize all the GUI components
public void jbInit() throws Exception {
  this.getContentPane().setLayout(m_gridBagLayout);
  this.setSize(new Dimension(856, 629));
  this.addWindowListener(new java.awt.event.WindowAdapter() {
    public void windowClosing(WindowEvent e) {
      m_parent.dispatchEvent("CLOSE");
    }
  });
```

continues

Listing 7.2　Continued

```
this.setTitle("Using SQLJ to perform DML in JavaStop");
m_jtable.setRowHeight(20);
m_jtable.setToolTipText("Table displays the rows");
m_clearButton.setMaximumSize(new Dimension(97, 29));
m_clearButton.setText("CLEAR");
m_clearButton.setPreferredSize(new Dimension(97, 29));
m_clearButton.setFont(new Font("Dialog", 1, 16));
m_clearButton.setToolTipText("Press to clear the text fields");
m_clearButton.setMinimumSize(new Dimension(97, 29));
m_statusField.setFont(new Font("Dialog", 0, 14));
m_statusField.setToolTipText("Status bar");
m_statusField.setEditable(false);
m_statusField.setBackground(Color.lightGray);
m_custidLabel.setText("Customer ID");
m_custidLabel.setFont(new Font("Dialog", 1, 14));
m_nameLabel.setText("Name");
m_nameLabel.setFont(new Font("Dialog", 1, 14));
m_custidTextfield.setToolTipText("Enter the Customer ID");
m_nameTextfield.setToolTipText("Enter the Customer Name");
m_addressTextfield.setToolTipText("Enter the Customer Address");
m_addressLabel.setText("Customer Address");
m_addressLabel.setFont(new Font("Dialog", 1, 14));
m_insertButton.setMaximumSize(new Dimension(97, 29));
m_insertButton.setText("INSERT");
m_insertButton.setPreferredSize(new Dimension(97, 29));
m_insertButton.setFont(new Font("Dialog", 1, 16));
m_insertButton.setToolTipText("Press to insert the record");
m_insertButton.setMinimumSize(new Dimension(97, 29));
m_selectButton.setMaximumSize(new Dimension(127, 29));
m_selectButton.setText("SELECT");
m_selectButton.setPreferredSize(new Dimension(127, 29));
m_selectButton.setFont(new Font("Dialog", 1, 16));
m_selectButton.setToolTipText("Press to select records");
m_selectButton.setMinimumSize(new Dimension(127, 29));
m_updateButton.setMaximumSize(new Dimension(97, 29));
m_updateButton.setText("UPDATE");
m_updateButton.setPreferredSize(new Dimension(97, 29));
m_updateButton.setFont(new Font("Dialog", 1, 16));
m_updateButton.setToolTipText("Press to update the record");
m_updateButton.setMinimumSize(new Dimension(97, 29));
m_delButton.setText("DELETE");
m_delButton.setFont(new Font("Dialog", 1, 16));
m_delButton.setToolTipText("Press to delete the record");
m_closeButton.setMaximumSize(new Dimension(147, 29));
m_closeButton.setText("CLOSE");
m_closeButton.setPreferredSize(new Dimension(147, 29));
m_closeButton.setFont(new Font("Dialog", 1, 16));
m_closeButton.setToolTipText("Press to exit the application");
m_closeButton.setMinimumSize(new Dimension(147, 29));
this.getContentPane().add(m_jScrollPane1, new GridBagConstraintsJstp
➥(0, 0, 12, 1, 1.0, 1.0
```

```
          ,GridBagConstraints.CENTER, GridBagConstraints.BOTH, new Insets
➡(19, 2, 0, 0), 291, -67));
          m_jScrollPane1.getViewport().add(m_jtable, null);
          this.getContentPane().add(m_custidLabel, new GridBagConstraintsJstp
➡(0, 1, 1, 1, 0.0, 0.0
          ,GridBagConstraints.WEST, GridBagConstraints.NONE, new Insets(20, 2, 0, 0),
➡ 4, 19));
          this.getContentPane().add(m_custidTextfield, new GridBagConstraintsJstp
➡(1, 1, 1, 1, 1.0, 0.0
          ,GridBagConstraints.WEST, GridBagConstraints.HORIZONTAL, new Insets
➡(25, 0, 0, 0), 143, 11));
          this.getContentPane().add(m_nameLabel, new GridBagConstraintsJstp
➡(2, 1, 2, 1, 0.0, 0.0
          ,GridBagConstraints.WEST, GridBagConstraints.NONE, new Insets
➡(24, 9, 0, 0), 14, 14));
          this.getContentPane().add(m_nameTextfield, new GridBagConstraintsJstp
➡(4, 1, 4, 1, 1.0, 0.0
          ,GridBagConstraints.WEST, GridBagConstraints.HORIZONTAL, new Insets
➡(25, 0, 0, 0), 309, 10));
          this.getContentPane().add(m_addressLabel, new GridBagConstraintsJstp
➡(8, 1, 1, 1, 0.0, 0.0
          ,GridBagConstraints.WEST, GridBagConstraints.NONE, new Insets(25, 27, 0, 0),
➡ 4, 14));
          this.getContentPane().add(m_addressTextfield, new GridBagConstraintsJstp
➡(9, 1, 2, 1, 1.0, 0.0
          ,GridBagConstraints.WEST, GridBagConstraints.BOTH, new Insets(26, 0, 0, 0),
➡ 68, 9));
          this.getContentPane().add(m_selectButton, new GridBagConstraintsJstp
➡(1, 2, 2, 1, 0.0, 0.0
          ,GridBagConstraints.CENTER, GridBagConstraints.NONE, new Insets
➡(51, 44, 0, 0), 9, 18));
          this.getContentPane().add(m_updateButton, new GridBagConstraintsJstp
➡(5, 2, 1, 1, 0.0, 0.0
          ,GridBagConstraints.CENTER, GridBagConstraints.NONE, new Insets
➡(51, 0, 0, 0), 18, 18));
          this.getContentPane().add(m_delButton, new GridBagConstraintsJstp
➡(6, 2, 1, 1, 0.0, 0.0
          ,GridBagConstraints.CENTER, GridBagConstraints.NONE, new Insets
➡(52, 14, 0, 0), 8, 16));
          this.getContentPane().add(m_closeButton, new GridBagConstraintsJstp
➡(9, 2, 3, 1, 0.0, 0.0
          ,GridBagConstraints.WEST, GridBagConstraints.BOTH, new Insets
➡(51, -1, 0, 15), -14, 17));
          this.getContentPane().add(m_statusField, new GridBagConstraintsJstp
➡(0, 3, 12, 1, 1.0, 0.0
          ,GridBagConstraints.WEST, GridBagConstraints.HORIZONTAL, new Insets
➡(9, 2, 4, 0), 747, 43));
          this.getContentPane().add(m_insertButton, new GridBagConstraintsJstp
➡(3, 2, 2, 1, 0.0, 0.0
          ,GridBagConstraints.CENTER, GridBagConstraints.NONE, new Insets
➡(51, 0, 0, 13), 3, 18));
```

7

continues

Listing 7.2   Continued

```
    this.getContentPane().add(m_clearButton, new GridBagConstraintsJstp
➡(8, 2, 2, 1, 0.0, 0.0
    ,GridBagConstraints.WEST, GridBagConstraints.NONE, new Insets
➡(52, 10, 0, 14), 0, 17));
 }
}

/* Listing for file sqljDML.sqlj */

/**
 * @author  Megh Thakkar
 * @version 1.0
 *
 * Development Environment      :  JDeveloper 3.0
 * Name of the Application      :  sqljDML.sqlj
 * Application Notes      :
 *
 * This application shows how to use SQLJ to perform DML in JavaStop
 *
 */

//import the SQLJ runtime classes
import sqlj.runtime.*;
import sqlj.runtime.ref.*;

// import the JDBC classes
import java.sql.*;

public class sqljDML {
  //Create a context object for the database connection
  DefaultContext  m_connection = null;

  //The User Interface for this application is handled by SqljDMLGui
  sqljDMLGui m_SqljGui;

  //The customer records are represented by the SQLJ iterator
  #sql iterator SelRowIter(String customer_id, String name, String address);

  /**
   *  The Constructor is used to instantiate the User Interface
   **/
  public sqljDML() {
    m_SqljGui = new sqljDMLGui(this); //Instantiate GUI
    m_SqljGui.setVisible(true);
  }

  /**
   *  This is the main entry point that makes a database connection to JSTP
   **/
  public static void main(String args[]) {
    sqljDML Sdml = new sqljDML();
```

```
    Sdml.dbConnection();
}

/**
*  The various events that can occur are handled in this class
**/
public void dispatchEvent (String p_eventName) {
  // Store the values input by the user
  String l_custid = m_SqljGui.m_custidTextfield.getText();
  String l_name = m_SqljGui.m_nameTextfield.getText();
  String l_address = m_SqljGui.m_addressTextfield.getText();

  // Handle the various events
  if (p_eventName.equals("SELECT"))
      selectRecords(l_custid, l_name, l_address);
  else if (p_eventName.equals("INSERT"))
      insertRecords(l_custid, l_name, l_address);
  else if (p_eventName.equals("UPDATE"))
      updateRecord(l_custid, l_name, l_address);
  else if (p_eventName.equals("DELETE"))
      deleteRecord(l_custid);
  else if (p_eventName.equals("CLOSE"))
      exitApplication();
}

public void dbConnection() {
 try {
      m_SqljGui.putStatus("Connecting to the Database....please wait.....");

      //Register the JDBC driver
      DriverManager.registerDriver(new oracle.jdbc.driver.OracleDriver());

      m_connection = new DefaultContext(
                    "jdbc:oracle:thin:@"+
                    ConnectionSpecs.s_hostName+":"+
                    ConnectionSpecs.s_portNumber+":"+
                    ConnectionSpecs.s_databaseSID,
                    ConnectionSpecs.s_userName,
                    ConnectionSpecs.s_password,
                    false);

      // The above connection is now set as the default context
      DefaultContext.setDefaultContext(m_connection);

      m_SqljGui.putStatus("Successful Connection to " +
                    ConnectionSpecs.s_databaseSID+ " as "
                    +ConnectionSpecs.s_userName);


  } catch(Exception ex){
      m_SqljGui.appendStatus("Error during connection....."
                    +ex.toString());
```

7

continues

Listing 7.2   Continued

```
      }
   }

   /**
   *   Close the connection to JSTP and exit the application
   **/
   public void exitApplication() {
      try {
          m_SqljGui.putStatus("Disconnecting from JSTP.......");
          if(m_connection != null)
             // close the connection
             m_connection.close();
      } catch(SQLException ex){
         m_SqljGui.putStatus("Error during disconnection....."
                             +ex.toString());
      }
      //Exit the application
      System.exit(0);
   }

   /**
   *   Method to select records from the customers table using SQLJ, based on the
   *   query conditions entered by the user
   **/
   public void selectRecords(String p_custid,String p_name,String p_address){

      try{
         // If no condition is specified then we will retrieve all the records
         if(p_custid.equals(""))
            p_custid = "%";
         if(p_name.equals(""))
            p_name = "%";
         if(p_address.equals(""))
            p_address = "%";

         // An instance of SelRowIter is used to store the records retrieved
         SelRowIter l_selRow = null;

         // Use an embedded SQL SELECT statement to retrieve the rows
         #sql l_selRow   = { select customer_id, name, address from  ow_customers
                        where customer_id like :p_custid
                        AND    name like :p_name
                        AND    address like :p_address
                        };
         //Clear the Jtable and then populate it using the retrieved records
         m_SqljGui.m_tmodel.clearTable();

         while(l_selRow.next()) {
            String l_custid = l_selRow.customer_id();
            String l_name = l_selRow.name();
            String l_address = l_selRow.address();
```

```
            m_SqljGui.insertJTable(l_custid, l_name, l_address);
        }

        //Close the iterator
        l_selRow.close();

    } catch(Exception ex){
        m_SqljGui.putStatus("Error occurred during selecting from JavaStop... "
                            +ex.toString());
    }

}


/* Insert a new record into the customer table using SQL INSERT statement*/
public void insertRecords(String p_custid,String p_name,String p_address){
 try{
     // Use an embedded SQL INSERT statement to insert the record
     #sql { INSERT INTO ow_customers(customer_id, name, address)
            values(:p_custid, :p_name, :p_address)};

     m_SqljGui.putStatus("The Record is successfully inserted");

     // Update JTable with the new record so that it can be shown in the User
➡Interface
     m_SqljGui.insertJTable(p_custid, p_name, p_address);

 } catch (SQLException ex) {
     m_SqljGui.putStatus("Unable to insert new record... "
                         +'\n'+ex.toString());
 }
}


/* Update a record from the customer table using SQL UPDATE statement*/
 public void updateRecord(String p_custid,String p_name,String p_address){
  try{
     // Modify records using embedded SQL UPDATE statement
     int l_cnt;
     #sql { SELECT count(*) INTO :l_cnt FROM ow_customers
            WHERE customer_id =:p_custid };
     if (l_cnt>0) {
       #sql { UPDATE ow_customers
              SET name =:p_name,
                  address =:p_address
              where customer_id =:p_custid };

     // Update JTable to reflect the new record
        m_SqljGui.updateJTable(p_custid, p_name, p_address);
        m_SqljGui.putStatus("Record updated successfully ");

     } else
```

continues

Listing 7.2   Continued

```
            m_SqljGui.putStatus("No rows updated");

        m_SqljGui.m_insertButton.setEnabled(true);
    } catch (SQLException ex) {
        m_SqljGui.putStatus("Error in updating record..."
                            + '\n'+ex.toString());
    }
}

/* Delete a record from the customers table using SQL DELETE statement*/
public void deleteRecord(String p_custid){
    try{
        // Delete a record using embedded SQL DELETE statement
        #sql { Delete from ow_customers where customer_id= :p_custid };

        m_SqljGui.putStatus("Record deleted successfully");

        //Delete from JTable also
        m_SqljGui.deleteFromJTable();

        m_SqljGui.m_insertButton.setEnabled(true);
    } catch(Exception ex){
        m_SqljGui.putStatus("Error in deleting record.... "
                            +'\n'+ex.toString());
    }
  }

}
```

 Note

In addition to embedding SQL statements in Java code, SQLJ also enables you to use Java host expressions (also known as bind expressions). Each host expression is preceded by a colon (:), and in its simplest form it consists of a variable. For example

```
 #sql {select name into :name from customers where
customer_id=:custid);
```

Because of the use of host expressions, you don't need to use result sets when returning only a single record.

SQLJ uses a strong typed version of JDBC ResultSets called iterators. *Iterators* have a certain number of columns of specific datatypes and must be declared prior to their use. For example

```
#sql iterator SelRowIter(String customer_id, String name, String address);
```

creates a SQLJ iterator class called `SelRowIter`. Iterators of the `SelRowIter` class can store records with three columns, all of which match to Java Strings. Furthermore, the three columns are named customer_id, name, and address.

The SQLJ iterators have a `next()` method that functions similarly to the `next()` method of JDBC `ResultSets`—returning true and moving the next row of data.

SQLJ Runtime Packages

The *SQLJ runtime* is a thin layer of Java code that runs on top of the JDBC driver. When your SQLJ source code is translated by the SQLJ translator, embedded SQL statements are converted into calls to the SQLJ runtime. These runtime classes provide wrappers around these calls for equivalent JDBC calls. When your application is run, the SQLJ runtime reads information about the program from the profile and passes information back and forth between the JDBC driver and application.

 Note

> The SQLJ runtime requires a JDBC driver. However, the JDBC driver can be any standard JDBC driver. The Oracle JDBC driver should be used if you want to use the Oracle-specific database types and features.

7

The Oracle SQLJ runtime consists of several important packages that can be imported and used in your application. It should be noted that packages beginning with *oracle* are for Oracle-specific features. These packages are as follows:

- `sqlj.runtime`—This package contains the wrapper classes for various input streams such as binary, ASCII, and Unicode. It also contains interfaces and abstract classes implemented by Oracle SQLJ connection contexts and iterators.

- `sqlj.runtime.ref`—This package contains classes that implement the interfaces and abstract classes in the sqlj.runtime package. The `DefaultContext` class used to specify default connection and create default connection context instances is contained in this package.

- `sqlj.runtime.profile`—This package contains interfaces and abstract classes that define the SQLJ profile. Each entry in a profile corresponds to a SQL operation in your application, and each profile entry consists of an `EntryInfo` object (belonging to the `EntryInfo` class) that describes the entry. The parameters of the profile entry are of the `TypeInfo` object (belonging to the `TypeInfo` class).

- `sqlj.runtime.profile.ref`—This package contains classes that implement the interfaces and abstract classes of the sqlj.runtime.profile package.

- `sqlj.runtime.profile.util`—This package contains classes used to access and manipulate the profiles.

- `sqlj.runtime.error`—This package contains resource files for all non–Oracle-specific errors generated by the SQLJ translator.

- `oracle.sqlj.runtime`—This package contains classes used by the Oracle implementation of SQLJ—for example, classes used to convert to and from Oracle type extensions.

- `oracle.sqlj.runtime.util`—This package contains classes used by SQLJ to access and manipulate Oracle profiles.

- `oracle.sqlj.runtime.error`—This package contains resource files for all Oracle-specific errors generated by the SQLJ translator.

Next Steps

This chapter discussed the use of SQLJ for implementing e-commerce applications. SQLJ and the SQLJ preprocessor were used to embed SQL statements in JavaStop code, resulting in code that is much cleaner and more compact compared to a pure JDBC implementation. The next chapter will show you how to include exception handling code in JavaStop. Exception handling implementation in both JDBC and SQLJ code will be discussed.

Chapter 8

Handling Exceptions in JavaStop

Introduction

When writing Java programs to connect to JSTP using JDBC or SQLJ, you have to ensure that the application will be able to handle errors that occur during runtime. Several types of errors can occur, for example

- Incorrect connection information is provided and therefore the connection is not successful.
- JSTP database might not be available.
- The table you are trying to manipulate might not exist.
- The user of the application might not have enough privileges to perform the desired select, insert, update, or delete on the specified table.

Your application should include provisions to ensure that it can handle all these errors and not crash. In this chapter, we will discuss how exception handling can be implemented in JavaStop. Specifically, we will include exception handling capabilities to JdbcDml.java (the JDBC implementation of JavaStop) and SqljDml.java (the SQLJ implementation of JavaStop).

Trapping Exceptions in JDBC

Most errors that occur within a JDBC program can be trapped by using the exception handling capabilities provided by the Java programming language. This is done by using the `try..catch` statement block to catch the exception and the `printStackTrace()` method to print the stack trace.

The basic syntax to handle an exception is as follows:

```
Try {<code to execute>}
Catch(SQLException e){ e.printStackTrace(); }
```

The following is a code snippet from JdbcDml.java:

```
public void dbConnection() {
  try {
      m_JdbcGui.putStatus("Connecting to the Database....please wait.....");

      //Register the JDBC driver
      DriverManager.registerDriver(new oracle.jdbc.driver.OracleDriver());

      m_connection = DriverManager.getConnection(
                  "jdbc:oracle:thin:@"+
                  ConnectionSpecs.s_hostName+":"+
                  ConnectionSpecs.s_portNumber+":"+
                  ConnectionSpecs.s_databaseSID,
                  ConnectionSpecs.s_userName,ConnectionSpecs.s_password);

      /*
       * Setting autocommit to false will prevent actual changes
       * to the database
       */
      m_connection.setAutoCommit(false);

      m_JdbcGui.putStatus("Successful Connection to " +
                  ConnectionSpecs.s_databaseSID+ " as "
                  +ConnectionSpecs.s_userName);


  } catch(Exception ex){
      m_JdbcGui.appendStatus("Error during connection....."
                      +ex.toString());

  }
}
```

As seen from the previous example, an attempt is made to connect to JavaStop in the code within `try { }`. If the connection is not successful for some reason, the exception is handled in the `catch {}` code.

Note JDBC calls can be logged by using the `java.io.PrintStream.DriverManager.setLogStream()` method. This method sets the logging/tracing PrintStream used by the DriverManager and all drivers.

To handle exceptions, the Oracle JDBC drivers throw a `java.sql.SQLException()`. Two types of errors can be returned:

- **Oracle database errors**—These errors contain an error number and a text message describing the error.
- **JDBC driver errors**—These errors don't contain an error number but contain a text message that describes the error and method that threw the error.

Two methods are commonly used to deal with exception errors:

- `getMessage()`—It returns the error message associated with the object that threw the exception.
- `printStackTrace()`—It returns the object name and its stack trace to the specified print stream.

Exception Handling in SQLJ

SQLJ executable statements result in JDBC calls with the use of `sqlj.runtime`; therefore, SQLJ also needs to catch or throw SQL exceptions because of the SQL statements in SQLJ code blocks. In addition, SQLJ traps errors during compilation.

Handling SQLJ exceptions requires the use of the `java.sql.SQLException` class, which can be imported using either of the following import statements:

```
Import java.sql.SQLException
```

or

```
Import java.sql.*
```

The following is a code snippet from SqljDml.sqlj:

```
/* Delete a record from the customers table using SQL DELETE statement*/
public void deleteRecord(String p_custid){
  try{
     // Delete a record using embedded SQL DELETE statement
     #sql { Delete from ow_customers where cust_id= :p_custid };

     m_SqljGui.putStatus("Record deleted successfully");

     //Delete from JTable also
     m_SqljGui.deleteFromJTable();

     m_SqljGui.m_insertButton.setEnabled(true);
  } catch(Exception ex){
     m_SqljGui.putStatus("Error in deleting record.... "
                         +'\n'+ex.toString());
  }
 }

}
```

8

As can be seen from the previous example, an attempt is made to delete from the customers table by embedding the `delete` statement in Java. The `#sql` makes JDBC calls, so the exceptions that can result from the `delete` statement must be handled. The `catch` statement is used to handle any exceptions during the deletion of the record.

Processing SQLJ Errors

Errors that occur during a SQLJ program can be one of the following types:

- **Oracle database errors**—These errors are of the form ORA-xxxxx, where *xxxxx* is an error code that indicates the nature of the database error.

- **JDBC driver errors**—SQLJ makes JDBC calls; therefore, JDBC driver errors can occur. These are listed in the appendix of the *Oracle8i JDBC Developers Guide and Reference*.

- **SQLJ runtime errors**—SQLJ runtime errors that can occur are listed in the *Oracle8i SQLJ Developers Guide and Reference*. Some common errors that can occur are discussed later in this chapter.

Additional information about SQLJ errors can be obtained from the `java.sql.SQLException` class and its subclass. Three useful methods are `getSQLState()`, `getErrorCode()`, and `getMessage()`. Information provided by these methods depends on where the error occurred and how it was handled there.

- `getSQLState()`—This method doesn't return anything meaningful for Oracle errors or JDBC errors. For SQLJ runtime errors, however, it returns a five-digit string containing the SQL state.

- `getErrorCode()`—This method doesn't return anything meaningful for JDBC errors or SQLJ runtime errors. For Oracle database errors, however, it returns *xxxxx*, where *xxxxx* represents the Oracle error code for the ORA-xxxxx error.

- `getMessage()`—This method returns the error message. For Oracle database errors, it also includes the ORA-xxxxx code.

For example, the following `catch` along with the `try` statement for the delete operation also would give you the SQL State.

```
catch(SQLException ex){
      m_SqljGui.putStatus("Error in deleting record.... "
                          +'\n'+ex.toString());

      String sState = ex.getState();

      System.err.println("SQL State = "+sState);
  }
```

Using `SQLException` Subclasses

A more detailed exception handling can be achieved by using any available subclass of `SQLException`. One such useful subclass is the `sqlj.runtime.SQLNullException` class. Java primitives can't handle NULL values, but the `sqlj.runtime.SQLNullException` class can be used to trap a NULL value that might be returned in a Java primitive variable.

 Note   Java primitives can't handle NULL values.

A `SQLException` subclass exception can be handled as a `SQLException`, so if you handle a `SQLException` first, the execution won't drop to the subclass for any special handling. Hence, it is very important that you handle the `SQLException` subclass exceptions before handling the `SQLException`.

For example, examine the `try..catch` block in the following listing.

```
Try{...
...
...
}catch(SQLException ex){
      m_SqljGui.putStatus("Error in deleting record.... "
                           +'\n'+ex.toString());

      String sState = ex.getState();

      System.err.println("SQL State = "+sState);}
Catch(SQLNullException nex){
System.err.println("Null value encountered:   "+ nex);
  }
```

The previous example won't catch the NULL or perform any special processing, but the following code will.

```
Try{...
...
...
}
Catch(SQLNullException nex){
System.err.println("Null value encountered:   "+ nex);}
catch(SQLException ex){
      m_SqljGui.putStatus("Error in deleting record.... "
                           +'\n'+ex.toString());

      String sState = ex.getState();

      System.err.println("SQL State = "+sState);}
```

Common SQLJ Runtime Errors

The following are common SQLJ runtime errors that can occur:

- SQL State : 42122—This error in the java.sql.SQLException class indicates that you are executing a select statement that selects x columns but is assigned to an INTO-list containing y columns or is assigned to an iterator that has y columns. You should revisit the select statement and INTO-list/iterator and modify them to select the correct number of columns.

- SQL State : 08003—This error in the java.sql.SQLException class indicates that a connection context instance used for an executable SQL statement was NULL. You should initialize the connection context instance to a non-NULL value and then retry it.

> **Note**   SQL statements of SQLJ can use an implicit context. This implicit context is initialized using the setDefaultContext method of the sqlj.runtime.ref. DefaultContext class.

- SQL State : 08000—This error in the java.sql.SQLException class indicates that a execution context instance used for an executable SQL statement was NULL. You should initialize the execution context instance to a non-NULL value and then retry it.

- SQL State : 46121—This error in the java.sql.SQLException class indicates that there is a mismatch between the column names in the iterator and its underlying result set. You should change either the iterator's column name or its underlying result set to match.

- SQL State : 21000—This error in the java.sql.SQLException class indicates that executing a SELECT INTO statement returned more than one row when it should have returned only one row. You should modify the SELECT INTO statement so that it returns only one row.

- SQL State : 02000—This error in the java.sql.SQLException class indicates that executing a SELECT INTO statement returned a result set with no rows when it should have returned only one row. You should modify the SELECT INTO statement so that it returns exactly one row.

- SQL State : 08000—This error in the java.sql.SQLException class indicates that a NULL SQLJ connection context or JDBC connection object was passed to the constructor of a connection context class. If you are using a JDBC connection, you should establish a database connection using a JDBC connection object before passing it to a connection context constructor.

The `getConnection` method of the `java.sql.DriverManager` class can be used for this purpose. On the other hand, if a connection context is used, make sure that it is properly initialized before passing it to the connection context constructor.

- **SQL State: 22002**—This error in the `sqlj.runtime.SQLNullException` class indicates that an attempt was made to store a SQL NULL in a Java primitive iterator column type, result, OUT, or INOUT parameter. You should use a NULLable Java wrapper type instead of a primitive type because Java primitives can't handle NULL values.

Handling NULLs

Java primitive types such as int, double, and float can't store NULL values, so you should be careful when using these for your result sets of host expressions. When you retrieve data from the database, SQL NULL values are converted into Java NULL values. Therefore, you should not use Java primitive types for storing SQL results that can contain NULL values. Using primitive Java types for such cases will throw a `sqlj.runtime.SQLNullException`. Instead of using primitive types, you should use one of the following approaches:

- **Use `SQLException` subclasses such as `SQLNullException`**—This technique was discussed earlier.

- **Use wrapper classes instead of primitive classes**—Wrapper classes allow NULL values. Examples of wrapper classes that can be used include

```
java.lang.Boolean
java.lang.Byte
java.lang.Short
java.lang.Integer
java.lang.Long
java.lang.Double
java.lang.Float
```

The following code snippet from SqljDml.sqlj shows the use of a wrapper. We can modify the code as shown in boldface to check for customers with no address:

```
/**
 * Method to select records from the customers table using
 * SQLJ, based on the
 * query conditions entered by the user
 **/
```

```
public void selectRecords(String p_custid, String p_name, String p_address){

   try{
      // If no condition is specified then we will retrieve all the records
      if(p_custid.equals(""))
         p_custid = "%";
      if(p_name.equals(""))
         p_name = "%";
      if(p_address.equals(""))
         p_address = "%";

      // An instance of SelRowIter is used to store the records retrieved
      SelRowIter l_selRow = null;

      // Use an embedded SQL SELECT statement to retrieve the rows
      #sql l_selRow = { select customer_id, name, address from  customers
                        where customer_id like :p_custid
                        AND    name like :p_name
                        AND    address like :p_address
                        };
      //Clear the Jtable and then populate it using the retrieved records
      m_SqljGui.m_tmodel.clearTable();

      while(l_selRow.next()) {
         String l_custid = l_selRow.cust_id();
         String l_name = l_selRow.name();
       if (l_selRow.address() == null)
        String l_address = " No address available";
       else
         String l_address = l_selRow.address();


         m_SqljGui.insertJTable(l_custid, l_name, l_address);
      }

      //Close the iterator
      l_selRow.close();

   } catch(Exception ex){
      m_SqljGui.putStatus("Error occurred during selecting from JavaStop... "
                          +ex.toString());
   }

}
```

Translator Error Messages and Exit Codes

During the SQLJ translation phase, you can encounter four main types of SQLJ messages: errors, non-suppressable warnings, suppressable warnings, and information.

Error Messages

Messages in this category are the most critical and can't be avoided. Error messages are prefixed by `Error:` and indicate that one of the following has occurred:

- A condition has occurred that will prevent compilation from being successful. An example is having a public class that doesn't match with its base filename.

  or

- A condition has occurred that will almost certainly result in a runtime error (for example, an untrapped exception).

You have to take care of error messages before any output (.java or profiles) is generated.

Non-Suppressable Warnings

Messages in this category, although not as critical as errors, are still important enough that they can't be ignored. Non-suppressable warnings are prefaced by `Warning:` and indicate that one of the following has occurred:

- A condition has occurred that has a huge potential to result in a runtime error (for example, a SELECT statement for which the output is not really stored in a result set or an iterator).

  or

- A condition has occurred that makes SQLJ code verification unreliable (for example, being unable to connect to the database to verify schema).

  or

- Suspect code.

When non-suppressable warnings occur, SQLJ compilation completes, but you should analyze the problem and fix it before running the application.

Suppressable Warnings

Suppressable warnings indicate that there is some abnormality in the application, but it is not very critical. These warnings can be suppressed by using the various -warn options of SQLJ:

- `precision/noprecision`—The default is `precision`. When `noprecision` is specified, it will suppress warnings related to possible data loss during precision relation conversions.
- `nulls/nonulls`—The default is `nulls`. When `nonulls` is specified, it will suppress warnings related to the possible occurrence of runtime errors due to nullable columns.

- `portable/noportable`—The default is `portable`. When `noportable` is specified, it will suppress warnings related to the use of Oracle-specific features that might not be available on other systems.
- `strict/nostrict`—The default is `strict`. When `nostrict` is specified, it will suppress warnings related to the use of iterator(s) with fewer columns than that in the statement used to retrieve values into it.
- `verbose/noverbose`—The default is `noverbose`. When `verbose` is specified, it will provide more informational messages related to the translation process.

The `-verbose` flag is different from the `-status` flag. The `-verbose` flag displays additional information about only the translation phase. On the other hand, the `-status` flag displays information about all phases of SQLJ translation: translation, semantics-checking, compilation, and profile-customization.

- `all/none`—This global flag takes precedence over all the other settings. It determines whether or not to show all (suppressable) warnings. There is no default for this setting.

The global flag `all` is equivalent to the settings `precision`, `nulls`, `portable`, `strict`, and `verbose`. The global flag `none` is equivalent to the settings `noprecision`, `nonulls`, `noportable`, `nostrict`, and `noverbose`.

There is no restriction on the ordering of the `-warn` flags except for the `all/none` flags, which should be the first flag.

For example

- If you want the `null` and `strict` warnings only, the command-line syntax would be the following:

  `-warn=none,null,strict`

  The Properties file syntax would be

  `sqlj.warn=none,null,strict`

- If you want to see all suppressable warnings, the command-line syntax would be the following:

  `-warn=all`

And, the Properties file syntax would be

```
sqlj.warn=all
```

In addition to the `-warn` flags, there are two more flags that are important:

- `status` flag—This can be true or false. The default is false. When it is set to true, it indicates that you want to see informational messages about all aspects of the SQLJ translation process.

- `explain` flag—This can be true or false. The default is false. When it is set to true, it indicates that you want to see cause and action information, if available, for the first occurrence of each error message output.

Next Steps

This chapter discussed the important issue of how to ensure that JavaStop can handle runtime exceptions that occur while connecting to JSTP. We looked at various JDBC provided classes that can help in exception handling. We also discussed how exception handling code can be added to both the JDBC and SQLJ implementation of JavaStop. The next chapter will show you various techniques that can be used to debug Oracle8i and Java code. In addition to debugging JavaStop code, we will look at debugging performance problems that can occur while running JavaStop in a demanding environment.

8

Chapter 9

Writing Java Stored Procedures for JavaStop

Introduction

In Oracle8i, the Aurora JVM is seamlessly integrated with the SQL and PL/SQL engine. Prior to Oracle8i, developers were able to write stored procedures using only PL/SQL. However, Oracle8i enables you to write stored procedures using either PL/SQL or Java. This enables you to pool your programming resources both from Java as well as the PL/SQL world and improve productivity and performance. The integration of the JVM with the PL/SQL and SQL engine enables you to write Java programs that call PL/SQL procedures via JDBC or SQLJ. In addition, both SQL and PL/SQL engines can call the *published* Java stored procedures.

Oracle8i gives you a lot of flexibility in the use of Java stored procedures. You can debug and compile all your Java source files at the client-side, which is the preferred option because most people are familiar with their IDEs, and then load/publish them into the database. Or, you can load the Java source files into the database and let the JVM compile and publish them.

 Note   The `jdbc:oracle:kprb` URL indicates the server-side JDBC driver (also known as Oracle KPRB JDBC driver), which provides direct access to the Oracle database.

One of the restrictions of a Java stored procedure is its incapability to materialize a GUI from the java.awt package. This is because the Java stored procedures run in the Oracle8i server and have no access to a default display device. It is, however, possible to call methods in the java.awt package that do not result in updates to the display. Any attempt to materialize a GUI will result in an `Unsupported feature` exception.

Library Units

Oracle8i can be informed to use a piece of Java code by loading the Java programs directly in it as a library unit. When you load .java, .class, or uncompressed .jar files in the database kernel, they are loaded as a library unit. After Java is loaded, the library units become database components and are managed by Oracle. Oracle maintains a comprehensive set of properties for each library unit in the data dictionary. When the developer wants to run the program, he will use the Java naming standards, and the Java VM will perform all the tasks of locating the program, loading it in memory, and executing it. It should be understood that such library units cannot be called from SQL, as is. However, SQL data can be extracted from the database. In order for the library unit to be called from SQL you have to publish the Java program to SQL using a call specification. Call specifications enable the SQL and PL/SQL programs to know the manner in which the Java program interacts with the other programs (for example, the data types that are passed and received by it). In a typical situation, you might load a large number of Java programs as library units, but only a few of them are exposed for SQL and PL/SQL. The majority of the Java units are called only by other library units. For example, if you have a Java class called `addCustomer`, the following SQL DDL extension provided by Oracle8i shows you how to publish it as a Java stored procedure:

```
Create or replace procedure add_customer(
Cust_id          varchar2,
Cust_name        varchar2,
Address          varchar2,
City             varchar2,
State            varchar2,
Country          varchar2,
Zip              varchar2,
Area_code        varchar2,
Phone_num        varchar2,
Comments         varchar2)
```

As language Java

```
Name 'addCustomer.main(java.lang.strong[]);
```

Types of Library Units

Three types of database program units are common in Oracle8i:

- **Java stored procedures**—A stored procedure is a unit of code that can be called within an SQL program. It performs the specified program logic, and Oracle8i enables you to write this program logic using SQL or Java. Java stored procedures are written using JDBC and SQLJ. Writing a Java stored procedure is similar to writing a Java class that is later loaded into the database. A Java stored procedure benefits from Oracle's caching and compilation techniques just like other database components.

- **Java stored functions**—Java stored functions are similar to Java stored procedures, with the main difference being that the stored functions are required to return a value.

- **Java database triggers**—A database trigger is a piece of code that executes when a certain event occurs, such as an INSERT, UPDATE, or DELETE operation against a database table. Oracle8i enables you to write such database triggers using PL/SQL or Java.

 **Note** Oracle8i enables you to write methods associated with abstract data types in Java.

Steps Required to Create a Java Stored Procedure

9

To develop a Java stored procedure, follow these steps:

1. Write the stored procedure
2. Load the procedure in the Oracle database
3. Publish the procedure in the Oracle data dictionary
4. Call the procedure

Write the Stored Procedures

Any Java IDE such as Oracle's JDeveloper and Symantec's Visual Café can be used to write your stored procedure.

Load the Procedure in the Oracle Database

In order for the Java files to be available to the Aurora JVM, they must be loaded into the Oracle database as schema objects. Each Java class is stored as a schema object and the object name is derived from the fully qualified name of the class (including the package name).

> Oracle accepts Java names of up to 4,000 characters long but the name of the Java schema object can't be more than 30 characters long. Therefore, for schema object names greater than 30 characters, a short name (alias) is created.

Java schema objects can be loaded and unloaded automatically using the loadjava and dropjava utilities, respectively. They also can be manually loaded by using the CREATE JAVA statement. Loadjava and dropjava can be used to upload and drop (respectively) the following:

- Java source files
- Java class files
- Java resource files
- SQLJ input files
- Uncompressed Java archives (JAR) or ZIP files. These files are not loaded as schema objects; instead, the archived files are loaded individually.

> Although Java source files can be loaded into the Aurora VM and then compiled by Aurora, it is better to compile them at the client side and then load the resulting class file into the Aurora VM.

Before you can use any loaded class, you need to resolve all the external references. Otherwise, the class is marked as invalid and any attempt to load an invalid class throws a ClassNotFound exception. The -resolve option of loadjava can be used to force early resolution. It also can force the resolution to be implicitly performed at runtime.

After a class is loaded, a resolver spec is created for it. The resolver spec is a list of schemas that need to be searched by the Aurora VM to find the classes referenced by that class. If any referenced class is not found in the resolver spec of a class, an error is generated. It is important to understand that loadjava resolves references to classes but not to resources, and therefore it is important to make sure that the resource files are loaded correctly.

Using loadjava

loadjava is a command-line utility that performs the following tasks:

- Uses a built-in package LOADLOBS to upload the specified Java files into a BLOB column of the database table CREATE$JAVA$LOB$TABLE.
- Uses the SQL Create Java statement to load the Java files as Oracle schema objects.

loadjava has the following syntax:

```
loadjava {-user ¦ -u} username/password[@connectstring]
➥[-options] filenames(s)
```

Where

- username/password[@database] specifies the authentication information.
- -options specifies the various loadjava options listed in Table 9.1.

Table 9.1 loadjava Options

Option	Description
andresolve ¦ a	Compiles source files and resolves each class file as it is loaded. This mode of resolution is not recommended because it can potentially leave the unresolved classes invalid, causing runtime errors.
debug	Generates debugging information.
definer ¦ d	By default, methods of classes execute with the privilege of the invoker. This specification indicates that they will execute with the privilege of the definer.
encoding ¦ e	Sets or resets the encoding option on the JAVA$OPTIONS database table. All uploaded Java files should have the same encoding as this table.
force ¦ f	By default, the loadjava utility loads only newer files. This option forces the loading of all files whether or not they were loaded earlier.
grant ¦ g	Grants EXECUTE privilege on the loaded classes to the specified users and roles.
oci8 ¦ o	This is the default option. It indicates that communication with the database should occur using the JDBC OCI driver.
oracleresolver	Newly created class schema objects are bound to the following predefined resolver spec:"((* Definer's_schema) (* public)).

continues

Table 9.1   Continued

Option	Description
resolve ¦ r	After all classes are loaded (and compiled if necessary), it resolves all of them for external references.
resolver ¦ R	Newly created classes are bound to the user-created resolver spec.
schema ¦ S	Binds newly created classes to the specified schema. By default, the logon schema is used.
synonym ¦ s	Creates a public synonym for the uploaded classes.
thin ¦ t	Indicates that communication with the database should occur using the thin driver.
verbose ¦ v	Displays progress messages.

If the thin driver is used, the connect string format used should be
@host:port:SID.

where

- host specifies the name of the host computer
- port specifies the port number (default 5521)
- SID specifies the Oracle database system identifier

The user_objects table can be checked to verify the result of uploading the Java files.

If neither -andresolve nor -resolve are specified, the resolution of classes is deferred to the runtime.

For example

- loadjava -u scott/tiger@mthakkar:5521:JSTP -t myjavaclass.jar—
  Connects to JSTP with the username scott and the thin driver. It then loads
  the files in the myjavaclass.jar JAR file into the JSTP database. All resolution is
  deferred to the runtime.

- loadjava -u scott/tiger@JSTP -resolve myjavaclass.jar—Connects to
  JSTP with the username scott and the JDBC OCI driver. It then loads the
  files in the myjavaclass.jar JAR file into the JSTP database. After all the classes
  have been loaded, the external references are resolved.

Using dropjava

The dropjava command-line utility is complementary to the loadjava utility. It can be used to remove Java classes that are no longer needed. Dropping a class invalidates other classes that directly or indirectly refer to it. Similarly, dropping a source file invalidates classes derived from it.

dropjava has the following syntax:

```
dropjava {-user ¦ -u} username/password[@connectstring] [-options] filenames(s)
```

where

- `username/password[@database]` specifies the authentication information.

- `-options` specifies the various dropjava options listed in Table 9.2.

Table 9.2   dropjava Options

Option	Description
oci8 ¦ o	This is the default option and indicates that communication with the database should occur using JDBC OCI driver.
schema ¦ S	Drops Java schema objects from the specified schema.
thin ¦ t	Indicates that communication with the database should occur using the thin driver.
verbose ¦ v	Displays progress messages.

For example

- `dropjava -u scott/tiger@mthakkar:5521:JSTP -t -S john`—Connects to JSTP with the username `scott` and the thin driver. It then drops all Java schema objects from the schema `john`.

Resolver Specification

The syntax for a RESOLVER is as follows:

```
RESOLVER ((<match_string> <schema_name>)...)
```

where

- `schema_name` specifies the schema that needs to be searched for finding the library unit.

- `match_string` is a Java name or a wildcard name that can appear in a Java import statement. It can even be a single * in which case it matches any name.

For example

```
RESOLVER (("com.jstp.customers.*" SCOTT) (* PUBLIC))
```

Publishing Java Procedures

After the Java classes have been loaded in the Oracle database, they are not immediately available for being called from SQL. This is because Oracle does not know which classes are safe entry points and which are not meant to be called from SQL. You have to specify this to Oracle by publishing your loaded Java procedures/classes in the Oracle data dictionary. When you publish your classes, you are essentially mapping Java method names, types, and parameters to their SQL equivalents.

It is important to understand that, unlike client-side connections, the server-side JDBC driver runs in a default session and default transaction context. Therefore, you don't need to use the `getConnection()` method. Instead, the `defaultConnection()` method should be used to get the default connection. Consequently, you also don't need to use the `close()` method because you are always connected (when using the server-side JDBC driver) with the default connection.

For server-side SQLJ execution, you don't need explicit connection handling. Similarly, the SQLJ runtime is automatically available and doesn't need to be imported.

The server-side JDBC driver does not support auto-commit, so the application is responsible for making commits and rollbacks.

Writing Call-Specs

A call-spec can be defined using the CREATE FUNCTION (for Java methods that return a value) or CREATE PROCEDURE (for Java methods that don't return a value). The call-spec can be defined as being in one of the following forms:

- Stand-alone PL/SQL function or procedure. The following syntax can be used:
```
CREATE [OR REPLACE]
{ PROCEDURE proc_name [param1, param2,...]
¦ FUNCTION func_name [param1, param2, ...] RETURN sql_type }
[optional_specs]
{IS ¦ AS} LANGUAGE JAVA
NAME 'method_fullname {java_type_fullname,[java_type_fullname]…}
[return java_type_fullname]';
```

where

paramN specifies the parameter#N as IN, OUT, or INOUT sql_type

The following optional_specs are allowed:

AUTHID can be DEFINER or CURRENT_USER. It specifies whether the stored procedure executes in the privileges of its definer or its invoker.

PARALLEL_ENABLE specifies that the stored function can be safely used in the slave sessions of a parallel DML statement.

DETERMINISTIC provides a hint to the optimizer to use the resultset from previous calls to the same function using the same arguments, which improves performance.

The NAME clause uniquely identifies the Java method.

- Packaged PL/SQL function or procedure. The following syntax can be used:

```
/* This is the Package specification*/
CREATE [OR REPLACE] PACKAGE package_name
[AUTHID {CURRENT_USER ¦ DEFINER}]
{IS ¦ AS} [optional_specs]
END [package_name];

/* This is the package body*/
[CREATE [OR REPLACE] PACKAGE BODY package_name
{IS ¦ AS} [optional_specs]
[BEGIN
    statements]
END [package_name];]
```

where

The package specification contains public declarations that are visible to your application.

The package body contains private declarations and implementation details that are hidden from your application.

AUTHID can be DEFINER or CURRENT_USER. It specifies whether the stored procedure executes in the privileges of its definer or its invoker.

Optional_specs can be used to specify type definitions, subprogram specifications, and cursor specifications.

For the complete syntax of the CREATE PACKAGE statement please refer to the *Oracle8i Server Reference Guide*.

- Member method of an object type. The following syntax can be used:

```
/* This is the Type specification*/
CREATE [OR REPLACE] TYPE type_name
[AUTHID {CURRENT_USER ¦ DEFINER}]
{IS ¦ AS} OBJECT {attribute_name datatype,....}
[{MAP ¦ ORDER} MEMBER {func_spec, call_spec},]
[{MEMBER ¦ STATIC} {subprogram_spec, call_spec}...]
);
```

9

```
/* This is the Type body*/
[CREATE [OR REPLACE] TYPE BODY type_name
{IS ¦ AS} [{MAP ¦ ORDER} MEMBER function_body
[{MEMBER ¦ STATIC} {subprogram_spec, call_spec}...]
);
```

For further details on using object types, please refer to the *Oracle8i Server Reference Guide*.

Calling Java Stored Procedures

After Java stored procedures have been loaded and published, you can call them from SQL as well as PL/SQL. They can be called in several ways:

- **From the top-level**—This can be done by using the CALL statement as follows:

```
CALL [schema_name.][package_name ¦ object_type_name][@db_link_name]
{ proc_name (params) ¦
func_name (params) INTO :host_variable };
```

  where params are parameters that are specified either as literals or host variables.

- **From a database trigger**—This can be done by using the CALL statement as in the previous bullet.

- **From SQL DML statements**—This is done similarly to calling any PL/SQL function or procedure.

- **From a PL/SQL block, subprogram, or package**—This is done similarly to calling any PL/SQL function or procedure.

 Note   Just as you can call Java stored procedures from PL/SQL, you also can call PL/SQL stored procedures from JDBC and SQLJ.

Using Java Stored Procedures—An Example

Let us consider an example that shows how Java stored procedures can be used with JavaStop. Suppose that we have a Java class manageOrder that has several methods that are used during order entry. One such method determineDiscount returns the amount of discount that should be given to a customer for any given order using two factors:

- **Amount of order**—The discount policy is as follows:

  Total order amount > 1000 then discount rate = 20%

  Total order amount < 1000 and > 500 then discount rate = 10%

- **Country of residence**—Customers in USA or Canada get an additional 5% discount

The backbone of this Java class can be written without using any SQL or PL/SQL code (see Listing 9.1).

Listing 9.1   The manageOrder Class

```
package com.javastop.orders;
public class manageOrder {

    public static void determineDiscount(float totamt, String country,
➥float discRate []) {

// We are using discRate as an array of size one.
// It will be a Java OUT parameter.
    float countryRate = 0;

    if (country == 'USA' ¦¦ country == 'CANADA')
        countryRate = 5;

    if (totamt > 1000)
        discRate[0] = 20;
    if (totamt < 1000 && totamt > 500)
        discRate[0] = 10;
    discRate[0] = discRate[0] + countryRate;


}
}
```

The next step is to load the preceding Java code into JavaStop. As mentioned earlier, you can load the Java source file and let the JVM compile it or you can compile the Java code outside and then load the .class file into the database. The name of the library unit will be derived from the fully qualified name of the class. If the above class is in the package com.javastop.orders, the name of the library unit will be com/javastop/orders/manageorder.

Several methods can be used to load the Java code into Oracle8i:

- Loading automatically by using loadjava
- Loading manually by using a binary file
- Loading manually by using a LOB column in the database

Note   Manual loading of the Java code in the database can be done using the CREATE JAVA CLASS... DDL statement.

Let us consider a manual approach using a binary file:

The following steps can be used:

1. Create a directory that will contain the Java code.

   ```sql
   SQL> create directory bfile_dir_ord as 'home/users/com/javastop/orders';
   ```

2. Using the Create Java class... statement, load the Java class file.

   ```sql
   SQL> create or replace java class using
   ➥bfile(bfile_dir_ord, 'manageOrder.class');
   ```

The loadjava utility can automate the previous procedure and will also take a RESOLVER spec as shown following:

```
C:\> loadjava -user scott/tiger@
➥mthakkar:5521:JSTP -r '(("orders.*" SCOTT) (* PUBLIC))'

manageOrder.class
```

The previous command connects to JSTP database on the host mthakkar with the username scott and password tiger. The resolver specifies that the Java classes in the orders package should be loaded in the SCOTT schema.

 Note   By default, loadjava and dropjava use the thin JDBC driver.

Now that we have loaded the Java class into the database, we need to publish the top-level class(es) and register it with SQL so that it can be called from SQL-PL/SQL. We need to consider several issues while publishing our Java classes:

- **Data type mapping between SQL and Java**—Java and PL/SQL interaction will result in data being passed back and forth between them in the form of parameters and return values. We need to map the SQL and Java values. The obvious mapping seems to be to map SQL native types with Java native types, but there are several problems with this:

  While mapping SQL NUMBER with Java int there is a possibility of data loss when extremely large numbers are involved.

  NULL values are allowed in SQL but Java scalar values can't be NULL and result in NULL CONSTRAINT exception.

  Several solutions are possible:

  Java provides classes corresponding to its scalar datatypes such as java.lang.Integer. These classes allow NULL values.

Use oracle.sql package. Oracle8i provides the oracle.sql package as an answer to the previously mentioned problems. Oracle.sql has a class definition for every SQL type that acts as a Java wrapper for native SQL types. These classes hold SQL data in SQL format instead of converting it to Java native types.

Use an array of size one to map SQL parameters to Java parameters. This is the approach we adopted in the preceding example of the `determineDiscount` method. SQL allows parameters to be `IN`, `OUT`, or `IN OUT`. Java, on the other hand, only allows `IN` parameters.

Another issue in using stored procedures is the privilege under which the stored procedure will run. Prior to Oracle8i, PL/SQL procedures ran under the *definer's privilege*. Definer's privilege means that the stored procedure will run under the definer's schema with the definer's visibility and privileges for accessing objects. Running a stored procedure in the definer's privilege enabled the programs to bind early to the tables they named. The disadvantage of this approach was that the PL/SQL code had to be loaded into every schema that would use it, in order to perform early binding. Oracle8i enables you to use the *invoker's privilege* for stored procedures so that the invoker or caller will determine the schema (their own schema) where the objects are accessed. In Oracle8i, PL/SQL calls to Java programs can be executed under the definer's or invoker's privileges. However, Java programs called from other Java programs always execute with the invoker's privilege.

 Note   By default, Java calls from PL/SQL execute under the definer's privilege.

Publishing Java stored procedures is done by using a call-spec that provides the following information:

- The language in which the program is implemented
- The fully qualified name of the method
- Mapping of SQL types to Java types
- Mapping of parameter modes
- Privilege under which the program will run

For example

```
SQL> create or replace procedure find_discount(total_amt IN number,
➥country IN varchar2, disc_rate OUT number) authid invoker
➥is language java name
➥'com.javastop.orders.manageOrder.determineDiscount(float,
 java.lang.String, float[])';
```

```
/
```

```
Statement processed.
```

The previous example publishes our Java class with the following specifications:

- The SQL interface is called `find_discount`
- The procedure is implemented in Java
- The name of the Java class is
  `com.javastop.orders.manageOrder.determineDiscount`
- An array of size one is used to map to a SQL OUT parameter
- The procedure will execute under the invoker's privilege

The Java stored procedure has been published and now can be called from SQL and PL/SQL. The call to a Java stored procedure can be made either as a regular procedure call or by using the CALL statement (new in Oracle8i):

Listing 9.2 shows the syntax for using a regular procedure call to call a Java stored procedure from PL/SQL.

Listing 9.2—Calling the Java Stored Procedure

```
declare
total_amt  number(8,2);
country    varchar2(10);
disc_rate   number(3);

begin
........
......
find_discount(total_amt, country, disc_rate);

total_amt := total_amt(1-disc_rate/100);
.....
....
End;
```

Listing 9.3 shows the syntax for using the CALL statement to accomplish the same task.

Listing 9.3—Calling the Java Stored Procedure Using the CALL Statement

```
SQL> variable total_amt number
SQL> variable country varchar2
SQL> variable disc_rate number
SQL> execute :total_amt := 800;
Statement processed
SQL> execute :country := 'USA'
```

```
Statement processed
SQL> call find_discount(:total_amt, :country, :disc_rate);
Statement processed
SQL> print disc_rate
DISC_RATE
----------
      15
```

The previous example demonstrated how to use Java stored procedures but did not make SQL calls from within Java. Let's now modify the determineDiscount method to determine the discount based solely on the order_id. The modified Java code is shown in Listing 9.4. It should be noted that Java stored procedures use the server-side JDBC driver to interact with the database.

 Note

Java stored procedures (with the help of the Java Virtual Machine) will automatically use the server-side JDBC driver. Unlike client-side thin and thick drivers, there is no need to explicitly load a JDBC driver or create connection objects.

Listing 9.4   The Java Class determineDiscount

```
package com.javastop.orders;
public class manageOrder {

    public static void determineDiscount(float ordid, float discRate []) {

    float totamt = 0;
    string country = "";
//
// We are using discRate as an array of size one.
// It will be a Java OUT parameter.
// The ordid parameter receives an order id.
// This order id is used to retrieve the country and
// total amount of the order.
    float countryRate = 0;

    #sql {select o.total, c.country
         into :totamt, :country
         from orders o, customers c
          where o.customer_id = c.customer_id and
             o.order_id = :ordid };

    if (country == 'USA' || country == 'CANADA')
        countryRate = 5;

    If (totamt > 1000)
        discRate[0] = 20;
```

continues

Listing 9.4 Continued

```
if (totamt < 1000 && totamt > 500)
    discRate[0] = 10;
discRate[0] = discRate[0] + countryRate;



}
}
```

As you can see from Listing 9.4, we easily can modify our Java code to use SQLJ and interact with the database. It should be noted that we didn't have to create special objects such as `Connection` and `PreparedStatement` because we intend to use this code as a Java stored procedure. Therefore, it will be run on the server and use the server-side JDBC driver.

The Java code in Listing 9.4 can be loaded into the database where the byte-code compiler will compile it into a Java class, or you can compile it and then load it into the database. The SQLJ translator embedded in the JVM will translate the SQLJ statements into JDBC calls.

Choosing Between Java and PL/SQL

We have seen that stored procedures in Oracle8i can be written in Java as well as in PL/SQL. The natural question is how to decide which one to use for my procedural logic and data access. When deciding between PL/SQL and Java, you should determine the strengths of each language and then make the choice based on your exact situation. PL/SQL is good for tasks that involve manipulation of SQL data. This is because the data type system doesn't need any translation. Also, PL/SQL provides a large number of functions that enable you to manipulate SQL data. Java, on the other hand, provides a lot of power for computational operations. Program logic that involves extensive looping, exception handling, and conditional logic can best benefit from the use of Java.

Several invocation methods can be used for Java stored procedures:

- A Java client application can call Java stored procedures using JDBC or SQLJ.
- Pro*C, Oracle Call Interface (OCI), and ODBC clients.
- Thick clients such as Oracle Developer FORMS clients.

Next Steps

This chapter demonstrated how Java stored procedures can be created in Oracle8i. These Java stored procedures use the server-side JDBC driver to communicate with the database.

So far in this book we have seen how to implement the e-commerce application. In the next chapter, we will look at various techniques for debugging the Java code as well as diagnosing database problems.

9

Diagnosing Problems and Debugging JavaStop Code

Introduction

When running an e-commerce application using Oracle8i and Java, the problems that you encounter can be caused by a variety of sources including:

- Oracle database
- Operating system
- Hardware
- Application (Java code)
- Middle-layer

A complete discussion of all the possible problems is beyond the scope of this book. In this chapter we will focus on diagnosing and debugging errors in Oracle8i and the Java code. (Refer to Chapter 8, "Handling Exceptions in JavaStop," for information about diagnosing JDBC problems.)

Common Problems in Oracle Systems

When running an Oracle system, the following types of errors are commonly encountered:

- **Database Crash**—A database crash can be evidenced in the form of an error message such as ORA-600 errors, an access violation, or other error messages that may appear in the alert log or the application. The actual process of diagnosing the error will depend on the exact error you encounter. An ORA-600 error or access violation normally (99 percent of the time) generates a trace file in the dump destination and an entry is placed in the alert log (this entry can help in finding out the name and location of the trace file). The trace file contains important diagnostic information such as the stack trace, memory dump, process state dumps, and other information that can help in fixing the problem.

The location of the alert log and the user_dump_destination can be obtained by querying v$parameters.

Events can be set to generate a trace file containing diagnostic information when a particular Oracle error occurs.

- **Process hang**—When a process is waiting for an event that will never happen, it is considered to be *hung*. It is important to note that hung processes don't consume CPU cycles. Usually, a hung process indicates that there is no problem with the process itself but that the problem is somewhere else and the effect is being seen by this process. Hung systems can be diagnosed by analyzing System state dumps and the output of v$session_wait.

- **Endless Looping process**—A process can get in an endless loop if it is in a loop whose exit criterion is a condition that will never become true. A process stuck in such an endless loop will keep repeating the same task and consume all available CPU. These types of problems are the most difficult to diagnose because the target keeps moving. In order to diagnose such problems you will have to get multiple stack traces and process state dumps.

- **Slow process**—A slow system indicates that the system performance is not optimal. System state dumps can be used to determine whether the system is slow or hung. (Please refer to Chapter 13, "Optimizing JavaStop Performance," for techniques that can help in improving performance.)

Oracle provides the UTLBSTAT/UTLESTAT scripts, which can be used to generate a report that gives you an idea of how the system is performing in the specified period of time.

- **User errors**—It is common to have user errors due to improper configuration or use of the system. Oracle will generate appropriate error messages that can help you in diagnosing these problems.

Getting Help from Oracle Support Services

If you have a support contract with Oracle then you will be able to tap into the resources provided by Oracle Support Services. On numerous occasions you will find yourself dealing with Oracle Support Services and the following simple but important guidelines will help you get a quick resolution to your problem:

- **Keep your Customer Support information handy**—Various types of support contracts are provided by Oracle to help customers with different needs. Be sure that you understand your support contract and keep the contact telephone numbers and your Customer Support Identification (CSI) number handy. If you are calling back on an existing Technical Assistance Request (TAR), you should have the TAR number (or PMS number in some countries) ready.

- **Understand the problem and ask for the appropriate group**—Oracle Support Services has a large number of highly trained professionals, but these professionals are divided into different groups and handle different kinds of issues such as database (generic), networking, desktop, languages, and so on. Understand the nature of the problem you are experiencing and ask for the appropriate group so that you don't get passed around from one group to another.

- **Prioritize your problem correctly**—When working with a support analyst, be sure that you explain how critical the problem is and the impact it is having on your system.

- **Obtain the environmental and configuration information**—Gather as much information about the environment as possible so that the support analyst helping you can diagnose the problem quickly. This information includes

  The hardware and operating system release number on which Oracle and the application(s) are running

  The release number of all the Oracle products involved in the problem

  Any third-party vendor and version in use

  A testcase (if possible)

  The nature of the problem such as crash, hang, performance, and so on

  The alert log

  The trace files you have obtained in relation to the error

  Backup strategy in use

10

Administrator account and password

Any system changes performed recently (consult with the system administrator to determine these)

Oracle Data Block Corruption

Oracle data blocks are written in a proprietary binary format. Prior to using a data block, Oracle checks it for possible corruption. A block is considered to be corrupt if its format doesn't match the expected format. Corruption for data blocks is checked at the cache and higher layers of the Oracle code. If corruption is detected at the cache layer then the object is marked as media corrupt, whereas if the corruption is detected at higher layers then it is marked as software corrupt.

Several causes can lead to database corruption, including

- Bad hardware
- Operating system bugs
- I/O or caching problems
- Running unsupported disk repair utilities
- Memory problems
- Oracle bugs
- Computer viruses

 **Note**   Information in corrupt blocks is basically lost and has to be recreated by using either a valid backup or a valid export.

Oracle has several tools, such as the data unloader (DUL), that can be used to extract data out of bad blocks, but it is not guaranteed to succeed completely. In addition, it is a very costly solution, so it is important to have a good backup and recovery strategy in place.

Handling Data Block Corruptions

When Oracle identifies a block corruption, it sends an error message such as ORA-1578 or ORA-600's. Several techniques are available to deal with data block corruptions and quickly make the system usable again:

- **Analyze the table and its associated objects**—A detailed check of the suspect table and its associated objects can be performed to determine the extent of corruption (if any). This can be done using the following SQL command:

```
analyze table <table_name> validate structure cascade;
```

The previous command checks data blocks at the cache and higher levels. It also checks index blocks to verify the one-to-one association between the table data and its index rows.

- **Use the DB_VERIFY utility**—Db_verify is an external command-line utility provided by Oracle that can be used to validate data files even when the data file is offline or the database is unavailable.

> **Note**
>
> The executable of db_verify that comes with Oracle8i is `dbv.exe` and is located in the `$ORACLE_HOME\bin` directory (for Windows NT).

The syntax is

```
dbv [parameters]
```

Where `parameters` can be one of the following:

- `FILE`—The data file against which db_verify is to be run.
- `START`—The starting block address. The first block of the file is the default start address.
- `END`—The ending block address. The last block of the file is the default end address.
- `LOGFILE`—The output of running db_verify is logged in this file.
- `BLOCKSIZE`—Logical block size. The default block size is 2048 bytes.
- `FEEDBACK`—0 indicates that there is no feedback, but if a number n is used then a `.` is displayed for every n pages verified.
- `HELP`—Provides online help for using db_verify.
- `PARFILE`—Parameters used at the command line can alternatively be placed in a parameter file. `PARFILE` indicates the parameter file to use for db_verify.

For example, suppose that you want to check the file `d:\oracle\oradata\orcl\data1.dbf` for possible corruption.

At the operating system prompt, type the following:

```
C:\> d:\oracle\ora81\bin\dbv file=d:\oracle\oradata\orcl\data1.dbf
➡ logfile=c:\dbvlog.out feedback=10

DBVERIFY: Release 8.1.5.0.0 - date
Copyright......
```

10

```
DBVERIFY - Verification starting: FILE = meghdata1.ora
.................................................................................
.............................................................................
```

The logfile can be opened using any editor, such as Notepad, and can contain

```
DBVERIFY - Verification starting : FILE = d:\oracle\oradata\orcl\data1.dbf
```



```
DBVERIFY - Verification complete

Total Pages Examined        : 8762
Total Pages Processed (Data) : 995
Total Pages Failing   (Data) : 0
Total Pages Processed (Index): 747
Total Pages Failing   (Index): 0
Total Pages Processed (Other): 183
Total Pages Empty           : 6837
Total Pages Marked Corrupt  : 0
Total Pages Influx          : 0
```

A number of checksum facilities provided by Oracle can be used to check for corruption of various types. Checksum facilities are enabled by setting parameters in the init.ora file.

- db_block_checksum—Setting this parameter to TRUE causes checksums to be calculated for all data blocks on their next update.
- log_block_checksum—Setting this parameter to TRUE causes checksums to be calculated for all redo log blocks.
- Event 10210—Adding the following line in the init.ora file and then restarting the database instance will enable this event:

```
event = "10210 trace name errorstack forever, level 10"
```

By setting event 10210, the data blocks are checked for corruption by checking their integrity. Data blocks that do not match the expected format are marked as soft corrupt.

- Event 10211—Adding the following line in the init.ora file and then restarting the database instance will enable this event:

```
event = "10211 trace name errorstack forever, level 10"
```

By setting event 10211, the index blocks are checked for corruption by checking their integrity. Index blocks that do not match the expected format are marked as soft corrupt.

- Event 10212—Adding the following line in the init.ora file and then restarting the database instance will enable this event:

  ```
  event = "10212 trace name errorstack forever, level 10"
  ```

  By setting event 10212, the cluster blocks are checked for corruption by checking their integrity. Cluster blocks that do not match the expected format are marked as soft corrupt.

- Event 10225—Adding the following line in the init.ora file and then restarting the database instance will enable this event:

  ```
  event = "10225 trace name errorstack forever, level 10"
  ```

  By setting event 10225, the fet$/uset$ dictionary tables are checked for corruption by checking their integrity. Blocks that do not match the expected format are marked as soft corrupt.

- _db_block_cache_protect—This is a hidden parameter that protects the cache from becoming corrupted and writing the corrupted data to disk.

Salvaging Data

We already have seen that database corruption can be the result of a variety of non-database problems and that the most common cause of database corruption is bad hardware. After you have resolved all the hardware and other non-Oracle issues, you can use the following steps to recover a corrupt Oracle8i database:

1. Determine the extent of the damage. When a database corruption is encountered, Oracle will generate error messages and trace files indicating the file(s) and block(s) that are involved in the corruption.

   Using file# (F) and block# (B), you can determine the extent of the database corruption as follows:

   1. Connect to server manager as internal.

   2. Determine the file that is identified as corrupt:

      ```
      svrmgrl> SELECT name
                 FROM v$datafile
                 WHERE file# = F;
      ```

   3. Determine the corrupt object:

      ```
      svrmgrl> SELECT owner, segment_name, segment_type
                 FROM dba_extents
                 WHERE file_id = F
                 AND  B BETWEEN block_id AND block_id  + blocks - 1;
      ```

10

2. The type of object that is corrupt (as determined in the preceding code) will determine the recovery procedure:

- **Rollback segment corruption**—This is a critical situation, and the recovery process requires the use of some hidden parameters that should not be changed without help from Oracle Support Services. Please contact Oracle Support Services in this situation.

- **Index segment corruption**—Use the following query to determine the table to which the index belongs:

```
svrmgrl>SELECT table_owner, table_name
        FROM dba_indexes
        WHERE index_name = 'segment_name';
```

- **Cluster segment corruption**—Use the following query to determine the table associated with the cluster:

```
svrmgrl> SELECT owner, table_name
        FROM dba_tables
        WHERE cluster_name = 'segment_name';
```

- **User table corruption**—Note the owner and table name.

- **Data dictionary table**—This is a critical situation, and the recovery process requires the use of some hidden parameters that should not be changed without help from Oracle Support Services. Please contact Oracle Support Services in this situation.

3. Run the ANALYZE command at least twice to ensure that the problem is not intermittent.

4. Salvage data from the corrupted object. Several techniques can be used to salvage the data from the corrupted object:

- **Media recovery**—Media recovery is the easiest method to resolve block corruption problems. However, you will lose the data that was not backed up.

- **Drop and recreate the object**—This technique should be used if the corrupt object easily can be recreated. This method works well for index segment corruption.

- **Select/copy around the corruption**—If the file(s) and block(s) numbers are known for the corrupted blocks, you can select around the bad data as follows:

```
Step#1: CREATE TABLE salvage AS
SELECT * FROM corrupt_table WHERE 1 = 2;
```

```
Step#2: INSERT INTO salvage
SELECT /*+ ROWID(corrupt_table) */ *
FROM corrupt_table
WHERE rowid <= 'low_rowid_of_corrupt_block';

Step#3: INSERT INTO salvage
SELECT /*+ ROWID(corrupt_table) */ *
FROM corrupt_table
WHERE rowid >= 'high_rowid_of_corrupt_block';
```

- **Use event 10231**—Setting this event in the Oracle initialization file will cause Oracle to skip software and media corrupted blocks when performing full table scans and thereby enable you to extract the good data.

  Its syntax is

  ```
  event="10231 trace name context forever, level 10"
  ```

- **Use event 10233**—Setting this event in the Oracle initialization file will cause Oracle to skip software and media corrupted blocks when performing index range scans and thereby enable you to extract the good data.

  Its syntax is

  ```
  event="10233  trace name context forever, level 10"
  ```

Performance Tuning Using UTLBSTAT/UTLESTAT Reports

Performance of the system is of utmost importance for an e-commerce application. Oracle supplies you with two scripts, `utlbstat.sql` and `utlestat.sql`, that can be used to tune the performance of your database. (Please refer to Chapter 13 for additional performance improvement techniques.)

The `utlbstat` and `utlestat` scripts work by gathering performance statistics before and after a specified period of time and then analyze the results based on a set of tuning recommendations (provided by Oracle) to indicate performance problems. The `utlbstat` component gathers the initial performance statistics and places them in temporary tables. The `utlestat` component gathers the performance statistics at the end of the observation period and places them in temporary tables. After `utlestat` finishes, it compares the information in the two sets of temporary tables and places the result in another set of temporary tables. The final result of running `utlbstat.sql` and `utlestat.sql` is a report placed in a file called `report.txt`, which is in the current directory.

10

`Report.txt` gives you a summary of your system performance, the results of which are shown in various categories:

- Library cache statistics
- Systemwide statistics
- Wait events
- DBWR statistics
- I/O statistics
- Latch statistics
- Dictionary cache statistics

The `utlbstat/utlestat` report can be generated using the following steps:

1. Determine the analysis period. `utlbstat` and `utlestat` should be run during normal working conditions. They should not be run right after the database has started because the report generated will not represent the true workload and environment.

2. Set the initialization parameter called `TIMED_STATISTICS`. The initialization parameter `TIMED_STATISTICS` should be set to `TRUE` so that you get timing information. One way this can be achieved is by setting it in the `init.ora` file:

   `TIMED_STATISTICS = TRUE`

   It also can be achieved by using the `ALTER SYSTEM` command at the server manager prompt:

   `ALTER SYSTEM SET TIMED_STATISTICS = TRUE;`

3. At the appropriate time, run `utlbstat.sql`:

   `svrmgrl> @$ORACLE_HOME\rdbms\admin\utlbstat`

4. At the end of the period, run `utlestat.sql`:

   `svrmgrl> @$ORACLE_HOME\rdbms\admin\utlestat`

   The output from `utlbstat` and `utlestat` is placed in an ASCII file called `report.txt`, which is located in the current directory.

 Note   Running `utlbstat` and `utlestat` has minimal impact on system performance.

Analyzing Java Exceptions

A lot of Java programs use the `getMessage()` method of the `IOException` class to debug Java exceptions during development. This is usually accomplished as follows:

```
try {

    //"try" some piece of Java code here
}
catch (IOException e){

    System.out.println("Exception encountered: " + e.getMessage());
}
```

The previous technique doesn't give a lot of information about debugging the error. A better technique is to use the method `printStackTrace()` of the `IOException` class. This technique can be used to generate a stack trace from the exception. The stack trace provides more valuable information than a simple error text returned by `getMessage()`.

Performing OS-Level Diagnosis from Java Applications

It is possible to run external operating system commands from within Java programs, but it is not recommended because it will affect the portability of your Java application. For example, if you write a Java program that runs the UNIX command `ps -ef`, it will provide valuable information on UNIX systems but unfortunately won't run on Windows platforms.

For the sake of discussion, let's assume that portability is not a factor for your Java application. In this situation, you can run operating system commands from your Java applications using two Java classes:

- `Runtime` class—The `exec()` method of the `Runtime` class can be used to run the operating system command as a separate process. It returns an object of the `Process` class.

- `Process` class—The `Process` class has several methods that can be used for managing the processes. Three commonly used methods are

  `getInputStream()`—Can be used to read the normal output of the command.

  `getErrorStream()`—Can be used to read the error output of the command.

  `getOutputStream()`—Can be used to write to the process.

10

The following sample code shows how you can do this:

```
public class RunOSCommand {

    public static void main(String args[]) {
      try {
        Process p = Runtime.getRuntime().exec("ps -ef");

            BufferedReader sin = new BufferedReader(new
InputStreamReader(p.getInputStream()));

            BufferedReader serr = new BufferedReader(new
InputStreamReader(p.getErrorStream()));

// Read the command output

// Read any errors

System.exit(0);

}
catch (IOException e) {

    System.out.println(" Exception occurred: ");
    e.printStackTrace();
    System.exit(-1);
}
}
}
```

Forcing Garbage Collection to Avoid Memory Leaks

One of the best features of Java is that it performs automatic garbage collection, or memory management. Other languages such as C++ don't perform garbage collection automatically; instead they leave this task to the developers. Generally, the Java VM performs garbage collection when it needs more memory to continue execution. Even though you might write a program that loses an object reference, thereby making it a candidate for garbage collection, there is no guarantee that the garbage collection will occur at that time. This can be a problem for systems with memory constraints.

Java makes it possible for you to force garbage collection when needed. It is a simple process that involves using the Runtime object.

Runtime objects enable you to interface with the environment in which your application is running.

The following Java code demonstrates how to force garbage collection.

Listing 10.1   Forcing Java Garbage Collection

```java
/*
 * This Java program shows you how to force garbage collection
 * Author: Megh Thakkar
 */
public class CollectGarbage {

   int ASIZE = 1000000;

   void useMemory() {

      int[] intA = new int[ASIZE];

      for (int i=0; i<ASIZE; i++) {
        intA[i] = i*2;
      }

   }

   public static void main (String[] args) {

      CollectGarbage gct = new CollectGarbage();

      // Get a Runtime object
      Runtime r = Runtime.getRuntime();

      // Collect garbage at the start of the program
      r.gc();

      // Let's see how much memory we have at the start
      long availMem = r.freeMemory();
      System.out.println("At program start we have : " + availMem + " bytes");

      // Let's use some memory
      gct.useMemory();

      // Let's see how much memory is left
      long availMem1 = r.freeMemory();
      System.out.println("After running the program,
      ➥we have :  " + availMem1 + " bytes");

      // Collect garbage
      r.gc();

      //Let's see what we have now
      long availMem2 = r.freeMemory();
      System.out.println("After collecting garbage
      ➥we have :    " + availMem2 + " bytes");
```

continues

Listing 10.1   Continued

```
long freedMem = availMem2 - availMem1;
System.out.println("Garbage collection
➥freed :     " + freedMem + " bytes");


    }


}
```

As seen from the previous Java code, there are two main steps involved in forcing garbage collection:

1. Create a `Runtime` object.

2. Invoke the garbage collector `gc()` method of the `Runtime` object.

Decompiling Java Classes

Sometimes you might want to decompile Java classes. Decompiling will change a Java class back to its equivalent source file. The source file is not necessarily an exact replica of the original source file, but it gives you an indication of how the Java Virtual Machine might be treating your Java program. This knowledge can be a powerful debugging feature. Two steps are required for decompiling Java classes:

1. Obtain the Java class(es) to decompile.

2. Use a decompiler to decompile the class.

Obtaining Java Classes for Applets

If you want to decompile a Java class corresponding to an applet, you need to download the Java class and save it using the following steps:

1. Make sure that you are looking at the applet in your browser (Netscape or Internet Explorer).

2. From the View menu of your browser choose Page Source (for Netscape 4.x), Document Source (for Netscape 3.x), or Source (for Internet Explorer 3.x).

3. In the source code for that page, search for the APPLET tag. This will indicate where the class file for this applet is located.

4. Close the source page and enter the location of the class file in the URL field of the browser.

5. Press the Return key when asked to save the file. Save the file on your local filesystem in a directory where the JDK is stored. Make sure that the file is saved with the extension .class.

Now you have a class file that can be decompiled.

Using Decompilers to Decompile Java Classes

Several decompilers are available, including javap (provided by the JDK). Mocha probably was the first decompiler available in the market and is still one of the most popular decompilers today. A beta version of the Mocha software is available from the Macmillan Web site at `http://mcp.com/product_support`. This version is beta and can be freely distributed as licensed by the original developer Hanpeter van Vliet, who died of cancer before copyrighting it. However, modifications have been made to the original Mocha by various vendors (including Borland, who incorporated a superior version of Mocha in their JBuilder software).

Two other Java decompilers include

- DejaVu
- WingDis

These can be downloaded from `http://www.download.com`.

You easily can see the potential security threats that can occur by allowing someone to decompile your Java code and see your source file. To avoid the decompiling of your Java classes, you should use obfuscators, which obfuscate your source file and prevent the decompiling of your Java classes. Several popular obfuscators include

- Crema
- Hashjava
- Jmangle
- Jshrink
- SourceGuard

These can be downloaded from `http://www.download.com`.

Debugging with JDB

The JDK contains a useful debugging facility called JDB. JDB is similar to the DBX debugger found on UNIX systems. It is a command-line–oriented debugger that enables you to interact with a running application for debugging purposes. It provides several commands that can be used to perform a variety of debugging tasks such as setting breakpoints and tracking variables.

> Advanced Java programmers can gain a better understanding of how the debugger works by looking at the source code of JDB. The JDB source code is found in the SRC.zip file, which is under the JDK root directory. Unzipping this source file will create two directories. The JDB source is based on the sun.tools.ttydebug.TTY class.

The JDB debugging facility is based on a client/server architecture. You start the application to debug in one session and debug it by launching JDB in another session on either the same machine or a different machine.

Three different ways in which JDB can be started are

- Start JDB and create a Virtual Machine instance without any classes loaded. Execute the following at the command line:

  ```
  jdb [-dbgtrace] [<java-arguments>]
  ```

  where

  - -dbgtrace specifies that you want to enable the verbose messages from the virtual machine.
  - <java-arguments> specifies an optional set of arguments to use when the java command is used to start a Virtual Machine.

- Start JDB and create a Virtual Machine with the specified classes loaded. Execute the following at the command line:

  ```
  jdb [-dbgtrace] [<java-arguments>] <classname> [<class-arguments>]
  ```

  where

  - -dbgtrace specifies that you want to enable the verbose messages from the virtual machine.
  - <java-arguments> specifies an optional set of arguments to use when the java command is used to start a Virtual Machine.
  - <classname> is the .class file to load initially into the Virtual Machine.
  - <class-arguments> specifies any arguments that might be needed by the classname's main method.

- Start JDB and connect to a remote Virtual Machine instance that is already running a class. Execute the following at the command line:

  ```
  jdb [-dbgtrace] [-host <hostname>] –password <password>
  ```

where

- -dbgtrace specifies that you want to enable the verbose messages from the virtual machine.
- -host <hostname> specifies the DNS name or IP address of a computer running the host JVM for the Java application or applet you are debugging. By default, the host is assumed to be localhost.
- -password <password> is the password that was generated when the host JVM containing the application or applet to be debugged was loaded. This password is generated at the console by java or appletviewer when the -debug flag is used with them.

JDB also can be made to run a specific set of commands from an input file. This technique is useful if you plan to run the same debugging session on a particular application or applet repeatedly. JDB looks for the existence of one of the following files:

- JDB.INI in the directory specified by the USER.HOME system property.
- JDBRC in the directory specified by the USER.HOME system property.
- STARTUP.JDB in the directory specified by the USER.DIR system property.

If one of the preceding files is found, JDB reads each line and executes the command as if it were typed at the JDB console.

JDB Commands

JDB provides a large number of commands to control the debugging process and query information from the Virtual Machine. The JDB commands can be categorized into different groups based on their functionality.

General Commands

These commands are used to control the debugger and query the remote VM:

- help—Displays the list of documented commands supported by the JDB. You can also use the ? to get the same result.
- memory—Displays the total amount of free and used memory in the remote JVM.
- gc—Causes the garbage collection task to run on the remote VM.
- !!—Causes the last command to be re-executed.
- exit/quit—Terminates the debugging session. If the debugging session is local then the VM is shut down, and if it is remote then the connection between the remote VM and JDB is broken.

- `itrace`—An undocumented command that enables (on) or disables (off) the tracing of bytecode instructions on the remote JVM.
- `trace`—An undocumented command that enables (on) or disables (off) the tracing of method calls on the remote JVM.

Context Commands

This category consists of commands that are used to set the context for the debugging session:

- `load`—Causes the remote JVM to search for the specified class.
- `run`—Loads and executes the specified class or the last class specified on the previous call to the `run` command.
- `threadgroup`—Sets the specified thread group as the default thread group. In order to use any JDB command associated with breakpoints, exceptions, and thread management, you need to have a default thread group.
- `thread`—Sets the specified thread as the current thread associated with the current thread group. In order to use any JDB command associated with breakpoints, exceptions, and thread management, you need to have a default thread group.
- `use`—Displays the path used by the remote JVM to find .class and .java files.

Information Commands

This category of commands is used to obtain information about the loaded classes and uses the context established:

- `classes`—Shows you the classes and interface names that are known to the remote VM.
- `dump`—Dumps the detailed description of the specified thread, stack-based variable, class, field, named local variable, or named argument.
- `list`—Displays one or more source files for the current thread's current method.
- `locals`—Displays all the arguments to the current method and local variables that are defined in this stack frame.
- `methods`—Displays all the methods in the specified class.
- `print`—Displays a description of the specified thread, stack-based variable, class, field, named local variable, or named argument.
- `threadgroups`—Displays the name and description of all the active thread groups in the remote JVM.

- threads—Displays the list of threads for the current or specified thread group.
- where—Displays the call stack for the current thread, specified thread, or all threads.

Breakpoint Commands

The commands in this category enable you to set, remove, and control program flow in association with breakpoints.

 Breakpoint—A point in the program at which you want execution to stop so that you can debug the program.

Several commands belong to this category:

- clear—Clears an existing breakpoint.
- stop—Sets a breakpoint.
- step—Executes the next instruction of the currently stopped thread. If the next instruction is a method call, execution stops at the first instruction of the method being invoked.
- cont—Continues the execution of all the suspended threads in the default thread group.
- next—An undocumented command used to execute the next instruction of the currently stopped thread. If the next instruction is a method call then the method is called and control returns to the debugger upon return from the method.

Exception Commands

This category includes commands that are used to control which exception classes should be caught or ignored by JDB:

- catch—Causes the debugger to catch occurrences of the exception class thrown by the remote JVM for the specified class.
- ignore—Causes the debugger to stop catching occurrences of the exception class thrown by the remote JVM for the specified class.

 Exception—A special situation that is not supposed to occur under normal processing. Java enables you to code exception handling into the application.

Thread Commands

Commands in this category are used to control the execution state and stack of currently active threads:

- suspend—Suspends the execution of the specified thread(s) or all non-system threads if no thread is specified.

10

- resume—Resumes the execution of the specified thread(s) or all non-system threads if no thread is specified.

- up—Moves the context of the current stack frame from its current position up one or more frames.

- down—Moves the context of the current stack frame from its current position down one or more frames.

- kill—An undocumented command that can be used to permanently stop the specified thread or all threads in the default thread group.

 Frame—Represents the execution state for a method.

Steps Required to Use JDB

JDB is best used as a client/server tool with the application being debugged running in a remote JVM (that acts as a server) and JDB running in a different process space (running as a client). Supposing that you want to debug the JdbcConnection application, the following steps can be used:

1. Compile JdbcConnection with debug information.

   ```
   javac -g JdbcConnection.java
   ```

2. Open up two command-line sessions. One will be used for the remote JVM and the other for JDB. From the first command window, start up the JVM:

   ```
   java -debug JdbcConnection
   ```

   The previous command will display a password that will be used for launching JDB.

   ```
   Agent password=XXXXXX
   ```

3. In the second command window, start JDB and connect to the remote JVM (started in the first command window) using the password obtained from the remote JVM.

   ```
   jdb -host <hostname> -password XXXXXX
   ```

Now you can use all the JDB commands that we discussed earlier to debug the application.

Next Steps

Several debugging techniques and tools were discussed in this chapter that can help you in debugging Oracle8i as well as Java code. Debugging e-commerce applications is much more difficult than debugging other application types because e-commerce applications involve a lot more components that can cause problems.

In the next chapter we will focus on the security concerns related to e-commerce applications and understand the various options available with Oracle8i and Java.

10

Chapter 11

Securing JavaStop Using Database Security and Firewalls

Introduction

The explosion of the Internet has opened new opportunities for companies. An increasing number of companies need access to the Internet for a variety of purposes such as the World Wide Web (WWW), Internet mail, telnet, ftp, and so on. A secure environment is very important for continued customer confidence. Lack of security can destroy any organization over night. Security issues become a bigger challenge in e-commerce applications due to the access-anywhere characteristics of such applications. We need to regulate the network traffic that occurs between the company and the Internet and vice versa. In this chapter, we will address the important issue of end-to-end security. End-to-end security is essential in e-commerce applications in order to protect the information and the customer details from unauthorized usage.

Understanding the Security Challenges in JavaStop

Web-enabling JavaStop requires that you understand the accompanying security threats and the options available. Let us revisit the application design of JavaStop. We are planning to use a three-tiered application design:

- A thin client
- A Web server
- A database server

The thin client connects to a Web server; the Web server connects to the database. The typical computer hacker is a very well-organized individual. Hackers do not really pursue nine-to-five jobs, and they even have conferences they attend at which they learn how to better themselves at their job—hacking into *your* system. Several types of tools are used by computer hackers that enable them to guess passwords, read network packets, and emulate IP addresses to trick your database server into believing that they are the authentic port that has been authorized to access data and so on.

Attacks from the Internet can be thwarted by using a firewall. In addition to the protection obtained by using firewalls, we also have to secure the database from attacks that can occur within the firewall. Database security is essential so that none of the client applications—whether they are created using Java or any language—can bypass the security and obtain unauthorized access.

 firewall—A mechanism used to prevent unauthorized entry into a company's internal network.

When implementing security, the principle of least privilege should be followed. This principle means that any user should only be given the permissions that are needed for him to perform his duties.

Understanding Firewalls

Most companies that use e-commerce implement an Internet firewall. A *firewall* is essentially a system that enforces a security policy for data transfer between the company and the Internet. In order for a firewall to be effective, it is important that all data transfer between the company and the Internet occurs through the firewall. The firewall intercepts, scrutinizes, and verifies each and every network packet that passes through it. It is important to understand that the firewall is not a substitute for other security measures. In fact, the firewall should be part of a comprehensive security strategy that includes physical protection as well as user awareness of the need to protect passwords and so on. Firewalls must reflect the level of security used throughout the organization. For example, highly sensitive data should be isolated from the rest of the corporate network and, in fact, classified data should not even be connected to the Internet.

Generally, a firewall is a combination of hardware and software. Leading firewall vendors use one of the following two approaches for implementing firewalls:

- **IP filtering**—This approach allows access or denies access between networks or specific machines based solely on information contained in the IP packet headers.

- **Application proxy**—This approach allows the flow of information through the firewall but not the packets. In other words, direct communication between the inside and outside is not allowed; however, the firewall acts as a data relay between the inside and outside hosts.

Security is often confused with data encryption. Data encryption is just a part of the overall security strategy. Most system hackers don't spend a lot of time and energy in trying to crack your encrypted data. Instead, it is usually easier for them to identify and crack a weak security strategy. As a system administrator you should periodically run some tool such as SATAN (Security Analysis Tool for Auditing Networks) to identify weaknesses in the security policy of your system and take appropriate measures to resolve any issues. At the same time, it is important to understand that firewalls can't protect against attacks that don't go through the firewall—attacks made by insiders in the form of a report, stealing data on a floppy disk, and so on.

You ideally should have some sense of the security policy that will be used during the design phase itself because the type of security used might have an influence on the application design. Specifically, it would be useful to know beforehand whether your application will be transferring data via a firewall or not. In other words, the answer to the following question must be known—the earlier the better:

Is my application going to run within the perimeter of a firewall or will it run through the firewall?

The answer to the preceding question will determine your options for communicating between the client and server.

Running Applications Within the Firewall

If your application will run within the perimeter of the firewall, your range of options for communicating between the client and server are extensive—from Remote Method Invocation (RMI) to sockets. Usually the use of RMI also requires the use of sockets access because it uses TCP/IP sockets at the network layer.

Running Applications Through the Firewall

If your application will run through the perimeter of the firewall, your range of options for communicating between the client and server are relatively limited—some sort of an HTTP solution. Firewalls typically allow TCP/IP traffic through port 80—the port traditionally dedicated to HTTP. When implementing a firewall, two diverse philosophies are popular:

- **Deny access to anything that is not specifically allowed access**—This technique results in high security because it blocks traffic from everything except a few chosen services. Commercial organizations generally implement this type of firewall.

- **Allow access to anything that is not specifically denied access**—This technique results in a system that is easy to use but not very secure. Academic institutions generally benefit from this type of firewall.

When choosing a firewall policy it is important to understand the overall security policy of your organization. Large corporations are usually very strict about the firewall requirements and will not allow you to digress even on an exceptional basis and allow, for example, a small hole in the firewall to allow sockets access. If RMI is used through the firewall, the firewall must allow access to specifically known ports. These ports can't be denied access by the firewall.

SOCKS is a network protocol that allows hosts from one side of the SOCKS server to access hosts on the other side of the SOCKS server without requiring direct IP accessibility between them. SOCKS was the result of a project at NEC and is freely downloadable from www.socks.nec.com. Commercial versions of SOCKS are also available from several vendors such as Sun Microsystems. SOCKS provides a partial solution to the use of RMI through firewalls because it protects outgoing RMI calls, but incoming RMI calls as well as RMI callbacks are not protected. Bidirectional RMI implementation through the firewalls requires the use of specific settings that can relax the security or application-level proxy servers, which can increase the administrative overhead.

Another alternative implementation for the RMI through the firewall approach is to use an HTTP proxy server. When used with an HTTP proxy server, RMI attempts two types of HTTP tunneling:

- HTTP-to-port or
- HTTP-to-CGI

Both of the preceding HTTP tunneling methods introduce performance and security issues. It should be clear by now that the use of the RMI through firewall approach has several performance and security concerns associated with it. It is therefore beneficial to limit the use of RMI to intranet-based applications only.

Types of Firewalls

Firewalls are basically one of the following types:

- **Screening router**—This firewall uses a host/server to direct network traffic to a specific network. This type of router can look only at packet header information and therefore can't enforce complex rules.

   Note   Enforcing complex rules with a screening router might result in performance degradation.

Screening routers can be configured to determine the address from which a packet originated. This can be used to block traffic from a specific address or network. It also can be used to restrict the usage of specific ports.

- **Proxy gateway**—The biggest disadvantage of a screening router is its incapability to read non-header information. This allows a potentially harmful transaction to interact with the internal application as long as it passes the screening test. Proxy gateways are a more secure component. The proxy server sits between the Internet and the internal application. All commands are screened by the proxy gateway, and it only allows commands defined as allowed to go through.

- **Guard**—This type of firewall incorporates all the features of a proxy firewall and also can be used to implement complex rules about the manner in which data flows through it.

   Note   Several firewall vendors such as Checkpoint Software, IBM, and Hewlett-Packard provide a SQL*Net proxy; meaning that when a port is opened for SQL*Net traffic, only SQL*Net traffic is allowed to use that port.

Firewall Configuration for JavaStop

Oracle does not have a preferred configuration for using client/Web server/database server. However, it is quite common to put a Web server outside the firewall and protect the database inside the firewall. It also is advisable to use subnetting or some other means to protect the database from the rest of the network in the event of a firewall breach. The host on which the database resides also should be protected by disabling features such as .rhosts, NFS mounting, and so on. For further details on these issues, refer to D. Brent Chapman's *Building Internet Firewalls*.

11

> **Note** If you use the Web server outside the firewall, you should use it on a higher assurance (B1 security or higher) operating system such as Trusted Solaris, HP-UX CMW, and so on.

For JavaStop, we could use the Web server outside the firewall as shown in Figure 11.1 and allow the Web server to pass data to the database server through the firewall. The firewall should have the following goals:

- Lock down ports. An open port is one of the easiest ways for a computer hacker to break into your system. You might have ports open for a variety of reasons—for example, SQL*Net needs port 1521 available for SQL*Net traffic. You might be using other operating systems and gateways that might require other ports to be open. A firewall ensures that open ports are used in a secure manner.

- Isolate the database server or network the database resides on from unauthorized usage.

- Restrict the direction of traffic.

Firewalls can be set up to allow network traffic to be only inbound or outbound. Figure 11.1 shows two firewalls in a typical Internet configuration. Firewall A is used by the e-commerce application that allows traffic flow inbound as well as outbound on a specific port. Firewall B, on the other hand, allows outbound traffic so that the company employees can access the Internet. Inbound traffic can be only SQL*NET.

> **Note** Optional services such as mail, FTP, Telnet and NFS should be turned off when using a Web-enabled database server. This will reduce the risk of a break-in to the system.

We have seen various ways in which a firewall can be used. The actual implementation should consider the overall security policy of your company. The security policy should clearly define the role of the firewall and up to what extent it is supposed to protect the data. You should carefully analyze how much risk is acceptable and the amount of protection that can be obtained by using the firewall.

Implementation of firewalls is beyond the scope of this book, so you should refer to the documentation provided by your firewall vendor for implementation details.

Understanding the Oracle Advanced Security Option

The Oracle Advanced Security Option (ASO) provides a range of options for data integrity and security. Some of the functionality is enabled in the Oracle software; however, the majority of the functionality is obtained by integrating Oracle networking with other third-party products. The Advanced Security Option comes in two versions:

- **Domestic use version**—This version is valid in USA and Canada only and can use the highest level of encryption currently available.
- **Export use version**—This version is used in other countries and the law requires that the lowest level of encryption be used.

The most important functionality provided by the Oracle ASO includes:

- **Data encryption and checksumming**—Data transmitted between the client and server can be encrypted so that it is secure during transmission. Furthermore, you can enable the transmission of checksum packets along with data packets so that data is not modified during transmission.
- **Authentication and single sign-on**—The Oracle environment can be integrated with other authentication solutions, for example, Net8 supports adapters for Kerberos, CyberSAFE, SecurID, and so on.
- **Integration with SSL**—Secured Sockets Layer (SSL) is an Internet standard that can be integrated with the Oracle Advanced Security Option.
- **Support for RADIUS protocol**—All devices that comply with the RADIUS standard (Remote Authentication Dial-In User Service) can be used with ASO.
- **Support for Oracle wallets**—Use of Oracle wallets enables the management of public keys.
- **Integration with DCE environment**—Oracle network and resources can be used with OSF's Distributed Computing Environment (DCE).

Configuring third-party products is beyond the scope of this book and you should refer to the *Oracle Advanced Security Option Administrator's Guide* as well as the documentation of the third-party product you are planning to work with.

Figure 11.1 shows a configuration that would work for us. We will use RADIUS protocol authentication to ensure that the connections to the database server are made from the Web server. Also, digital certificates can be used for authentication of connection requests. Firewall A allows both inbound and outbound traffic, so the e-commerce application works without any problem. Firewall B allows outbound traffic while inbound traffic is only via port 1521 (SQL*Net), so the employees can have access to the Internet and the administrators can perform remote administration of the database, perform backups and recovery, and so on.

11

Figure 11.1

Using firewalls to secure JavaStop.

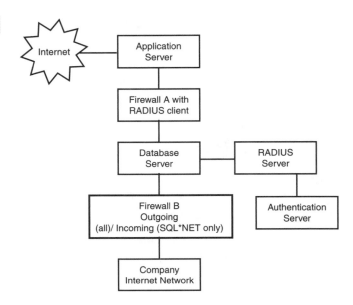

Authenticating Connections to JavaStop

Generally, Internet applications use multitiered architectures and access the databases via multiple networks. JavaStop is one such example, as shown in Figure 11.1. The database servers need to be able to trust that the client is who it says it is, and the application server is who it says it is.

Two methods are commonly used for such authentication: Passwords and Digital Certificates.

Authentication Using Passwords

Password management is enhanced in Oracle8i. Oracle8i allows you to manage and protect user passwords by specifying several characteristics such as

- **Password lifetime and expiration**—A time limit can be associated with the use of a password. Once the time limit is reached, the password has to be changed. After the password expires a grace period is given to the user within which the account is locked if the password is not changed.

- **Password history**—A password history prevents users from choosing the same password for the specified amount of time or for the specified number of password changes.

Note   Rules for password reuse can be configured by using the CREATE PROFILE statement.

- **Enforcement of password complexity verification to prevent it from being easily guessed**—Oracle8i provides a default password complexity verification routine that requires that each password satisfy the following:
    - Contain a minimum of four characters in length
    - Should not equal the UserID
    - Should equal at least one alphabetic character, one numeric character, and one punctuation mark
    - Should not equal any word on an internal list of simple words
    - Should differ from the previous password by at least three characters
- **Account lockup after a certain number of unsuccessful attempts**—In order to have a highly secure environment, you might be tempted to set a low value for the number of unsuccessful attempts after which the account locks up, but don't do it. Otherwise, you might receive many calls from users who tend to forget their password easily and frequently.

Authentication Using Digital Certificates

Digital certificates provide a better means of authentication than passwords. Digital certificates of the type X.509 version 3, an Internet standard–based public key infrastructure (PKI), can be used to authenticate users or machines. A digital certificate can contain the following information:

- Name of the certificate owner
- Name of the certificate authority
- Public key of the certificate owner
- Range of date for which the certificate is valid
- Signature of the issuer
- Serial number of the certificate

An *Oracle wallet* stores the certificate and private key. Oracle wallets are published in the Oracle directory server by the Oracle certificate authority or another certificate authority. A centralized tool—the Oracle Wallet Manager—simplifies the management of Oracle wallets.

In order to achieve security for data transmission across the network, you should use digital certificates with the Secure Sockets Layer protocol (SSL). SSL provides data integrity checking and data encryption across the network. With the help of ASO, you can use the RADIUS protocol, which has become an Internet standard. The RADIUS protocol allows the use of a variety of authentication techniques, such as

- Passwords
- Tokens devices—This technique uses a physical device that the user must have to establish connection. A commonly used method is challenge/response. It works as follows:
  1. The user enters the username.
  2. A number is sent back to the user (challenge).
  3. The user enters the number on a device.
  4. The token device used is specifically configured for the user and it generates another number (response) that is used as the password.

  For each connection a separate challenge/response sequence is used.

- Biometrics—Biometric devices use a physical characteristic that is unique to the individual, such as fingerprints. Currently, the Oracle8i ASO only allows the use of a fingerprint scanning device. It works as follows:
  1. The fingerprint of the user is first recorded on the system.
  2. When a connection is desired, the user specifies the Oracle service and places her finger on the fingerprint reader.
  3. The finger placed on the reader is compared with the fingerprint stored in the database, and if there is a match, the user is allowed access.

- Smartcards
- Network authentication services (such as Kerberos and SESAME)—In this technique, the user is created on each database she will use and database privileges are assigned to the user, but the password is the reserved word *external*. When a connection is desired, an external source is enabled to authenticate the user. An authentication server stores usernames, passwords, and hostnames. This authentication server is used for password verification.

External Authentication

External authentication refers to the authentication of the user by some means external to the database. External authentication is usually performed by the operating system or network authentication service.

 **Note** During external authentication, the database still identifies the user, but a database password is not required for login.

External authentication requires that the init.ora parameter OS_AUTHENT_PREFIX be set to a value that serves as the prefix for users authenticated externally. In other words, this parameter tells Oracle that any user who has the same prefix as this value is to be authenticated externally. For example, if OS_AUTHENT_PREFIX is set to ops$ and you have two Oracle users—ops$smith and johnson—external authentication is performed for ops$smith while database authentication is performed for johnson. It is not necessary to set OS_AUTHEN_PREFIX to a non-null value; it can be set to null by using "".

Another parameter that is commonly used with external authentication is REMOTE_OS_AUTHENT. When set to TRUE it enables Oracle to use the username from a nonsecure connection.

Enterprise Authentication

Enterprise authentication can be performed with the help of Oracle Security Service (OSS). OSS interfaces with the Oracle Enterprise Manager to centralize security management. In this technique, the user is called a *global* user and must be created on each database that she will use with the password *globally*. The user is identified by Oracle but is authenticated by Oracle Security Services.

Encrypting the Data

Secure user connections and encryption algorithms can be used to maintain data integrity. A modified data encryption standard (DES) algorithm can be used to encrypt passwords using the following steps:

1. On the database server, set the init.ora parameter DBLINK_ENCRYPT_LOGIN to TRUE.

2. On the client machine, set the environment variable ORA_ENCRYPT_LOGIN to TRUE.

A further step along this line can be taken by encrypting all the data. Currently, OAS provides two encryption algorithms—RSA and DES—with different key lengths. Different key lengths are used within the USA/Canada and outside it:

- 56-bit RSA RC4, 56-bit DES, and 128-bit RSA are used in the USA and Canada.
- 40-bit RSA RC4, 40-bit DES40, and 3DES are available for export outside the USA and Canada.

11

The preceding encryption algorithms can ensure data integrity during the transmission from the client workstation to the database server.

Securing the JSTP Database

Oracle8i provides various security mechanisms for controlling access to the data. These security features include user logons, passwords, privileges, auditing, and fine-grained access control. The Oracle Enterprise Manager can be used to simplify the administration of database security by allowing you to manage users, privileges, roles, profiles, and so on.

Database Users

Before any information can be accessed in the database, you should log in to the database using a valid username and password. This username is different from the operating system username. The GUI Oracle Enterprise Manager or the SQL command CREATE USER can be used to create users. Refer to Chapter 1, "Introduction to the Internet Capabilities of Oracle8i," for a list of the users that are automatically created with the starter database. For example, the following SQL command creates a user csmith with the password coffee.

```
SQL> create user csmith identified by coffee;
```

System Privileges

System privileges specify the tasks that a user can perform in the database. A large number of system privileges can be assigned to users.

> When granted to a user with the Admin option, a system privilege gives the user the ability to grant the privilege to other users.

A system privilege is not linked to a schema object. It is a permission to perform certain activities in the database. System privileges might affect more than one object. For example, if the system privilege select any table is granted to sjones, she can select from all tables defined in all schemas, even if the other schemas have not explicitly granted select privileges on their table to sjones.

> In order to connect to an Oracle instance, the create session system level privilege must be granted.

System level privileges exist in two forms:

- **Single schema**—These system level privileges allow the grantee to perform the task in a single schema. For example, the `create procedure` privilege allows the grantee to create a table in his or her own schema.

- **Any schema**—These system level privileges allow the grantee to perform the task in a single schema. For example, the `create any procedure` privilege allows the grantee to create a table in any schema.

For example, the following SQL command grants permissions to `csmith`, allowing him to connect to the database, create procedures in any schema, and use storage:

```
SQL> grant connect, resource, create any procedure
2    to csmith;
```

Discussion of all the available system and object level privileges is beyond the scope of this book and is probably more relevant to DBAs. If you are interested in knowing more about these, you might want to refer to the Oracle SQL Reference guide. However, an understanding of how security is implemented in Oracle databases is useful to developers so that security can be implemented properly.

Object Privileges

Object privileges control a user's access on various database objects such as tables, views, procedures, and synonyms. Object privileges can be used to specify whether a user can SELECT, INSERT, UPDATE, or DELETE from a table, or execute a procedure.

The concept of a schema can help in understanding how database security is implemented. A *schema* is a collection of objects, such as tables, indexes, views, and stored procedures. An Oracle database maintains a list of users who are allowed to access the data. Associated with each database user is a schema by the same name. For example, a user account `csmith` is created by a database administrator to allow a user Charles Smith to access the database. When this user logs in to the database, the schema `csmith` is accessible by him. Another user `sjones` can access the objects in the `csmith` schema using the dot notation. For example, a table `products` created in the schema `csmith` is accessed as `csmith.products`. User `sjones` cannot access objects defined in other schemas (such as `csmith`) unless she has been granted privileges to do so. Object level privileges allow a schema owner to control access to objects they own.

11

> Both object level and system level privileges are granted through the GRANT command, whereas privileges are revoked through the REVOKE command. For example, from SQL*Plus the following command allows sjones to select from the products table in the schema csmith:
>
> `SQL> grant select on csmith.products to sjones;`

The following object level privileges are commonly used:

- SELECT—Allows external schema to select from specified tables
- ALTER—Allows external schema to alter the structure of specified tables
- UPDATE—Allows external schema to update the specified tables
- DELETE—Allows external schema to delete from the specified tables
- INDEX—Allows external schema to create indexes on the specified tables
- INSERT—Allows external schema to insert into the specified tables
- EXECUTE—Allows external schema to execute the specified stored procedures

We have to pay special attention to the EXECUTE privilege. Stored procedures or stored functions are code modules that perform database actions, such are accessing or modifying data. Oracle8i enables you to write stored procedures and functions using either Java or PL/SQL. In addition, result sets can be returned by these procedures, enabling developers to get the result sets from stored procedures instead of using JDBC or SQLJ calls to submit SQL statements to the database. As a result, users can indirectly interact with the data even though they might not have been explicitly given permission to do so. Consider a client application written in Java that enables users to manipulate the database in a controlled manner. The security is built into the application. The user can, however, install a client tool such as SQL*PLUS and then directly execute DML statements against the database and completely bypass the application security. On the other hand, if we implement security using stored procedures and revoke any direct DML activity from users, then the application as well as SQL*PLUS would have to call the stored procedure to perform DML activity. This provides a more robust and reliable security environment.

Roles

Oracle8i provides many privileges and therefore the task of assigning individual user privileges can become tedious. Roles can be used to group privileges based on user functionality. Suppose that your organization has users who perform different functions such as clerks, managers, developers, and salespersons. Each role requires a certain set of privileges in the database so that the role can successfully perform the task. Database roles enable you to group privileges and then assign the role (instead of individual privileges) to the users. Several roles are created by Oracle during the installation, such as the DBA role that, when granted, allows the user to perform database administrator-type functions in the database. Roles can be managed by using the Oracle Enterprise Manager or using SQL commands (refer to the Oracle Reference manual guide).

> **Note**
>
> When granted to a user with the Admin option, a role gives that user the ability to grant the role to other users and to alter or drop the role.

For JavaStop, we can create several roles to simplify administration:

- **jstp_admins**—This role will have the necessary permissions to administer JSTP. Permissions include

    all (select, insert, update, and delete) on products

    all (select, insert, update, and delete) on customers

    all (select, insert, update, and delete) on orders

    all (select, insert, update, and delete) on items

    all (select, insert, update, and delete) on price

- **jstp_users**—This role will have the necessary permissions to use the JSTP database. Permissions include

    select from products

    select from price

    select, insert, update, and delete from orders (only for orders that they have placed)

    select, insert, update, and delete from items (only for orders that they have placed)

    no permission on the customers table

    execute on all procedures that are used to implement database functionality

Profiles

Profiles enable you to restrict the system resources a user can access. Several types of resource usage can be restricted, such as

- CPU time
- Connect time

11

- Idle time
- Number of concurrent sessions per user
- Number of database blocks that can be read

Controlling resource usage can prevent problems because of runaway processes in the system. During the installation of Oracle, a DEFAULT profile with unlimited resource usage is created. All newly created users are assigned this default profile unless specified otherwise. Profiles can be associated with users during the creation of a user.

For example

```
create profile jstp_admins
limit_sessions_per_user unlimited
cpu_per_session unlimited
cpu_per_call    5000
connect time 50
composite_limit 8000000;
```

creates a profile jstp_admins with the following specifications:

- No limit on the number of session
- No limit on the CPU usage per session
- The total elapsed time of each session is limited to 50 minutes
- The composite limit for resource usage is fixed to 8000000

Refer to Chapter 2, "Creating and Populating the JavaStop Database," where we have seen the necessary GRANT commands to implement database security. In the next sections we see how to implement application-level security and implement complex rules using fine-grained access control and application contexts.

Securing Applications

Views can be used to control access to the information stored in the database.

Suppose that you have an employees table containing information about all employees. The principle of least privilege would require that any employee should be able to see only information that pertains to her. The following view can be used for this purpose:

```
Create view employees_v as
   Select * from employees
   Where emp_name = USER
```

Similarly, the following view allows a user to access only those records that are modified by him:

```
Create view orders_v as
   Select * from orders
   Where last_modified_by = USER
```

The preceding example assumes that in the orders table we are using a last_modified column to indicate the user who last modified that particular record.

However, using views as a security mechanism has several problems associated with it:

- It can make the database inflexible and difficult to maintain. If views primarily are used for security purposes, it can become an administrative nightmare. For example, you might want to implement function-based security where an employee can view only his records, a manager can view the records of all employees in her department, and an HR manager can view the records of all company employees. Using a views-only approach would require you to either create different views to satisfy all these requirements (resulting in a lot of views) or create a complex and inefficient view that encompasses all the different scenarios.

- Security based on runtime parameters can't be easily implemented. For example, you might want the nature and extent of the access to an object to be related to the time of day, the IP address of the machine, and the task currently being performed by the application. A views-only approach makes this very difficult.

- Experienced and knowledgeable users might be able to access the information directly from the base tables.

Oracle8i features such as application contexts and fine-grained access control provide a more robust and reliable approach.

Using Application Contexts

Oracle8i provides a new database object type called *application context*, which enables you to cache session information securely. Application contexts can be created using the following syntax:

```
CREATE OR REPLACE CONTEXT namespace using package;
```

Attributes of the application context can be extracted using the SQL function SYS_CONTEXT:

```
SYS_CONTEXT(namespace,attribute);
```

11

A primitive context can be used to store certain information for a session such as the username, session ID, and IP address. The primitive context is stored in the name-space USERENV.

The following example demonstrates how to use SYS_CONTEXT to manipulate attributes of an application context:

```
SYS_CONTEXT('userenv','username');
```

The DBMS_SESSION.SET_CONTEXT procedure can be used to set nonprimitive contexts, as shown in the following:

```
DBMS_SESSION.SET_CONTEXT(namespace,attribute,value);
```

Using attributes stored in a context can be useful because the attribute values are stored in the private memory of the session. Also, each application can have its own context, and SYS_CONTEXT() is treated as a bind variable during query execution, resulting in performance improvement.

 Note   Attributes of a context are transient and, when set or reset, are valid for the entire duration of the user session.

Using Fine-Grained Access Control

The *fine-grained access control* (FGAC) feature of Oracle8i allows you to define security policies on tables and views. Any access to the table or view after the policy has been implemented causes the server to call a function that is enforcing the policy. The policy then dynamically generates predicates on those operations. As a result, each user accessing the database can access only information they have been authorized to access.

 Note   Different policies can be set for different DML statements on the same table or view.

The interfaces necessary to manage policies are contained in the DBMS_RLS package:

- add_policy(*object_schema*, *object_name*, *policy_name*);
- drop_policy(*object_schema*, *object_name*, *policy_name*);
- enable_policy(*object_schema*, *object_name*, *policy_name*, *enable*);
- refresh_policy(*object_schema*, *object_name*, *policy_name*);

 **Note**   Don't use security policies as an alternative to constraints.

Several benefits can be obtained by using FGAC:

- **Security**—FGAC is implemented at the server level and therefore can't be bypassed by the client software.
- **Flexibility**—Predicates are generated dynamically, allowing you to implement complex security requirements.
- **Transparency**—A change in security requirements can be easily implemented by changing the policy without any application change.
- **Scalable**—The SQL statements are parsed, optimized, and stored in the shared pool, making them available to other users. These SQL statements don't really depend on the policy that is in place.

Consider an example of the orders table in which a customer should see only the orders that she has placed. The orders table has the following description:

order_id is a unique ID for an order and serves as the primary key for this table

order_date specifies the date when the order was placed

customer_id refers to the customer_id column of the customers table

ship_date specifies the date when the order was fulfilled

total specifies the total dollar value of the order placed

The customers table has the following description:

customer_id specifies a unique ID for each customer and acts as the primary key for this table

name

address

city

state

country

zip_code

area_code

phone_number

comments specifies particular customer needs, characteristics, and so on

11

The following steps can be used to implement this security requirement:

1. Connect to Server Manager (or SQL*Plus) as internal.

2. Create the application context:

```
create or replace context order_ctx
using sec_admin.ord_ctx;
```

3. Create the trusted package specification:

```
Create or replace package sec_admin.ord_ctx as
    Procedure set_cust_number;
End ord_ctx;
```

4. Create the package body:

```
CREATE PACKAGE BODY ord_ctx IS
  PROCEDURE set_cust_number IS
    custnum NUMBER;
    BEGIN
      select customer_id into custnum
      from customers
      where name = sys_context('userenv', 'session_user');
      dbms_session.set_context('order_ctx', 'customer_id', custnum);
    END set_cust_number;
  END ord_ctx;
```

5. Grant permissions to everyone to execute the package:

```
GRANT EXECUTE ON ord_ctx TO PUBLIC;
```

6. Create the policy function:

```
CREATE PACKAGE sec_admin.order_security AS
    FUNCTION custnum_sec(owner VARCHAR2, object_name VARCHAR2)
    RETURN VARCHAR2;
    END order_security;
```

7. Create the package body for the policy function:

```
CREATE PACKAGE BODY order_security IS
    FUNCTION custnum_sec(owner VARCHAR2, object_name VARCHAR2)
    RETURN VARCHAR2 IS
    BEGIN
        RETURN ('customer_id =
            sys_context("order_ctx",  "customer_id")');
        END custnum_sec;
    END order_security;
```

8. Add the new policy to the orders table:

```
execute DBMS_RLS.ADD_POLICY('apps','orders', 'order_policy',
'sec_admin', 'order_security.custnum_sec');
```

where, apps and sec_admin are valid usernames in the database.

When this policy is associated with the orders table, any access to the orders table causes the predicate `'where customer_id = sys_context("order_ctx",` `"customer_id")'` to be added to the query.

Understanding Definer and Invoker Rights

Whenever you execute a stored procedure or an object method, the success of the execution depends on whether appropriate permissions have been granted. The user whose permissions are checked depends on whether definer's rights or invoker's rights are in effect. By default, stored procedures and SQL methods are executed with the definer's rights. For example, suppose that we have a standalone procedure called `add_customer` in the schema `csmith`:

```
SQL> create procedure add_customer(new_custname varchar2(10),
2 new_custdesc varchar2(20)) as
3 begin
insert into customers(customer_id, name, comments)
values(custno_seq.nextval, new_custname, new_custdesc);
end;
```

If another user `sjones` has been given the permission to execute this procedure and decides to execute it, the following is true:

- The procedure will execute with the privileges of the definer (in this case, `csmith`).
- The unqualified reference to the customers table is resolved in the schema `csmith`. Consequently, new customers get added in the customers table in the schema `csmith`.

In several situations including our JavaStop project, we might have procedures that modify objects in some schema other than the definer's schema. There are several alternative ways to achieve this result:

- Use fully qualified references. This is undesirable because it will make the procedure not portable.
- Copy the same procedure in every schema that will use this procedure. This solution is undesirable because it will create an administrative nightmare.
- Use invoker's rights.

Oracle8i allows the use of the AUTHID clause in procedures. AUTHID can be used to specify that the procedure should execute with the invoker's rights instead of the definer's rights. Making use of invoker's rights has several advantages:

- Portability of procedures is increased.
- The management of permissions is simplified.

11

- Procedures are not bound to a particular schema.
- Data retrieval can be centralized.

The following syntax shows how the AUTHID clause can be used:

- Functions

```
CREATE [OR REPLACE] FUNCTION [schema_name.]function_name
➥[(parameter_list)] RETURN datatype [AUTHID {CURRENT_USER ¦ DEFINER}] {IS
➥¦ AS}
```

- Procedures

```
CREATE [OR REPLACE] PROCEDURE [schema_name.]procedure_name
➥[(parameter_list)] [AUTHID {CURRENT_USER ¦ DEFINER}] {IS ¦ AS}
```

- Packages

```
CREATE [OR REPLACE] PACKAGE [schema_name.]package_name
➥[AUTHID {CURRENT_USER ¦ DEFINER}] {IS ¦ AS}
```

- Object types

```
CREATE [OR REPLACE] TYPE [schema_name.]object_type_name
➥[AUTHID {CURRENT_USER ¦ DEFINER}] {IS ¦ AS} OBJECT
```

In all the preceding uses, CURRENT_USER specifies that you want the execution to be performed with the invoker's rights.

 Note   By default, procedures, functions, packages, and object methods execute with the definer's rights.

The procedure add_customers can be modified as follows to specify that it should be executed with the invoker's rights:

```
SQL> create procedure add_customer(new_custname varchar2(10),
2 new_custdesc varchar2(20))
3 AUTHID CURRENT_USER as
4 begin
5 insert into customers(customer_id, name, comments)
6 values(custno_seq.nextval, new_custname, new_custdesc);
7 end;
```

When using invoker's rights, the invoker's rights are checked at runtime, and the external references are resolved in the schema of the invoker. However, it is important to understand the following:

- The PL/SQL compiler must resolve the references at compile time, and therefore the definer must create template objects that match the actual invoker objects.

- The external references are resolved in the schema of the invoker for only the following cases:

  SELECT, INSERT, UPDATE, and DELETE statements

  The transaction control statement LOCK TABLE

  The cursor control statements OPEN and OPEN-FOR

  The dynamic SQL statements EXECUTE IMMEDIATE and OPEN-FOR-USING

  SQL statements that are parsed by using DBMS_SQL.PARSE()

- When invoker-rights routines are used within a view or database trigger, the view owner (not view user) is considered the invoker.

There might be some instances when you want to mix the rights usage. In other words, you might want to use the invoker's rights for the procedure but use definer's rights to resolve certain external references. This can be achieved using one of the following alternatives:

- Use a public synonym. You can create a public synonym for the procedure (in the definer's schema). This will cause the definer's procedure to be used unless the invoker has also defined a procedure or private synonym with the same name.
- Fully qualify the external reference.

Auditing JavaStop Activity

Oracle8i provides an auditing facility that can be used to audit database access. Both successful and unsuccessful attempts can be audited for the following actions:

- Login attempts
- Access to objects
- System privileges and statements without regard to the object being accessed

Note Auditing is enabled by using the AUDIT command and disabled by using the NOAUDIT command.

11

In order to use auditing, the following steps must be taken:

1. Connect to server manager as the SYS account.
2. Run CATAUDIT.SQL.

3. In the init.ora file, set the parameter AUDIT_TRAIL to the appropriate value:

> **DB (for database)**—This enables systemwide auditing and causes audited records to be written to the database's audit trail (SYS.AUD$ table). If this option is used, the SYS.AUD$ table should be placed in a tablespace with a lot of free space.

> **OS (for operating system)**—This enables systemwide auditing and causes audited records to be written to the operating system's audit trail.

4. Restart the database instance.

Auditing Logins

The AUDIT SESSION command can be used to audit successful as well as unsuccessful login attempts. Use the following variations if you want to audit only successful or only unsuccessful login attempts:

- AUDIT SESSION WHENEVER SUCCESSFUL—Audits only successful login attempts
- AUDIT SESSION WHENEVER UNSUCCESSFUL—Audits only unsuccessful login attempts

 **Note**   The AUDIT ANY privilege is required to audit login attempts.

The data dictionary view DBA_AUDIT_SESSION can be used to query audit records.

For example, the following query

```
Select os_username, username,
    To_char(timestamp, 'DD-MON-YY HH24:MI') logon_time,
    To_char(logoff_time, 'DD-MON-YY HH24:MI') logoff_time
From dba_audit_session;
```

can result in the following output:

```
OS_USERNAME    USERNAME    LOGON_TIME         LOGOFF_TIME
MEGHT          MEGHT    02-OCT-99 13:24    02-OCT-99 18:30
```

Auditing Database Actions

Using the command AUDIT statement-option, you can audit database actions at the statement or system privilege level without reference to any particular database object being accessed. Both successful and unsuccessful attempts can be audited. See Table 11.1 for a list of statement options that can be audited.

Table 11.1   Audit Options for SQL Statements

AUDIT Statement Option	SQL Statements Audited
ALTER SYSTEM	ALTER SYSTEM
CLUSTER	CREATE CLUSTER, ALTER CLUSTER, TRUNCATE CLUSTER, DROP CLUSTER
DATABASE LINK	CREATE DATABASE LINK, DROP DATABASE LINK
INDEX	CREATE INDEX, ALTER INDEX, DROP INDEX
NOT EXISTS	SQL statements that return an Oracle error that the specified object does not exist
PROCEDURE	CREATE [OR REPLACE] FUNCTION, CREATE [OR REPLACE] PACKAGE, CREATE [OR REPLACE] PACKAGE BODY, CREATE [OR REPLACE] PROCEDURE, DROP PACKAGE, DROP PROCEDURE
PUBLIC DATABASE LINK	CREATE PUBLIC DATABASE LINK, DROP PUBLIC DATABASE LINK
PUBLIC SYNONYM	CREATE PUBLIC SYNONYM, DROP PUBLIC SYNONYM
ROLE	CREATE ROLE, ALTER ROLE, SET ROLE, DROP ROLE
ROLLBACK SEGMENT	CREATE ROLLBACK SEGMENT, ALTER ROLLBACK SEGMENT, DROP ROLLBACK SEGMENT
SEQUENCE	CREATE SEQUENCE, DROP SEQUENCE
SESSION	Session connects and disconnects
SYNONYM	CREATE SYNONYM, DROP SYNONYM
SYSTEM AUDIT	AUDIT, NOAUDIT
SYSTEM GRANT	GRANT, REVOKE
TABLE	CREATE TABLE, ALTER TABLE, DROP TABLE
TABLESPACE	CREATE TABLESPACE, ALTER TABLESPACE, DROP TABLESPACE
TRIGGER	CREATE TRIGGER, ALTER TRIGGER, ENABLE or DISABLE TRIGGER
USER	CREATE USER, ALTER USER, DROP USER
VIEW	CREATE [OR REPLACE] VIEW, DROP VIEW

Auditing DML Activity

The AUDIT command has options that enable you to audit DML activity on a specific object. The following syntax can be used:

```
AUDIT obj_option on schema.object
BY SESSION/ACCESS WHENEVER [NOT] SUCCESSFUL;
```

11

where

- `obj_option` specifies the activity, such as `UPDATE`, `DELETE`, and so on, for which the auditing is to be performed. The keyword `ALL` specifies that all activity on the specified object is to be audited.

- `schema.object` specifies the object for which the `obj_option` is to be audited.

- `SESSION` or `ACCESS` specifies whether the auditing is for the entire session or per access. Auditing `BY SESSION` causes Oracle to write a single record for all SQL statements (at the same time) used during the same session, whereas auditing `BY ACCESS` causes Oracle to write one record for each audited statement.

For example, the following will audit unsuccessful updates and deletes on the products table:

```
AUDIT update, delete
   ON products
   WHENEVER NOT SUCCESSFUL;
```

Note Auditing can be a very space-consuming and time-consuming task and you should be selective in determining the activities that you want to audit.

If audit records are written to the sys.aud$ table, you should restrict access to this table. In fact, you also should audit this table, as follows:

```
AUDIT select, insert, update, delete
ON sys.aud$
BY ACCESS;
```

Next Steps

In this chapter, we have discussed a very important issue in e-commerce application development: security. We have seen how various types of security can be implemented in JavaStop. Keep in mind that no security mechanism is completely foolproof; you have to determine how important the data is, and then take the appropriate measure to protect it. The next chapter discusses another important issue in e-commerce applications: scalability.

Improving the Scalability of JavaStop

An e-commerce application potentially has the whole world as its customer base. Special consideration has to be made to ensure that your application will be capable of handling the concurrency and workload. Having said that, we also have to realize that not all these users will be logging on at the same time; however, we have to make a realistic assumption about the amount of concurrency based on the expected workload and the nature of the application. For JavaStop, we might not have a particular timeframe when the workload is greater than other times. We have to make provisions for a reasonably high level of concurrency. When we are looking at ways to improve concurrency, we have to also be careful not to sacrifice performance.

Challenges in Developing a Scalable Java Environment

One of the key features of the Java language is the support of multithreading. However, it is still quite difficult to write reliable and scalable multithreaded Java applications. The Oracle8i Aurora Java Virtual Machine can efficiently and concurrently schedule Java execution for thousands of users. Although Oracle8i supports Java language level threads, all Java code in Oracle8i executes as a call within a session. Therefore, it is not necessary to write server-resident Java code that uses Java's multithreading capabilities to obtain scalability. Instead, the Java programs can use the same scalability architecture used by Oracle internally. This can be achieved by writing Java programs that execute within a server (the JVM).

It should be understood, however, that Oracle JServer allows you to write multi-threaded Java applications if you desire. In any case, the JVM and Oracle8i are responsible for managing all the processes and threads (even the O/S threads).

When using the multithreading capabilities of Java to obtain a scalable Java platform, the interaction of threads and automated storage management or garbage collection is an issue. Unlike languages such as C and C++, garbage collection is a major aspect of the Java language's automated storage management mechanism.

The automatic garbage collection in Java eliminates the need for Java developers to allocate and free memory explicitly. Several advantages are obtained by this approach:

- Development is simplified because the developers don't have to worry about the memory management aspects of programming.
- Fewer errors.
- Improved program speed.
- Reduced footprint.

The garbage collector executing in a Virtual Machine has no knowledge of which Java threads are executing or how they are scheduled. In a non-Oracle8i model, a single user maps to a single Java language level thread and the same single garbage collector manages the garbage from all users. This approach limits the scalability of the multithreaded application. The garbage collector used in the Oracle8i Aurora Java Virtual Machine is more reliable and efficient because it never collects garbage from more than one user at any time. The Virtual Machine coordinates with the operating system for management of the O/S processes and threads. As a result of this, even though a large number of users connect to the server and execute the same Java code, each user experiences it as if she is executing her own Java code in her own Virtual Machine.

 **Note**   You do not have to write multithreaded Java code to achieve scalability when working with Oracle8i.

Consequently, when writing your Java programs, you don't have to worry about the inefficiency and overhead that is normally generated by the use of a garbage collector. In the Oracle8i Aurora Java Virtual Machine, the memory manager always deals with the allocation and collection of objects within a single session (see Figure 12.1). This enables you to use sophisticated allocation and collection schemes tuned to the types and lifetime of objects, for example

- New objects are allocated in fast and cheap call memory that can be allocated and accessed quickly and efficiently.
- Objects held in Java static variables are migrated to session space.
- Different garbage collection algorithms are applied in the various memory areas, making the overall process very efficient.

Figure 12.1

Each Virtual Machine shares most of its implementation and read-only data with other JServer sessions.

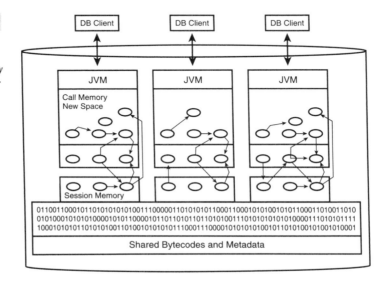

 Note   When using Oracle8i, garbage collection is transparent to the Java programmers.

Footprint

The footprint of an executing Java program refers to the amount of resources being used by the program and it depends on several factors:

- **Program Size**—Size of a Java program is determined by the number of classes and methods it uses. The use of core Java libraries can help in the sharing of Java bytecodes and minimizing program size.
- **Program complexity**—Use of core class libraries can reduce the complexity of the Java program and reduce footprint.
- **State objects used by Aurora**—State objects refer to the preservation of object states across calls. Excessive use of state objects can increase the footprint.

- **Efficiency of the garbage collector**—In Java, the garbage collector is automatically invoked. It is also possible to manually invoke the garbage collector on demand if your program requires excessive memory management. Refer to Chapter 10, "Diagnosing Problems and Debugging JavaStop Code,") for details on how manual garbage collection can be achieved.

A minimum incremental per-user session footprint is a key factor in achieving high scalability. In Aurora, read-only data that all users employ, such as Java bytecodes, is placed in shared memory. In addition, different garbage collection algorithms are used depending on the type of memory. This helps in keeping call and session memory under control.

> Oracle JServer is architected for scalability because the JServer sessions are garbage collected independently, resulting in no multiuser garbage collection bottleneck.

Keep in mind that as a developer you won't have to worry about all the garbage collection that goes on because it is handled automatically by Aurora. However, it is important to understand that Aurora preserves the state of your Java programs between calls by migrating objects reachable by static variables into session space at the end of the call. This indicates that you should use static variables carefully. Improper and unnecessary use of static variables can place a heavy burden on the memory manager and effectively reduce the scalability. Session space usage can be controlled by avoiding the use of static variables for instance-specific data. The EndOfCallRegistry notification provided by Aurora can be used to clear static variables at the end-of-call.

> Sharing resources across Java processes will allow each individual Java process to use fewer resources and have reduced overhead for resource management. Consequently, its footprint will be reduced.

Configuring Memory Usage for the JavaStop Database (JSTP)

Two main `init.ora` parameters affect the memory usage and performance of Java code:

- `Shared_pool_size`—The shared pool is consumed transiently when you use loadjava. It is also used when call specifications are created and dynamically loaded Java classes are tracked by the system.

The database initialization process performed by executing `initjvm.sql` against a clean database requires that the `shared_pool_size` be set to 50MB as it loads the Java binaries for more than 4,000 classes and resolves them.

- `java_pool_size`—The shared in-memory representation of the Java method and class definitions are stored here. These are shared by all the user sessions. In addition, the Java objects that are migrated to session space at end-of-call are also stored here. The `java_pool_size` must be adjusted based upon the amount of state held in static variables for each session.

Two more `init.ora` parameters that can affect memory usage per session are as follows:

- `java_soft_sessionspace_limit` (default 1MB)—Specifies the "soft" limit for the memory usage per session. If this limit is exceeded, a trace file containing a warning is generated.
- `java_max_sessionspace_size` (default 4GB)—Specifies the maximum limit for the memory usage per session. It this limit is exceeded, Aurora kills the session with an out-of-memory failure message. This is a hidden parameter and should not be modified without consulting Oracle support. Improper setting can make your database unstable.

End-of-call Memory Management

As you enhance JavaStop to make use of Enterprise Java Beans (EJBs), the application will end up retaining a significant amount of state in static variables across multiple calls. This significantly increases the size of the footprint for a large number of users. A simple technique to minimize footprint is to release large data structures at end-of-call. Aurora provides a mechanism for calling a specified Java method when a session is about to become inactive that can help in achieving this result. Such end-of-call optimization is provided by Oracle in the oracle.aurora.memoryManager package. The `EndOfCallRegistry` class and the Callback interface are used for this purpose.

 Data structures that are candidates for end-of-call optimization include

- Buffers or caches
- Static fields
- Dynamically built data structures

12

The `EndOfCallRegistry` class maintains a table of thunk/value pairs known as end-of-call callbacks. At the end of a call, the thunk.act (value) is invoked for every thunk/value pair in the table. However, if the end-of-call is also the end of session, the callback is not invoked. After the callback is invoked, it is removed from the table. Several important methods of the `EndOfCallRegistry` class include

- `public static void registerCallback(Callback thunk, Object value)`— This method installs *thunk* as an end-of-call callback. At the end-of-call, *thunk.act (value)* will be called for every end-of-call callback. A common variation is to not use the *value*:

  ```
  public static void registerCallback(Callback thunk)
  ```

- `static void runCallbacks()`—This method should not be called from your code. It is called by the Virtual Machine at the end-of-call for every thunk/value pair registered using `registerCallback`.

- `public void act(Object value)`—This method can be written to do whatever you want for callback purposes such as notification of end-of-call.

  Chapter 15, "Enhancing JavaStop Using EJBs and CORBA," shows an example of how end-of-call optimization can be used with Enterprise JavaBeans.

 Note   Any object that you want to register using EndOfCallRegistry.registerCallback must implement the oracle.aurora.memoryManager.Callback interface.

Speed of Execution

Java executes platform-independent bytecodes on top of a Virtual Machine. The Virtual Machine then deals with the specific hardware platform, which makes the execution slightly inefficient. A popular approach to resolving this issue is to use *Just In Time* (JIT) compilers. JIT compilers quickly compile Java bytecodes to native machine code, enabling frequently run Java code to be executed efficiently. Oracle makes use of a *Way Ahead of Time* (WAT) approach. In the WAT approach, Aurora translates Java bytecodes to platform-independent C code. This C code is then translated by a standard C compiler for the target platform. This is suitable for server-side Java applications because they are not updated and deployed frequently. In addition, the WAT approach can be used across all platforms while the JIT approach requires a low-level, processor-dependent code to be written and maintained for each platform.

Note | When working with the Oracle8i Aurora Java Virtual Machine you don't have to worry about building scalability into your Java code by writing multithreaded Java code. The scalability aspect is handled at the server level.

Using Natively Compiled Code

Oracle JServer provides all the core Java class libraries and Oracle-provided Java code natively compiled (see Figure 12.2). Java classes exist as shared libraries in the $ORACLE_HOME/javavm/admin directory. Each shared library corresponds to a Java package and is used by the Aurora Virtual Machine as needed. In general, the use of natively compiled code instead of bytecode interpretation improves speed (by two to ten times), but it also takes up more memory (two to three times more). The current release of Oracle doesn't provide native compilation for your Java code. In the current JServer release, Java code loaded in the server is interpreted, whereas the core classes such as `java.lang.*` are fully compiled. As a result, the more Java code used from core classes and the more Oracle-provided class libraries used, the more speed benefit that can be obtained.

Figure 12.2

Core Java class libraries and Oracle-provided Java code are natively compiled and their use improves the execution speed.

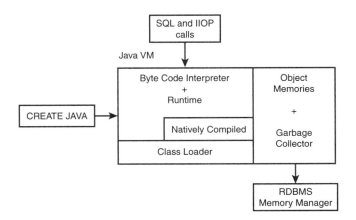

Understanding the Oracle Multithreaded Server Architecture

By default, whenever a user attempts to make a connection to the database, the connection is made using dedicated server processes. In other words, for each user connection there is a shadow process created that performs all the work on behalf of the user process. This includes loading the desired data from the database files into the database block buffers and returning the results of the query back to the user

12

process. Such dedicated connections are very fast and would be desirable, but they happen to have a problem: You can't have too many of them without quickly making the overhead prohibitive. This is particularly true for JavaStop if we are planning to support at least a couple hundred connections. In addition, the dedicated servers take up the same amount of resources on the database whether they are active or not, and this can be inefficient if the user connections access the database infrequently.

Multithreaded server is a technique that can be used to support a large number of concurrent users without requiring a large amount of resources. It enables the user processes to share a smaller number of server processes and thereby conserve resources. Further, the overall idle time for server processes is reduced. For example, if you have 1,000 simultaneous connections but at any time a maximum of 50 user connections are active, you can allocate 50 shared servers so that they are active most of the time, instead of having 50 active and 950 idle server processes.

Several processes are involved in a multithreaded configuration:

- **A network listener process**—This functionality, provided by Net8, connects user processes to dispatchers or dedicated servers as requested.
- **One or more dispatcher processes**—Dispatchers are protocol-specific handlers associated with a particular instance.
- **One or more shared server processes**—Shared servers satisfy the requests submitted by the dispatchers.

In addition to the preceding server processes, several enhancements are made to the SGA in order to support the MTS architecture:

- *Request queues* that contain the requests placed by the dispatchers
- A *Response queue* that is used by the shared servers to place the response to the requests
- Session information is migrated from the PGA into the SGA (this section of the SGA is known as the UGA, or *user global area*)

Initialization Parameters for MTS

When using the multithreaded server configuration, the following `init.ora` parameters must be set:

- `MTS_SERVERS` specifies the number of shared server processes to be created at instance startup.

      Setting `MTS_SERVERS` = 0 disables multithreaded servers.

- `MTS_MAX_SERVERS` specifies the maximum number of shared server processes that can exist for an MTS instance.
- `MTS_DISPATCHERS` specifies the number of dispatchers created at instance startup, the protocol associated with the dispatchers, and the number of clients that can connect to a particular dispatcher.
- `MTS_MAX_DISPATCHERS` specifies the maximum number of dispatchers that can be created on an MTS instance.
- `SHARED_POOL_SIZE` specifies the shared pool size. As discussed earlier, when using an MTS configuration, additional memory structures such as request queues and response queues are created in the SGA and you have to increase the shared pool size to make provisions for extra memory structures. You should add about 1KB for each user who will connect by using MTS.

The following is a sample init.ora file making use of MTS parameter settings:

```
Sample init.ora file with MTS parameters

mts_dispatchers= "tcp, 1"
mts_max_dispatchers=8
mts_max_servers=10
mts_servers=6
```

The corresponding listener.ora file should be like the following:

```
LISTENER =
(ADDRESS_LIST =
(ADDRESS=(COMMUNITY= TCP.world)(PROTOCOL= TCP)(Host= your_machine)
➥(Port= 1521))
)

SID_LIST_LISTENER = (
SID_LIST =(SID_DESC =(SID_NAME = YOUR_SID)))
```

The tnsnames.ora file used for client machines should be as follows:

```
YOUR_SID_TCP.world=
(DESCRIPTION =(ADDRESS=(PROTOCOL=TCP) (HOST=your_machine) (PORT=1521))
(CONNECT_DATA= (SID=YOUR_SID)(SERVER=SHARED)))
```

MTS Connection Mechanism

When you use multithreaded servers, the connection mechanism is as follows (see Figure 12.3):

1. When the listener is started, it opens and establishes a communication pathway and starts listening on the addresses listed in the listener.ora file. This channel is utilized by users to communicate with Oracle.

12

2. When an MTS-configured Oracle instance is started, each dispatcher (specified in the init.ora file) receives its random listen address.

3. The dispatchers call the listener and notify the listener about the address at which the dispatcher listens for connection requests.

4. The listener updates its list of known services by adding the address of the dispatchers.

5. The listener process now waits for incoming connection requests.

6. A user requests a connection to the database. This could be a connection request from any type of client, including a Java application.

7. The user connection request is intercepted by the listener. If the user requests a dedicated server process, the listener creates a dedicated server process and connects the user process to it. The user communicates with Oracle through this dedicated connection.

On the other hand, if an MTS connection is needed, the following steps occur:

The listener gives the user process the address of a dispatcher process with the lightest load.

The user process connects to the dispatcher.

The dispatcher creates a virtual circuit that is used by the user process (throughout its lifetime) to communicate with the shared servers.

Figure 12.3

Multithreaded Server connection mechanism.

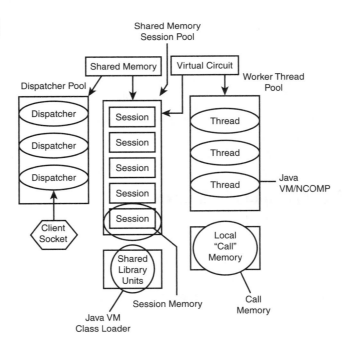

In an MTS connection, when the user process issues a request, the dispatcher places the request in the request queue (part of the SGA). The request queue is common to all dispatchers, but each dispatcher has its own response queue. The user request is eventually picked up by an available shared server. The shared server process does all the necessary processing and returns the results to the dispatcher's response queue in the SGA. The dispatcher returns the result back to the user process.

Note All dispatchers share a common queue but they have their own response queues.

Configuring JavaStop for MTS Connections

When using MTS, not only do you get load and user balancing, but you can also configure different connection types and protocols.

In order to configure JavaStop for MTS connections, we need to perform several steps:

1. Configure the TNS listener.

   The initial connection request comes to the TNS listener. A basic listener.ora file follows:

```
LISTENER=
    (DESCRIPTION_LIST =
        (DESCRIPTION =
            (ADDRESS_LIST =
                (ADDRESS = (PROTOCOL = IPC) (KEY = EXTPROC0))
            )
            (ADDRESS_LIST =
                (ADDRESS = (PROTOCOL = TCP) (HOST = myserv) (PORT = 1521))
            )
        )
    )
SID_LIST_LISTENER =
    (SID_LIST =
        (SID_DESC =
            (SID_NAME = PLSExtProc)
            (ORACLE_HOME = c:\oracle)
            (PROGRAM = extproc)
        )
    )
```

   In the preceding listing, the PLSExtProc reference and the EXTPROC0 entry indicates that you want to allow PL/SQL code and the database to make calls to external C libraries. The TCP entry in the DESCRIPTION list indicates that you want to allow the listener to have TCP/IP access via port 1521.

12

2. Start the listener.

3. Use `LSNRCTL SERVICES` to determine whether the listener is running or not.

```
C:\> lsnrctl services
```

The following output might be generated:

```
Services Summary
      ORCL       has 1 service handler(s)
          DEDICATED SERVER established: 0, refused: 0
              LOCAL SERVER
      PLSExtPROC    has 1 service handler(s)
DEDICATED SERVER established: 0, refused: 0
              LOCAL SERVER
```

4. Edit the init.ora file to use the MTS parameters. A sample init.ora file using MTS is shown earlier.

5. Shut down and start up the database.

Now, JavaStop is configured to use MTS. If you want to use EJBs or CORBA, you also will have to enable Internet Inter-Orb Protocol (IIOP) support. IIOP support can be achieved by adding the following entry to your listener.ora file:

```
(DESCRIPTION =
    (PROTOCOL_STACK =
        (PRESENTATION = GIOP
        (SESSION = RAW)
    )
    (ADDRESS = (PROTOCOL = TCP) (HOST = myhost) (PORT = 2481))
)
```

Now the listener has to be restarted. The next step is to add the following lines to the init.ora file:

```
mts_dispatchers = "(PROTOCOL=TCP) (PRE=oracle.aurora.server.SGiopServer)"
#mts_dispatchers = "(PROTOCOL=TCP) (PRE=oracle.aurora.server.GiopServer)"
#mts_dispatchers = "(PROTOCOL=TCPS) (PRE=oracle.aurora.server.SGiopServer)"
```

In the preceding code, the first line configures the dispatcher to handle session-based GIOP connections. The second line configures the dispatcher for standard GIOP connections. The third line configures the dispatcher for SSL connections.

Common Problems with MTS

Generally, problems experienced with MTS configurations fall into one of the following categories.

Connection Problems

It is possible to get a dedicated connection even though you had asked for an MTS connection. Also, an MTS connection might be hung. Several data dictionary views can be checked to verify that a particular connection is an MTS connection or whether it is having any connection problems:

- v$circuit lists all the virtual circuits in the instance.
- v$session displays session information. The SERVER field of this view displays SHARED or NONE if it's an MTS session.
- v$dispatcher displays information about the dispatchers. The ACCEPT field of this view determines whether the dispatchers are accepting any more connections.
- v$shared_server displays information about the shared server processes.

In addition to checking data dictionary views, the following steps can be taken to diagnose connection problems in an MTS configuration:

- Check the alert log and the trace files of the dispatchers, shared servers, and PMON for any errors.
- Check the link between the listener and dispatcher for problems. Problems with the listener can occur as a result of the dispatcher not registering with it or the address used by the dispatcher to call the listener (MTS_LISTENER_ADDRESS) not matching the actual address on which the listener is listening.
- Verify that the correct listener address is being used by the client connections.

Performance Problems

It easily can be seen that the path from the user processes to the database is longer in an MTS connection compared to a dedicated connection. This is because the dispatcher is also involved and server processes are shared. As a result of this, the main sources of contention in an MTS configuration are the shared servers and the dispatchers.

Managing Contention for Dispatcher Processes

All communication in an MTS connection occurs through a dispatcher. If you don't use the proper number of dispatchers, they can get overworked. Contention for dispatchers can be identified by very busy dispatchers (v$dispatcher) or by a steady increase in the wait time for responses in the response queues of the dispatchers (v$queue).

12

In order to determine the efficiency of your dispatchers, run your application for some time, and then run the following query:

```
Svrmgrl> SELECT name, owned, status, (busy /(busy + idle)) * 100
     2>         "% of time busy"
     3> FROM  v$dispatcher;

NAME    STATUS    % of time busy
-----   -------   --------------
D000    WAIT      .082074981
D001    CONNECT   .781903784
D002    WAIT      .037892708
```

The preceding output indicates that this instance uses three dispatchers, of which two are in the WAIT state while D001 is servicing a client request. The percentage of time for which the dispatchers are busy is very low, indicating that we might be able to do with fewer dispatchers.

If the output of the preceding query indicates that the dispatchers are very busy, you should reduce the contention for dispatchers using one of the following techniques:

- **Add more dispatcher processes**—The ALTER SYSTEM command can be used to add more dispatchers.

- **Enable connection pooling**—Connection pooling can be enabled by using the optional attribute POOL (or POO) with the MTS_DISPATCHERS parameter. For example, in the init.ora file

  ```
  MTS_DISPATCHERS = "(PROTOCOL=TCP) (DISPATCHERS=3) (POOL)"
  ```

  enables the connection pooling feature and starts three TCP dispatchers. Connection pooling is a Net8 feature that uses a time-out mechanism to temporarily release an idle transport connection while maintaining its network session. Consequently, the bandwidth is used more efficiently.

Managing Contention for Shared Server Processes

In an MTS configuration, server processes are shared by the user processes and if you don't use a proper number of shared server processes, they might get overworked. A steady increase in the waiting time for requests in the request queue of shared servers (as shown by v$queue and v$shared_servers) indicates contention for shared servers.

One of the biggest performance gains in an MTS configuration can be obtained by identifying connections that would benefit by using a dedicated connection instead of an MTS connection. The following query can be used to determine how efficiently the shared servers are being used:

```
Svrmgrl> SELECT name, status, requests, (busy /(busy + idle)) * 100
      2> "% of time busy"
      3> FROM v$shared_server;

NAME    STATUS            REQUESTS   % of time busy
------  ----------------  ---------- --------------
S000    WAIT(COMMON)      5810       .290847
S001    WAIT(COMMON)      210        .091730
S002    WAIT(ENQ)         1          97.187302
```

The preceding output indicates that servers S000 and S001 are pretty much idle, whereas server S002 is very busy servicing a client request that might benefit from a dedicated server connection rather than MTS.

The following query indicates the average wait time in the request queue. A steady increase in this value indicates that there is contention for shared server processes:

```
Svrmgrl> SELECT DECODE( totalq, 0, 'No Requests',  wait/totalq )
      2> "Avg wait time per requests  "
      3> FROM v$queue
      4> WHERE type = 'COMMON';

Average wait time per requests (hundredths of seconds)
----------------------------------------------------------------
                       0.829018942
```

Oracle automatically adjusts the number of shared server processes in an MTS configuration to improve performance, but as mentioned earlier, the greatest benefit can be obtained by identifying connections that should be dedicated instead of using shared servers. In general, short transactions that don't tie up the server for a long time are suited for MTS connections, whereas those that require prolonged connections and perform intensive operations are suited for dedicated connections.

Using Clusters to Improve Scalability

Clusters can exist in a variety of configurations:

- Tightly coupled systems use multiple CPUs that share memory through a common memory bus. Performance of such systems is limited by the bandwidth of the bus.
- Loosely coupled systems use a node that contains one or more CPUs and communicates with other nodes through a high-speed common bus. The nodes don't share memory, but they do share disk and other resources.

12

- Massively parallel processors are comprised of nodes that usually contain an inexpensive CPU. These systems achieve high scalability by making use of hundreds of nodes. The nodes communicate by using a high-speed interconnect. These systems are also referred to as shared-nothing architecture because neither memory nor disk resources are shared between nodes.

Oracle Parallel Server (OPS) is a clustering solution that provides not only reliability but also good scalability for well-designed applications. OPS runs on loosely coupled systems as well as massively parallel processors. When using a clustering approach to improve scalability, application design plays an important role in the overall system performance. OPS enables multiple Oracle instances running on multiple nodes to access a single shared Oracle database. A typical OPS environment has the following characteristics:

- An Oracle instance exists on each node.
- The nodes share the same physical database and have common datafiles and control files.
- Each instance has its own shared global area (SGA) and background threads.
- Each instance has its own redo thread accessible by other instances, because this redo is needed during instance recovery.
- Instances can use different init.ora files but must have some common parameters.
- Archived redo log files can be separate but must be available to all instances so that media recovery can be performed.
- Each node can support multiple users who can execute multiple transactions simultaneously.

A quick overview of the Oracle Parallel Server architecture is shown in Figure 12.4.

A set of operating-system–dependent (OSD) components is provided by various vendors to provide valuable service during the operation of OPS. Oracle has defined the requirements and interfaces for the OSD components. Some of the modules in the OSD layer are required, whereas others are optional and used by individual vendors for competitive advantage. The modules in the OSD layer provide a range of functionality:

- **Cluster Manager (CM)**—The Cluster Manager module is used to discover and access the cluster's state. The fault-tolerant capabilities of OPS depend on the fault-tolerant capabilities of the cluster manager. In case a cluster node fails, the CM reconfigures the cluster to work with the remaining nodes.

Figure 12.4

Oracle Parallel Server architecture.

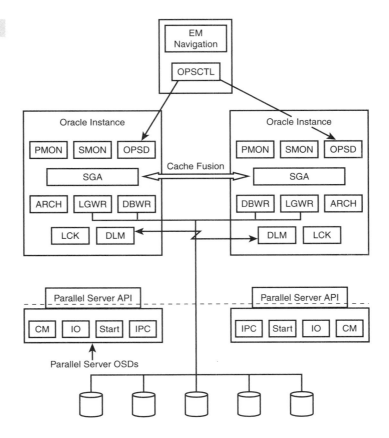

- **Inter-Process Communication (IPC)**—The Inter-Process Communication module provides reliable communication between instances. The performance of OPS depends heavily on the usage of a fast interconnect between the nodes. The distributed lock manager (DLM) performs all its functions using an asynchronous messaging model that is supported by the IPC.

- **Input/Output (I/O)**—The I/O module provides access to shared devices from all nodes to a cluster disk farm.

- **Startup**—The Startup module is responsible for initiating the OPS components in a particular order during instance startup. It also initializes vendor-specific structures and allocates the necessary resources.

 Note

A new Oracle8i feature, *cache fusion*, enables the transfer of requested blocks between instances via the high-speed interconnect between them, instead of writing the block to disk by one instance and then reading by another instance.

12

In an OPS system, the biggest cause of performance problems is *pinging*. Pinging occurs each time a data block is written to disk by one instance so that it can be read by another instance. In contrast, false pinging occurs when a block is written to disk by one instance not because the particular block is requested, but because another block that's managed by the same lock is requested. Pinging can be reduced by properly designing the applications.

 Note   Pinging always occurs in an OPS environment by virtue of the mechanism used to maintain data integrity in such an environment. Your goal shouldn't be to eliminate pinging but to minimize the pinging activity.

OPS provides several advantages:

- High performance. Use of OPS can improve the performance of well-designed applications. If an application doesn't perform well using a single instance, it will usually perform worse in an OPS environment. Therefore it is important to ensure that your application is designed properly so that the amount of pinging and false pinging is minimized.
- High availability. The various nodes that are part of an OPS are isolated from one another and therefore failure in one node doesn't affect other nodes. The other nodes can keep running and help in the recovery of the failed node.
- High scalability and support for a large number of users.

Each node has its own memory and can therefore support users. The addition of more nodes increases the number of users supported.

Oracle Parallel Server can potentially improve system performance tremendously, but it requires careful configuration, and a detailed discussion of using OPS is beyond the scope of this book. For further details on how to implement OPS in your system, please refer to the *Oracle Parallel Server Concepts and Administrators Guide*.

Application Features That Cause Contention in a Cluster

Several application features can cause contention in an OPS environment. Make sure that if your application is using the following features, appropriate steps are taken to minimize pinging:

- Multiple nodes inserting in the same table concurrently. Partition the application tables and use multiple free-list groups to minimize contention.
- Multiple nodes inserting in the same indexed table concurrently

- Caching sequence numbers in the SGA of multiple instances
- Performing full table scans at the same time that the blocks are being updated by another instance.

This causes excessive pinging of the rollback segment blocks and therefore you should avoid full table scans when running in an OPS environment.

- **Use of referential integrity constraints that propagate across nodes**—This refers to DML activity that cascades across nodes. Redesign your applications to avoid cascade operations across nodes.

- **Excessive use of tables that store transient information**—These tables have a lot of DML activity and could be the cause of false pinging. Revisit your application design to ensure that the tables are used properly.

Next Steps

In this chapter, we have addressed a very important issue that needs to be dealt with when developing e-commerce applications—scalability. We have seen how the multi-threaded server architecture of Oracle8i can be used for this purpose. In the next chapter, we will look at various techniques that can be used to optimize JavaStop code.

12

Chapter 13

Optimizing JavaStop Performance

Introduction

In any e-commerce application, including JavaStop, the overall system performance depends on tuning several components:

- Hardware
- Oracle server
- Middle-layer (for example, Web server)
- Operating system
- Application
- Network

Most of the performance gains in such a system can be obtained by tuning the application. Oracle8i as well as operating system tuning can provide significant performance improvement, but your primary focus should be on tuning the application. This chapter will focus on tuning the Java code and Oracle8i. It also shows you some basic strategies that can be used for tuning your operating system for an e-commerce application.

Tuning the Operating System

Several simple strategies can be used to improve the performance of the operating system you are using in your e-commerce architecture. Detailed operating system tuning is beyond the scope of this book. Please refer to the documentation that came with your operating system software for specifics on operating system tuning.

Basic Tuning of Windows NT

Several basic guidelines can be used to tune Windows NT, knowing that the particular machine is intended for use in an e-commerce application as an Oracle database server or as a Web server.

Choose Maximum Throughput for Network Applications

The Oracle server uses its own memory management for caching file and network I/O. In addition, the Web server won't be doing a lot of operating system caching. Therefore, you can optimize server memory by changing the relationship of memory allocated to network connections compared to that allocated to applications. This can be done as follows:

1. In Control Panel, go to the Network tool's Services page.
2. Select the Server service and click Properties.
3. In the Server dialog box, select Maximize Throughput for Network Applications.

Don't Give Performance Boost to Foreground Applications

For Windows NT Server, the default choice of throughput setting devotes much memory for filesystem buffers, which is unnecessary because you will use the system as a database server, not as a file server. You should not give any performance boost to foreground applications. This can be set as follows:

1. In Control Panel's System Properties tool, go to the Performance page.
2. Choose None for the performance boost for foreground applications.

Disable Unnecessary Services

Several services are unnecessary and take up system resources. The services that can be disabled include the following:

- License Logging Service
- Remote Access AutoDial Manager
- Remote Access Connection Manager
- Remote Access Server
- Telephony Service

13

Several services shouldn't be disabled, including the following:

- Alerter
- Browser
- EventLog
- Messenger
- OracleService*XXXX* (where *XXXX* is an instance name)
- OracleTNSListener
- Server
- Spooler
- Workstation

Use Only One Oracle Instance per System

Ideally, you should use only one instance of Oracle8i per system. This not only simplifies administration but also helps troubleshoot performance problems.

Don't use the Oracle database server and Web server on the same machine because they will compete for resources. In addition, don't use the machine for other purposes, such as

- Network file server
- Primary or backup domain controller
- Print server
- Router
- Bridge
- Remote access server
- Active workstation for desktop processing

Disable Screen Savers

Use of screen savers should be minimized on the server because they take up valuable system resources. The OpenGL versions of screen savers should be particularly avoided.

Apply Microsoft's Latest Service Pack

Service packs are a cumulative collection of bug fixes and product enhancements to the base Windows NT release. The service packs are free and can be downloaded from the Microsoft Web site at `http://www.microsoft.com`. You should also check with Oracle Support Services to ensure that the Oracle version you are using is certified by Oracle for that service pack.

Characteristics of an Optimally Tuned Oracle System

An optimally tuned Oracle system has several characteristics:

- Waiting on I/O should be minimal because this indicates that the CPU has work to do while there are outstanding I/Os.
- Most CPU usage should be allocated to shadow processes and threads, not to background processes and threads.
- Response time should be fast. Quick system response is dependent on several components of which application and network tuning play a major role.
- The system should be CPU bound. The performance of CPU-bound systems can be improved by adding more processors. The following guidelines can be used to ensure that the system isn't I/O bound:
  - Isolate sequential I/Os to their own controller volumes. Components such as redo logs are accessed sequentially in a write-only manner; therefore, it helps to place them on their own disks.
  - Balance random I/Os across drives. Data files are usually accessed randomly and should be spread across drives to avoid hot disks.
  - Redo logs should be mirrored.
  - I/O rate capabilities of disks should not be exceeded. Exceeding I/O rate capabilities can lead to very serious performance problems. No matter how much you tune the database it won't cause a dramatic increase in performance because the disks can handle only so much communication. Check with your hardware vendors about the maximum I/O rates for the disks that you are using.

Managing Contention in Oracle Memory Structures

Contention can occur when multiple processes try to access the same resource simultaneously, resulting in some processes waiting for access to the database structures.

An e-commerce application usually involves a lot of short transactions and tends to resemble an online transaction processing (OLTP) type environment more than a decision support system (DSS).

OLTP systems have several characteristics you must consider when dealing with OLTPs:

- High throughput
- Insert/update intensive

13

- Large number of concurrent users
- Rapidly increasing amounts of data

Several database memory structures can experience contention in an e-commerce system. Of these, the most notable structures are

- Rollback segments
- Database buffer cache LRU latches
- Redo log buffer latches
- Library cache latches
- Shared servers
- Dispatchers
- Free lists
- Parallel server processes

Contention for shared servers and dispatchers is discussed in Chapter 12, "Improving the Scalability of JavaStop."

Optimizing Rollback Segment Use

When a transaction begins, it's assigned to a rollback segment. The assignment of a transaction to a rollback segment can occur either automatically or manually. This assignment is for the duration of the transaction:

- **Automatic**—This occurs when the first DDL or DML statement is issued in the transaction.
- **Manual**—The SET TRANSACTION SQL command with the USE ROLLBACK SEG-MENT parameter can be used to manually specify a rollback segment to use for a transaction. Manually assigning a transaction gives you more control over the size of the rollback segment to which it is assigned.

 Note   Queries are never assigned to rollback segments; therefore, rollback segments are more important for OLTP-type situations.

Rollback segments are written in a circular manner. You should use large rollback segments so that the transactions do not wrap around; otherwise, a read-consistent view can't be constructed for long-running transactions. Also, one or more transactions can concurrently use the same rollback segment, so any delays caused by contention on rollback segments affect performance. You should carefully choose the number and size of rollback segments for your database.

Note   More transactions per rollback segment potentially can cause more contention but use space more efficiently. In contrast, fewer transactions per rollback segment can cause less contention but waste more space.

Table 13.1 shows the classes of blocks that provide information about rollback segments and can be analyzed through the v$waitstat view.

Table 13.1   Block Classes Showing Rollback Segment Information

Block Class	Description
System undo header	Buffers containing header blocks of the SYSTEM rollback segment
System undo block	Buffers containing blocks of the SYSTEM rollback segment other than header blocks
Undo header	Buffers containing header blocks of the rollback segments other than the SYSTEM rollback segment
Undo block	Buffers containing blocks other than header blocks of the rollback segments, other than the SYSTEM rollback segment

Use the following queries to determine the number of data requests and waits for different block classes:

- Determine the number of data requests:

Input

```
SELECT SUM(value)  "DATA REQUESTS"
FROM V$SYSSTAT
WHERE name IN ('db block gets', 'consistent gets');
```

Output

```
DATA REQUESTS
-----------------------
          491081
```

- Determine the waits per block class:

Input

```
SELECT class, count
FROM V$WAITSTAT
WHERE class LIKE '%undo%'
AND COUNT > 0;
```

13

Output

```
CLASS                COUNT
-----------------    ----------
system undo header   5910
system undo block    402
undo header          1049
undo block           390
```

From the previous output you can calculate the percentage of waits for the rollback segment block classes as follows:

- Wait for system undo header is (5910/491081)×100 = 1.2%
- Wait for system undo block is (402/491081)×100 = 0.08%
- Wait for undo header is (1049/491081)×100 = 0.21%
- Wait for undo block is (390/491081)×100 = 0.079%

Waits for system undo header blocks is greater than 1% of the total requests indicating contention for rollback segments.

Contention for rollback segments can be reduced by using the following guidelines:

- Add more rollback segments. These new rollback segments should be referenced in the init.ora ROLLBACK_SEGMENTS parameter and also brought online.
- Set the storage parameter NEXT to the same value as INITIAL.
- Set the storage parameter MINEXTENTS to be greater than or equal to 20.
- Set the storage parameter OPTIMAL to INITIAL * MINEXTENTS.
- Determine the amount of undo generated by transactions as follows:

  ```
  SELECT MAX(USED_UBLK)
  FROM v$transaction;
  ```

  and then set INITIAL to be greater than or equal to MAX(USED_UBLK).

- Interleave the order of the rollback segments in the initialization parameter ROLLBACK_SEGMENTS. In other words, the first rollback segment is in one tablespace, the second is in another, and so on.

An e-commerce system generally comprises numerous short transactions and can benefit from the use of numerous rollback segments. In such an environment, you can benefit from using unlimited rollback segments or a high value for MAXEXTENTS.

 Note Be sure that you have a lot of free space in the rollback tablespace.

As a rule of thumb, the number of rollback segments should be N/4, where N is the expected number of concurrent transactions.

Managing Latch Contention

Internally, Oracle uses various types of structures. Access to these structures is controlled using a variety of mechanisms:

- Latches
- Enqueues
- Distributed locks
- Global locks (used in parallel instance implementations)

Latches control the access to internal data structures and thereby provide a way to protect them. If a process can't obtain a latch immediately, it *spins* while waiting for the latch. Spinning processes should be minimized because they can lead to additional CPU use and a slowing of the system. There are various types of latches, which are commonly referenced by the data structure to which they control access. Table 13.2 lists the most important latches you should be concerned with. In general, you don't have control over which latch is used or when it is used. However, by setting certain init.ora parameters, you can optimize the use of these latches, resulting in improved system performance.

Several data dictionary views can be helpful in identifying latch contention:

- v$latch
- v$latchholder
- v$latchname

The following queries can provide useful information about latches:

- This query provides the name of the latch by using the latch address:

```
svrmgrl> SELECT name
2> FROM v$latchname ln, v$latch l
3> WHERE l.addr = '&addr'
4> AND l.latch# = ln.latch# ;
```

- This query provides systemwide latch statistics:

```
svrmgrl> SELECT ln.name, l.addr, l.gets, l.misses, l.sleeps,
2>         l.immediate_gets, l.immediate_misses, lh.pid
3> FROM v$latch l , v$latchholder lh , v$latchname ln
4> WHERE l.addr = lh.laddr (+)
5> AND l.latch# = ln.latch#
ORDER BY l.latch# ;
```

- This query provides statistics for any latch Z:

```
svrmgrl> SELECT ln.name, l.addr, l.gets, l.misses, l.sleeps,
2>        l.immediate_gets, l.immediate_misses, lh.pid
3> FROM v$latch l , v$latchholder lh , v$latchname ln
4> WHERE l.addr = lh.laddr (+)
5> AND l.latch# = ln.latch#
6> AND ln.name like '%Z%'
7> ORDER BY l.latch# ;
```

If either of the following is true for a latch, it indicates contention:

- The ratio of MISSES to GETS exceeds 1 percent.
- The ratio of IMMEDIATE_MISSES to the sum of IMMEDIATE_MISSES and IMMEDIATE_GETS exceeds 1 percent.

Table 13.2   Important Latches That Can Cause Contention

Latch Number	Name	Latch Number	Name
0	Latch wait list	22	Sequence cache
1	Process allocation	23	Sequence cache entry
2	Session allocation	24	Row cache objects
3	Session switching	25	Cost function
4	Session idle bit	26	User lock
5	Messages	27	Global transaction mapping table
6	Enqueues	28	Global transaction
7	Trace latch	29	Shared pool
8	Cache buffers chain	30	Library cache
9	Cache buffers LRU chain	31	Library cache pin
10	Cache buffer handles	32	Library cache load lock
11	Multiblock read objects	33	Virtual circuit buffers
12	Cache protection latch	34	Virtual circuit queues
13	System commit number	35	Virtual circuits
14	Archive control	36	Query server process
15	Redo allocation	37	Query server freelists
16	Redo copy	38	Error message lists
17	Instance latch	39	Process queue
18	Lock element parent latch	40	Process queue reference
19	DML lock allocation	41	Parallel query stats
20	Transaction allocation		
21	Undo global data		

The following recommendations can help reduce latch contention:

- The cache buffers chains latch is needed when the SGA is scanned for database cache buffers. Contention for this latch can be reduced by increasing the DB_BLOCK_BUFFERS init.ora parameter.

- The cache buffers LRU chain latch is needed when the LRU chain containing all the dirty blocks in the buffer cache is scanned. Contention for this latch can be reduced by increasing the DB_BLOCK_BUFFERS and DB_BLOCK_WRITE_BATCH init.ora parameters.

- The row cache objects latch is needed when the cached data dictionary values are being accessed. Contention for this latch can be reduced by increasing the SHARED_POOL_SIZE init.ora parameter.

- Minimize contention for library cache latches by using the following guidelines:

  Minimize the fragmentation of the shared pool.

  Increase the use of shared SQL statements, and thereby decrease the reloads. Identify the SQL statements that are receiving many parse calls with the following query:

  ```
  svrmgrl> SELECT sql_text, parse_calls, executions
  2> FROM v$sqlarea
  3> WHERE parse_calls > 100
  4> AND executions < 2*parse_calls;
  ```

  Then, try to use sharable SQL wherever possible.

  Set the CURSOR_SPACE_FOR_TIME init.ora parameter to TRUE to keep shared SQL areas pinned in the shared pool. This prevents them from aging out of the pool as long as an open cursor references them, which results in faster execution. However, be sure that your shared pool is large enough to hold all the cursors.

  Use fully qualified table names.

- The redo allocation latch controls the allocation of space for redo entries in the redo log buffer. Before an Oracle process can allocate space in the redo log buffer, it must obtain this latch. Contention for the redo allocation latch can be minimized by decreasing the value of the LOG_SMALL_ENTRY_MAX_SIZE init.ora parameter because this parameter determines the number and size of redo entries copied on the redo allocation latch.

- The redo allocation latch is released as soon as space is allocated. However, the copy is then performed under the redo copy latch. On multiple CPUs, the LOG_SIMULTANEOUS_COPIES parameter determines the number of redo copy latches. Contention for redo copy latches can be reduced by increasing the